LAW AND SEXUAL MISCONDUCT IN NEW ENGLAND, 1650-1750

For Nancy and Nathan Chandler, with love

Law and Sexual Misconduct in New England, 1650-1750

Steering Toward England

ABBY CHANDLER
University of Massachusetts Lowell, USA

Routledge
Taylor & Francis Group
LONDON AND NEW YORK

First published in paperback 2024

First published 2015 by Ashgate Publishing

Published 2016 by Routledge
4 Park Square, Milton Park, Abingdon, Oxon OX14 4RN

and by Routledge
605 Third Avenue, New York, NY 10158

Routledge is an imprint of the Taylor & Francis Group, an informa business

Publisher's Note
The publisher has gone to great lengths to ensure the quality of this reprint but points out that some imperfections in the original copies may be apparent.

British Library Cataloguing in Publication Data
A catalogue record for this book is available from the British Library

The Library of Congress has cataloged the printed edition as follows:
Chandler, Abby, 1974- author.
Law and sexual misconduct in New England, 1650-1750 : steering toward England / by Abby Chandler.
pages cm
Based on author's thesis (doctoral - University of Maine, 2008) issued under title: At the magistrate's discretion : sexual crime and New England law, 1636-1718.
Includes bibliographical references and index.
ISBN 978-1-4724-6192-6 (hardcover)
1. Sex and law–New England–History–17th century.
2. Sex and law–New England–History–18th century. 3. Sex crimes–New England–History–17th century. 4. Sex crimes–New England–History–18th century. 5. Law–New England–English influences–History–17th century. 6. Law–New England–English influences–History–18th century. 7. New England–History–Colonial period, ca. 1600-1775 I. Title.
KF9325.C43 2015
345.74'025309032–dc23

2015019032

ISBN 13: 978-1-4724-6192-6 (hbk)
ISBN 13: 978-1-03-292800-5 (pbk)
ISBN 13: 978-1-315-59151-3 (ebk)

DOI: 10.4324/9781315591513

Contents

Preface

Studying a historical subject in the places where it occurred comes with particular benedictions. My understanding of the landscape which has long surrounded my life has changed in the past 10 years as street names and gravestones came to hold the personalities of the families for whom they were named in the seventeenth and eighteenth centuries. Much of this book was composed on Osgood Street in North Andover, Massachusetts, which was named for the family who tangled most often with my own ancestors in the court rooms of Essex County.

More striking still was the discovery of the Chebacco graveyard, which lies a few yards away from a busy road in Essex, Massachusetts. Debora Proctor, whom you will meet later in this book, was unable to persuade the Essex County court system to convict Thomas Choat on charges that he had molested her daughter. One of the Chebacco gravestones announces that "Here lyes buried/the Body of Capt. Thomas Choate/Died March Ye 31st/in 1745/ in ye 74th year of his age." The stone for his wife, Mary Choat, stands next to it, along with their children and grandchildren. Forming a wider circle around the Choat gravestones are stones for the Burnham and Cogswell families, as connected in the New England landscape as their depositions were connected in the Proctor/Choat trial of 1705.

The court records which bring these stories to life are held in archives across New England and I am grateful to all the librarians and archivists who found them for me. I would especially like to thank The American Antiquarian Society, The Andover Historical Society, The Bangor Public Library, The Ipswich Historical Society, Tammy Marks at The Maine State Archives, Elizabeth Bouvier at The Massachusetts State Archives, The New England Historic and Genealogical Society, The Phillips Library at the Peabody-Essex Museum, and Andrew Smith at The Rhode Island Judicial Archives.

No major research project is ever completed without funding and I wish to acknowledge the following grants: The Phillips Library Research Fellowship from the Peabody-Essex Museum, and both the Charles J. Dunn Dissertation Research Grant and the University Graduate Research Fellowship from the University of Maine. I also wish to thank the University of Massachusetts Lowell who funded the research trips necessary for expanding my original dissertation's time frame of 1636–1718 to the book's time frame of 1650–1750.

I am equally grateful for all the feedback I have received while presenting my research at conferences hosted by The British Group in Early American History, The Massachusetts Historical Society, The New England Historical Association, The Omohundro Institute of Early American History and Culture, The Society of Early Americanists, and The Society for the Study of Early Modern Women. I particularly wish to thank Mary Sarah Bilder for inviting me to talk about my research at the Boston College Legal History Roundtable, and Rose Doherty and Will Holton for inviting me to talk at the Boston Charter Day celebration and for welcoming me into the community of The Partnership for the Historic Bostons.

Other responses have come my way as this book has made its way into print. Portions of the book were derived from an article titled "'And the author of wickedness Surely is most to be blamed': The Deposition of Debora Proctor" in *Legacy: A Journal of American Women Writers* and articles titled "'Incontinent Practices:' Women, Language and Sexual Crime Trials in Colonial Maine" and "From Birthing Chamber to Court Room: The Medical and Legal Communities of the Colonial Essex County Midwife" in *Early Modern Women: An Interdisciplinary Journal.* I also wish to thank Tom Gray at Ashgate Press both for his interest in my book and for his suggestion of the anonymous reader whose ideas led to a complete restructuring of the book manuscript in the summer of 2014.

I began teaching at the University of Massachusetts Lowell in the fall of 2010 and have been blessed ever since with many people who share my love of history, whether as written documents or historical objects. Kate DiTullio reminds me why we teach and what we pass on to our students as they become teachers themselves, while Marc Fountain reminds me of the worlds outside my classrooms, historic or otherwise. Dan Sweeney has read every single word of this book and, more importantly, has thought about every word in this book. I also wish to thank Michael Pierson, Christoph Strobel, Joe Lipchitz, Lisa Edwards, and the rest of the UMass Lowell History department, who are the best of colleagues and mentors and whose office doors are always open when needed.

Like many first books, this particular volume began as a dissertation at the University of Maine and I again wish to thank Liam Riordan and the rest of my dissertation committee, William TeBrake, Martha McNamara, Mazie Hough, and Stephen Miller, for all their feedback and support.

Graduate school for me began at the University of Massachusetts in the fall of 2000. While my studies in Amherst produced the initial questions which drew me to colonial New England's sexual misconduct trials, I also made friends who still widen my world on a daily basis. For over a decade, Bree Beal has read drafts, asked questions, listened to stories, and, most importantly, made the 3,000 miles between Massachusetts and Oregon feel like no distance at all.

I also wish to thank Wade Franck, with whom I shared both a love of history and a love of telling stories about history, whether in Iowa or in Massachusetts. You will be missed by all of us who have harvested wheat, or spun wool, or run a printing press at Living History Farms.

All historians should have the world's best librarian on call, who also edits manuscripts, cooks, washes dishes, and copes with lost weekends and vacations which closely resemble archival visits or conference presentations. There are not words enough to say thank you to my dear and loving husband, Jim Riordan, for this book would not exist without you.

Finally, this book is dedicated to the memory of my grandparents, Nancy and Nathan Chandler, from whom I gained my first understanding of the different country inhabited by the past and who long believed that I could write about that country. Because you could not hold the finished book in your hands, I offer this dedication on behalf of all your family. Thank you, with all my love.

Abby Chandler
North Andover, Massachusetts

Note on Transcriptions

Unless otherwise noted, all transcriptions from the original court records are my own. Where possible, I retained the original spelling, punctuation, and capitalization but did expand both abbreviations and contractions. For purposes of clarity, the older usages of "u" for "v," "y" for "th," and the long or descending "s" for "s" have all been modernized.

All dates are written in the New Style in which the calendar year begins on January 1 rather than on March 24. I also used the American style of dating which places the month before the day.

Introduction

The first snow arrived in October of 1641, taking the fall colors with it. Thomas Gorges sat in the "one pretty handsome roome & studdy" afforded by his uncle's house in Maine and considered the letter he was composing to family friend, Richard Bernard.[1] "Longe have these poor people groaned for want of government," he wrote, describing Sir Ferdinando Gorges's newly recreated Province of Maine.[2] Thomas Gorges and Bernard were Puritans, a religious affinity shared with the leaders of Massachusetts Bay Colony, though Massachusetts laws and government made both men uneasy. Massachusetts colonist John Wheelwright was banished in 1637 for religious heresy and wrote to Gorges in 1641 to ask what sorts of laws his family might find in Maine. "I told him," Gorges told Bernard, "for the civill we steared as neere as we could to the course of Ingland. For the ecclesiastical we forced noe man to the common prayer booke or to the ceremonies of the Church of Ingland but allowed the Liberties of Conscience." Gorges's planned legal code never came to fruition but his letters suggest an active interest in modeling Maine law on English law in the mid-seventeenth century.

The Anglicization Thesis

The many political, legal, and cultural exchanges between England and its North American colonies have received growing interest from scholars in the past half century. This research includes the Anglicization thesis or the argument that the American colonies were at their most English on the eve of the American Revolution. John Murrin's dissertation "Anglicizing an American Colony: The Transformation of Provincial Massachusetts" states that "this period marked, not

1 Thomas Gorges, *The Letters of Thomas Gorges, Deputy Governor of the Province of Maine, 1640–1643*, Robert E. Moody, ed. (Portland: Maine Historical Society, 1978), 1. Richard Bernard published books on theology and law and was criticized by Puritans and Separatists alike for his moderate views. His daughter, Mary Bernard, married Roger Williams in 1629. The personal connections between Gorges, Bernard, and Williams suggest a shared conversation on the topic of "Liberties of Conscience," though no further concrete evidence of such a connection survives.

2 Gorges, *The Letters of Thomas Gorges*, 17.

the Americanization of an English colony, but the Anglicization of an American colony."[3] Scholars who have expanded on Murrin's ideas include Richard Johnson, Joseph Conforti, Brendan McConville, Michael Meranze, James Henretta, and Owen Stanwood, though some of them have questioned whether "Anglicization" is the best term for describing this process.[4] Conforti suggests that "these developments should be more properly called 're-Anglicization,' a return to the region's English origins" while Meranze favors "Imperialization" and Johnson, "Royalization."[5] Henretta adds that "what Murrin describes as 'Anglicization' might better be called an attempt at centralization; that is the subordination to metropolitan control of legal institutions throughout the 'provinces'—whether English counties or American colonies."[6]

The dissenting colonies of Plymouth, Massachusetts Bay, and Connecticut created certain variations on English law and custom in the seventeenth century and their cultural and legal shift back toward England at the turn of the eighteenth century supports the timeline of the Anglicization thesis. The first laws created in the Provinces of Maine and New Hampshire and the colony of Rhode Island demonstrate an initial interest in "steering towards England," though Maine's

---

[3] John M. Murrin, "Anglicizing an American Colony: The Transformation of Provincial Massachusetts" (PhD diss., Yale University, 1966), 259.

[4] See Richard R. Johnson, *Adjustment to Empire: The New England Colonies, 1675–1715* (New Brunswick: Rutgers University Press, 1981), Joseph A. Conforti, *Saints and Strangers: New England in British North America* (Baltimore: The John Hopkins University Press, 2006), Brendan McConville, *The King's Three Faces: The Rise and Fall of Royal America, 1688–1776* (Chapel Hill: The University of North Carolina Press, 2006), Michael Meranze, "Penality and the Colonial Project: Crime, Punishment, and the Regulation of Morals in Early America," in *The Cambridge History of Law in America*, Volume 1, Michael Grossberg and Christopher Tomlins, eds (New York: Cambridge University Press, 2008), 178–210, James A. Henretta, "Magistrates, Common Law Lawyers, Legislators: The Three Legal Systems of British America," in *The Cambridge History of Law in America*, Volume 1, 555–92 and Owen Stanwood, *The Empire Reformed: English America in the Age of the Glorious Revolution* (Philadelphia: University of Pennsylvania Press, 2011). For another discussion on Anglicization and English identity, see Jack P. Greene, *Creating the British Atlantic: Essays on Transplantation, Adaptation and Continuity* (Charlottesville: University of Virginia Press, 2013). Cornelia Hughes Dayton's "Turning Points and the Relevance of Colonial Legal History," *The William and Mary Quarterly*, 50 no. 1 (1993): 7–17 provides an overview of the changing nature of law in the British North American colonies. Benjamin H. Irvin's 2008 review of McConville's *The King's Three Faces* provides additional discussion on the Anglicization thesis. See "Smashing Idols," Common-Place, accessed January 5, 2014, http://www.common-place.org/vol-08/no-04/reviews/irvin.shtml.

[5] Joseph A. Conforti, *Saints and Strangers: New England in British North America* (Baltimore: The John Hopkins University Press, 2006), 164, Meranze, "Penality and the Colonial Project," 200 and Johnson, *Adjustment to Empire*, 419.

[6] Henretta, "Magistrates, Common Law Lawyers, Legislators," 581.

absorption into Massachusetts in the late seventeenth century meant that Maine faced toward England, turned away, and then came back. These patterns suggest that in most of New England, at least, "Alternating Anglicization" may be a more appropriate term as each colony considered its own relationship with English law differently at different times.

The terms "Imperialization," "Royalization," and "Centralization" all suggest a process decided in London and imposed on English colonies in North America, though colonial leaders' carefully negotiated willingness to go along with the new regime is well documented. Less attention has been paid to the ways in which ordinary colonists responded to these changes, though Owen Stanwood has examined the impact these transitions had on popular political cultures in the North American colonies.[7] The evolving nature of law and its resulting legal cultures provide a particularly useful conduit for studying this process as law is, by its very nature, both prescriptive and reactive.[8] Political or ecclesiastical leaders create laws because they desire their subjects or parishioners to behave in a certain fashion and because they wish to convey larger messages about the societies they are creating. When those same laws are broken, lawbreakers must be tried and punished by a means intended to serve as a warning to other would-be lawbreakers, though lawbreakers and their witnesses did not always comply quietly with this process. My two-part analysis of changing sexual misconduct laws and the resulting trial depositions highlights the ways in which ordinary colonists across New England both interacted with and responded to the growing Anglicization of their legal systems and argues that these men and women saw themselves as taking part in a much larger process.

Using Sexual Misconduct Charges to Study Political and Legal Changes

European society in the medieval and very early modern periods recognized few distinctions between public life and private life and strictures governing personal

---

[7] Stanwood, *The Empire Reformed*.

[8] Richard Ross defines legal culture as the "values and attitudes which bind the system together, and which determine the place of the legal system in the culture of the society as a whole." Ross, "The Legal Past of Early New England: Notes for the Study of Law, Legal Culture, and Intellectual History, *The William and Mary Quarterly* 50, no. 1 (1993), 32. Christopher Tomlins adds that "rather than planting a template of 'English' law, the inside story of English colonizing is one of successive seedings of mainland North America with a plurality of legal cultures, each expressing the designs of projectors but also heavily influenced by migrants' regional English origins." Tomlins, *Freedom Bound: Law, Labor and Civic Identity in Colonizing English America, 1580–1685* (New York: Cambridge University Press, 2010), 294.

behavior were commonly enforced by both religious and political entities. Societal members were exhorted to refrain from public drunkenness, slander, blasphemy, and engaging in sexual relations outside of marriage, to name just a few.[9] Laws restricting all these activities existed in most, if not all, of the English colonies and so any or all of them could be used to study shifting relationships between colonial laws and English laws. Nevertheless, my study focuses in particular on the prosecution of sexual misconduct, a term chosen as it best encompasses the ambiguities created by the early modern custom of prosecuting sexual intercourse outside of marriage.[10] All crimes can threaten orderly society but no other crime posed quite the same long-term implications as individuals who engaged in such behavior. Unlike public drunkenness, blasphemy, and slander, illicit sex often resulted in illegitimate children who could then become their own societal challenges. All these factors made sexual misconduct a sore subject for early modern leaders, which makes it a particularly fruitful subject for studying the complex relationship between laws created in England and laws created in the English colonies.

Moving beyond the concerns of early modern leaders, the sheer mass of court records generated by sexual misconduct trials provided me with the range of data necessary for tracking the often subtle shifts toward more Anglicized legal systems in the British colonies. At the most basic level, sexual misconduct charges were filed in nearly every New England court session in the seventeenth and early eighteenth centuries. Both men and women were routinely charged with sexual misconduct which allowed me to examine these shifts from male and female perspectives. Finally, the overall prosecution of sexual misconduct was undergoing changes of its own in the early modern period. Traditionally tied to moral issues, English sexual misconduct trials were conducted first by the Catholic Church and later by the Anglican Church. But the early stages of moving from pastoral to urban societies and the eventual Industrial Revolution raised the question of financial support for illegitimate children and, increasingly, sexual misconduct prosecution came to be about economic

---

9 See Martin Ingram, *Church Courts, Sex and Marriage in England, 1570–1640* (Cambridge: Cambridge University Press, 1987), Jenny Kermode and Gartine Walker, *Women, Crime and the Courts in Early Modern England* (Chapel Hill: University of North Carolina Press, 1994) and Laura Gowing, *Domestic Dangers, Women, Words, and Sex in Early Modern London* (Oxford: Oxford University Press, 1996).

10 The other term considered was "sexual crime" but since it specifically connotes rape and incest to the modern ear, I decided that sexual misconduct was a more accurate way of describing the hundreds of fornication before marriage and bastardy trials and handful of rape, incest, and adultery trials which comprise my research.

rather than moral concerns. Other issues included the differences between consensual and nonconsensual sex, whether men and women who conducted in sexual acts outside the marriage bed should be considered differently, addressing homosexuality, and whether the regulation of illicit sex should favor the needs of the individual or the needs of the community. European global expansion in the sixteenth and seventeenth centuries added the additional category of race to these considerations. These decisions were made by political as well as ecclesiastical and legal leaders and, consequently, sexual misconduct trials can tell us as much about political cultures as they do gender roles.

Law and the Anglo-American Atlantic World

English leaders had to maintain a careful balancing act when creating their legal systems in North America. The disparate sea of common law, ecclesiastical, chancery, and prerogative courts comprising the English legal system in the early modern period meant that there was no easily labeled "English law" to serve as a model. Likewise, England's legal systems were undergoing transitions of their own in the seventeenth and eighteenth centuries, including the question of whether sexual misconduct should be addressed in the ecclesiastical or the common law courts. Finally, colonial laws "could not be contrary or repugnant to the laws of England" and the changes in the English legal systems meant there were no consistent answers to whether laws might be deemed repugnant or acceptable.[11] Despite these challenges, creating some form of legal order was an early piece of business in most settlements. Courts gave leaders an important institutional venue to assert their authority and moral values. In turn, court sessions gave ordinary colonists forums to air grievances and all of these needs intersected as charges were made, evidence presented and sentences dispensed.

---

[11] Mary Sarah Bilder, *The Transatlantic Constitution: Colonial Legal Culture and the Empire* (Cambridge: Harvard University Press, 2004), 3. Also see David H. Flaherty, "Introduction," *Essays in the History of Early American Law* (Chapel Hill: Institute of Early American History and Culture, 1969), Joseph H. Smith, "The English Criminal Law in Early America," in *The English Legal System: Carryover to the Colonies*, Joseph H. Smith and Thomas G. Barnes, eds (Los Angeles: University of California Press, 1975), Richard Scott Eckert, *The Gentleman of the Profession: The Emergence of Lawyers in Massachusetts, 1630–1810* (New York: Garland Publishing, Inc., 1991), *The Cambridge History of Law in America*, Volume I, Early America (1580–1815) eds Michael Grossberg and Christopher Tomlins (New York: Cambridge University Press, 2008), and G. Edward White, *Law in American History* (Oxford: Oxford University Press, 2012) for additional discussion of the challenges involved in crafting laws not repugnant to English law.

Sexual Misconduct Prosecution in New England

The prosecution of sexual misconduct in New England was discussed by Laurel Thatcher Ulrich and Cornelia Hughes Dayton in the 1980s and 1990s and, more recently, by Else Hambleton and M. Michelle Jarrett Morris.[12] Most of these studies, including Richard Godbeer's *Sexual Revolution in Early America*, focus largely on Puritan New England rather than the region as a whole, which tells only part of this story.[13] Religious differences led to the creation of multiple political systems and legal cultures within New England's small geographic area, including the ones in Essex County, Massachusetts, Maine, and Rhode Island comprising this study.[14] Essex County represents Puritan dominated Massachusetts Bay while Maine provides a case study for examining that same dominance since the colony was completely absorbed into Massachusetts as York County in the 1670s.[15] Unlike Maine, Rhode Island remained independent

---

[12] See Laurel Thatcher Ulrich, *Good Wives: Image and Reality in the Lives of Women in Northern New England, 1650–1750* (New York: Alfred A. Knopf, 1980) and *A Midwife's Tale, the Life of Martha Ballard, Based on Her Diary, 1785–1812* (New York: Vintage Books, 1990), Cornelia Hughes Dayton, *Women Before the Bar: Gender, Law, and Society in Connecticut, 1639–1789* (Chapel Hill: University of North Carolina Press, 1995), Else Hambleton, *Daughters of Eve, Pregnant Brides and Unwed Mothers in Seventeenth-Century Massachusetts* (New York: Routledge Press, 2004), and M. Michelle Jarret Morris, *Under Household Government: Sex and Family in Puritan Massachusetts* (Cambridge: Harvard University Press, 2013). Also see Mary Beth Norton, *Founding Mothers & Fathers: Gendered Power and the Forming of American Society* (New York: Alfred A. Knopf, 1996), Jane Kamensky, *Governing the Tongue, the Politics of Speech in Early New England* (Oxford: Oxford University Press, 1997), and Elaine Forman Crane, *Ebb Tide in New England, Women, Seaports, and Social Change, 1630–1830* (Boston: Northeastern University Press, 1998) and *Witches, Wife Beaters, & Whores: Common Law and Common Folk* (Ithaca: Cornell University Press, 2011).

[13] See Richard Godbeer, *Sexual Revolution in Early America* (Baltimore: The Johns Hopkins University Press, 2002). Studies on sexual misconduct in other English colonies include Kathleen Brown, *Good Wives, Nasty Wenches, & Anxious Patriarchs* (Chapel Hill: University of North Carolina Press, 1996), Kirsten Fischer, *Suspect Relations: Sex, Race and Resistance in Colonial North Carolina* (Cornell University Press, 2002), Clare Lyons, *Sex among the Rabble: An Intimate History of Gender & Power in the Age of Revolution, Philadelphia, 1730–1830* (Chapel Hill: University of North Carolina Press, 2006) and Sharon Block, *Rape And Sexual Power in Early America* (Chapel Hill: University of North Carolina Press, 2006).

[14] See Philip E. Gura, *A Glimpse of Sion's Glory: Puritan Radicalism in New England, 1620–1660* (Middletown: Wesley University Press, 1984) for further discussion on cultural diversity in New England.

[15] When discussing Maine, I will use the terms "Province of Maine" and "Maine" interchangeably when talking about Maine prior to the 1670s and the terms "York County" and "Maine" interchangeably after the 1670s.

of both Massachusetts Bay and Connecticut, though Joseph Conforti notes that "Rhode Island's weak civic culture, religious toleration and commercial individualism all had parallels in northern New England."[16] These distinctions allow the sexual misconduct trials of Essex County, Maine, and Rhode Island to provide a cross-section view of their colonies' disparate relationships with both England and with each other.

My consideration of the broader political and social contexts for Massachusetts, Maine, and Rhode Island's sexual misconduct trials provides a needed link between the political studies conducted by John Murrin, Richard Johnson, and others and the legal and gender studies conducted by Laurel Thatcher Ulrich, Richard Godbeer, and others. Ulrich's research has greatly widened our understanding of the lives of women like midwife Martha Ballard, but Ballard and her counterparts need to be seen in context with the wider political movements surrounding them. Likewise, Johnson's *Adjustment to Empire* does not answer the question of how growing English control of their colonies and their court systems affected the lives of ordinary New England women on a daily basis. By examining these connections, my research places these studies in dialogue with each other.

Methodology

My research included compiling a database containing all documented information for the 1,843 sexual misconduct trials conducted in Essex County, Maine, and Rhode Island court rooms between 1650 and 1750. Considering every individual sexual misconduct trial conducted by these courts provides the level of precision necessary for understanding how and when the considerations described in the previous paragraph became part of larger societal transitions in colonial New England. I divided the trials into nine categories: sexual intercourse outside of marriage, usually defined as fornication; fornication before marriage; bastardy; paternity; adultery; rape; incest; bestiality; and sodomy (defined as intercourse between two men). Information from the three jurisdictions was entered into spreadsheets which tracked numbers of court sessions, names and towns (if listed), types of charges and punishments, acquittals, defaults, repeat offenders, and whether any depositions or further documentation still survive. Analyzing *charges*, rather than colonists or trials, allows for a more accurate representation of the colonial court room. Couples charged with fornication

[16] Conforti, *Saints and Strangers*, 90.

before marriage were treated as a single entity rather than two separate charges. This decision reflects the consistent numbers of married couples who received the same charge and punishment as well as the lack of a separate legal identity for married Anglo-American women in the early modern period.[17] Couples charged with conceiving illegitimate children were treated as separate charges because the punishments for bastardy and paternity were different. Rape victims were noted, but not counted, while women who failed in their rape claims and were convicted for fornication were included in the numbers of fornication charges. Within jurisdictions, I organized the spreadsheets according to the individual courts. For example, Essex County had five spread sheets, covering the Salem Quarterly Court (1650–92), the Salem General Sessions of the Peace (1692–1750), the Ipswich Quarterly Court (1650–92), the Ipswich General Sessions of the Peace (1692–1750), and the Newbury General Sessions of the Peace (1692–1750).

Once I had completed my research, the spreadsheets for the individual jurisdictions were divided into four 25-year sections which covered the years between 1650 and 1674, 1675 and 1699, 1700 and 1724, and 1725 and 1750, which allowed for specific analysis of change over time within the jurisdictions and change over time for the overall time period between 1650 and 1750. All three colonies were firmly established by the end of the 1630s, but their societies evolved at very different rates. For example, Rhode Island's transition toward a highly commercialized, urban society in the late seventeenth century would not be matched in Massachusetts until the early eighteenth century and elements like these played out in each jurisdiction's sexual misconduct trials. Likewise, placing the trials into these four data sets allowed me to compare and contrast the rise and retreat of Anglicized legal systems in these three colonies.

My first four categories – sexual intercourse outside of marriage, fornication before marriage, bastardy, and paternity – were the most common types of sexual misconduct trials conducted in colonial New England and throughout the Anglo-American world. Early modern European society put enormous emphasis on ritual as children passed from birth and baptism to adulthood and marriage. "Ideally, as classic rites of passage, these ceremonies worked to

---

17 The seventeenth-century legal text *The Lawes Resolutions of Womens Rights* states that "As soone as a man and woman are knit, and fast linked together in bands of wedlocke, they are become in common parlance ... yoke-fellowes, that in an even participation, must take all fortunes equally." T.E., *The Lawes Resolutions of Womens Rights, or, The Lawes Provision for Woemen: a Methodicall Collection of Such Statutes and Customes, with the Cases, Opinions, Arguments, and Points of Learning in the Law, as doe properly concerne Women* (Clark: The Lawbook Exchange Ltd, 2006. Original edition: London: Printed by John More, 1632), 116.

bring people together or to assign everyone their place," writes historian David Cressy. However, as Cressy adds, "They also set up traps into which people could stumble, and tests which not everyone could pass. Ritual performance, in practice, revealed frictions and fractures that everyday local discourse attempted to hide or to heal."[18] Laws were consequently devised to punish those sexual acts which struck at the heart of the rituals surrounding birth and marriage, whether couples who had sexual intercourse before marriage or couples who conceived children out of wedlock.

Research Findings and Categorization

I found 1,334 fornication trials in Essex County, Maine, and Rhode Island between 1650 and 1750: 557 of these trials were identified as being for fornication before marriage, though this distinction affected neither the trial process nor the ultimate decision made by the justices. Another 166 colonists were tried for some other form of sexual misconduct, whether "incontinency," "lascivious carriage" or "uncleanness," to give a few examples.[19] The use of such charges changed drastically in the Anglo-American world between the sixteenth and seventeenth centuries and tracking their use was helpful for understanding the Anglicization of sexual misconduct laws in New England, a point that will be discussed further in Chapter 2. The second most common type of sexual misconduct trial was for colonists who conceived children out of wedlock. A total of 514 women were charged with bearing illegitimate children, while 244 men were charged with fathering those same children. Women convicted on bastardy charges were nearly always also convicted on fornication charges; men convicted on paternity trials were rarely tried on fornication charges after the 1660s.

The remaining categories of adultery, rape, incest, bestiality, and sodomy all carried severe penalties, including capital punishment, though it was rarely used. Most colonial New England courts refused to execute suspects who fell short of their definition of absolute proof: testimonies from two outside witnesses, a confession from the accused party or both for conviction in such trials.[20] Justices also sought ways to avoid capital punishment even for convicted defendants. All three jurisdictions had laws recommending capital punishment for colonists who committed adultery but none of the 22 colonists convicted on adultery

[18] David Cressy, *Birth, Marriage & Death: Ritual, Religion, and the Life-Cycle in Tudor and Stuart England* (Oxford: Oxford University Press, 1997), 2.

[19] See Appendix A for a complete list of Alternate Sexual Misconduct Charges.

[20] Godbeer, *Sexual Revolution in Colonial America*, 101.

charges were actually put to death. Most of these colonists came from Rhode Island, which reflects Rhode Island's decision to place both married men and married women on trial for adultery, while both Essex County and Maine tried married women on adultery charges and married men on fornication charges.

Rape and incest trials both raise questions about the differences between trials for consensual sex and nonconsensual sex. Early modern authorities understood that differences existed between consensual and nonconsensual sex, though they were undecided on how to punish convicted rapists. Michael Dalton's *The Countrey Justice* defined rape as a capital crime and suggested hanging as the best means of execution.[21] A 1650 English law prohibiting "the detestable sins of incest, adultery, and fornication" also recommended capital punishment for defendants convicted on incest charges.[22] Massachusetts Bay authorities briefly contemplated using Mosaic law which ordered men who raped married women to be stoned to death while men who raped single women were ordered to marry their victims.[23] The colony eventually decided to allow justices to choose their own punishment and the law states that men convicted on rape charges should "be punished either with death, or with some other greivous punishment according to circumstances as the Judges, or General court shal determin."[24] The Rhode Island legal code created in 1647 defined rape as "when a man through his wild & unbridled affection eth wth & Forceth A Woman against her will like unto him" and ordered defendants convicted on this charge to receive capital punishment "without remedy."[25]

All successful rape charges required two witnesses who could document that the women had been "forceth against her will." The small numbers of these trials, only 10 rape and six incest trials, suggest that some of the fornication and bastardy trials conducted in these jurisdictions were really rape trials without enough witnesses for the female defendant to be able to prove that she had been raped. It should also be remembered that unreported crimes were a part of life in the colonial period, particularly in the outlying settlements. Women raped by family members or family friends were wary about naming their attackers in court, recognizing there

21 Michael Dalton, *The Countrey Justice* (New York: The Legal Classics Library, Division of Gryphon Editions. Original edition, London: Company of Stationers, 1655), 355.

22 "May 1650: An Act for suppressing the detestable sins of Incest, Adultery and Fornication.," *Acts and Ordinances of the Interregnum, 1642–1660* (1911), 387–9. URL. http.// www.british-history.ac.uk/report.aspx?compid=56399 Date accessed: July 7, 2014.

23 Hambleton, *Daughters of Eve*, 136–8.

24 *The Laws and Liberties of Massachusetts, Reprinted from the Copy of the 1648 edition in the Henry E. Huntington Library* (San Marino: The Henry E. Huntington Library and Art Gallery, 1998), 6.

25 *The Earliest Acts and Laws of the Colony of Rhode Island and Providence Plantations, 1647–1719*, John D. Cushing, ed. (Wilmington: Michael Glazier Inc., 1977), 64.

would be repercussions within family structures and households. Likewise, justices ruling on accusations of incest were equally wary about executing household heads who would then leave their wives and children without financial support.[26]

English common law and the legal codes created in Massachusetts and Rhode Island in the 1640s all agreed that sodomy was "a vile Affection men given up thereto leave the Naturall use of women & burn in their lust one Towards Another," while bestiality or buggery was "a most Filthy lying with A beast as wth a woman & is Abomination & Confusion."[27] There were no colonists tried for bestiality or sodomy in Essex County, Maine, or Rhode Island between 1650 and 1750 so it is impossible to know how the justices would have responded to such an occurrence. If there was an equivalent of Thomas Grainger's alleged barnyard orgy in Plymouth Colony in any of these jurisdictions, it did not make it into their court records.[28]

The Anatomy of an Early Modern Sexual Misconduct Trial

While this book is focused on distinctions between sexual misconduct trials, there were certain commonalities between them. The first stage of trying a defendant in a sexual misconduct trial began in the community as a whole.[29] Political and religious leaders and local inhabitants alike kept a watchful eye on their family members and neighbors' sexual behavior, whether an out-of-

---

26 See Irene Quenzler Brown and Richard D. Brown, *The Hanging of Ephraim Wheeler: a Story of Rape, Incest, and Justice in Early America* (Cambridge: Belknap Press of Harvard University Press, 2003) for a rare example of an incest trial which did result in a conviction and Ann Taves, *Religion and Domestic Violence in Early New England: the Memoirs of Abigail Abbot Bailey* (Bloomington: Indiana University Press, 1989) for a close look at devastation wrought by one father's unprosecuted molestation of his daughter. In addition, see Block, *Rape & Sexual Power in Early America* for a more detailed discussion of the difficulties posed by finding and classifying rape trials in the American colonies.

27 *The Earliest Acts and Laws of the Colony of Rhode Island and Providence Plantations*, 64.

28 Thomas Granger was convicted in 1642 for sexual intercourse with a mare, a cow, two goats, five sheep, two calves and a turkey. While the Plymouth Colony court records barely mention the matter, William Bradford's *Of Plymouth Plantation* describes Granger's trial and eventual punishment in detail. See William Bradford, *Of Plymouth Plantation, 1620–1647*, Samuel Eliot Morison, ed. (New York: Knopf Press, 1952), 326.

29 This composite portrayal of the procedures used to prosecute sexual misconduct in the English courts is drawn from Ingram, *Church Courts, Sex and Marriage in England*, Cynthia Herrup, *The Common Peace: Participation and the Criminal Law in Seventeenth-Century England* (Cambridge: Cambridge University Press, 1987), Kermode and Walker, *Women, Crime and the Courts in Early Modern England*, and Anna Clark, *Desire: A History of European Sexuality* (New York: Routledge, 2008).

wedlock pregnancy or an overlong dalliance between an unmarried couple. Women threatened by potential rapists were expected to defend themselves by fighting off their assailants or by drawing community attention to their plights. Whether they had done so was then used during their trials to determine whether to treat them as victims or willing participants. Women who could not adequately demonstrate efforts to defend themselves or to obtain assistance were often charged with fornication, particularly if a child had been conceived.

Once some form of sexual misconduct had been identified, complaints were made to a local justice who dispatched the appropriate town sheriff with warrants for defendants and subpoenas for witnesses. Defendants were required to make their first statements before justices, while further information was gathered from witnesses. At this time, defendants were required to pay some form of "surety," an early modern equivalent of bail, which promised that the money put up would be forfeited if the defendant did not appear in court. Defendants who could not afford their surety charges were allowed to call on family members and friends until the full amount had been reached and the court records routinely list anywhere from one to four or five names as being responsible for these charges. If there was not enough time to build a case before the next quarterly court session, a "presentment" was read in court, ordering the defendants to appear at the next session. During the court session, charges against the defendant were read out, the defendant represented himself or herself, applicable witnesses gave their testimony, and the decision was made. Defendants were allowed to appeal court rulings, but few did.

Some form of punishment always followed conviction and these punishments evolved over time, as did English punishments for sexual misconduct. The earliest court records from the 1630s and 1640s occasionally mention ordering convicted defendants to stand in public while wearing a white sheet or a sign describing their actions, but the overall records make clear that such punishments were rarely implemented before 1650 and were not used after 1700.[30] Instead, most convicted colonists in Essex County, Maine, and Rhode Island were ordered to receive either a whipping or a fine, depending on their preferences, although whippings became less common in the eighteenth century.[31] Very

---

[30] See Appendix B for a complete list of Alternate Punishments.

[31] Punishments for sexual misconduct trials highlight a core economic difference between the New England and the Chesapeake Bay colonies. Defendants convicted on sexual misconduct trials in Virginia were fined, rather than choosing between a fine or a whipping. If the defendant was an indentured servant, his or her master paid the fine and additional time was added to the servant's indenture. The tobacco economy in the Chesapeake colonies created a system in which most colonists were either servants or wealthy masters and it was in the best interest of the masters

few trials specify which option was chosen and it is difficult to know whether colonists preferred monetary hardship or painful humiliation. For the most part, defendants who were whipped received anywhere from five to 10 lashings. Defendants convicted on charges such as rape which were deemed particularly horrific by justices or jury were not allowed to choose their punishments and were always whipped, generally anywhere from 20 to 40 times. These punishments often specified that the lashings be "severely laid" on the defendant's naked back, which suggests that lashings for ordinary sexual misconduct convictions were intended to be less painful and, perhaps, to cause less permanent damage.

The most common fine used in Essex County, Maine, and Rhode Island was 50 shillings, or two pounds and 10 shillings. Rapid fluctuations in colonial currencies and the frequent use of barter rather than cash make durable goods a more useful barometer for estimating the financial damage caused by such a fine.[32] A probate inventory done for the estate of Thomas Scott of Ipswich, Massachusetts, on July 7, 1657 listed "3 old kettels, a lettel Kettel, a scummer, a warming pan, too smal Iron potts and an old bras frying pan," which were collectively valued at two pounds, eight shillings and twelve pence.[33] Another probate inventory done for the estate of Thomas Woodbridge of Newbury, Massachusetts on June 3, 1681 listed "1 brass kettle, 1 warming pan, 2 skillets, skimmer & ladle" as being worth two pounds and five shillings.[34] These valuations suggest that 50 shillings was enough to buy the kitchen implements necessary for cooking a meal. Occasionally, the records will specify whether the fine could be paid in something other than cash, which again serves as a reminder that colonial economies were based as much on barter as exchanges of cash.[35]

Essex County, Maine, and Rhode Island's court records make clear that most colonial New England trials involving sexual acts were mundane in nature,

---

to keep their servants indentured for as long as possible. John Ruston Pagan, *Anne Orthwood's Bastard, Sex and Law in Early Virginia* (Oxford: Oxford University Press, 2003), 107.

32 James E. McWilliams, *Building the Bay Colony: Local Economy and Culture in Early Massachusetts* (Charlottesville: University of Virginia Press, 2007) and Ed Crews, "How Much is That in Today's Money?" *Colonial Williamsburg Journal* 24, no. 2 (2002). URL: http://www.history.org/Foundation/journal/Summer02/money2.cfm Date accessed: July 7, 2014.

33 *The Probate Records of Essex County, Massachusetts, 1635–1664*, Volume 1, George Francis Dow, ed. (Salem: Newcomb & Gauss, 1916), 258.

34 *The Probate Records of Essex County, Massachusetts, 1675–1681*, Volume 3, George Francis Dow, ed. (Salem: Newcomb & Gauss, 1920), 424.

35 Joseph Chandler was ordered in 1691 to "pay in Corn or other good provision at Currant price, toward the maintaining of the Child 2s per week." Essex County Quarterly Court trial for Elizabeth Sessions and Joseph Chandler, File Papers Box 2. Judicial Archives, Massachusetts State Archives, Boston.

resulting in punishments expensive or painful but rarely life-threatening or even life-altering. Nathaniel Hawthorne may have portrayed heroine Hester Prynne as a woman whose life was permanently damaged by her transgressions in his 1850 novel *The Scarlet Letter* but the historical record makes clear that Hawthorne greatly exaggerated Prynne's punishment.[36] Some young women who became pregnant out of wedlock never married, others went on to marry men who were not their original sexual partners. Martha Proctor, Mary Osgood and Elizabeth Sessions were all convicted on fornication and bastardy charges in the Essex County court system. While Proctor never married, Osgood and Sessions both made successful marriages in the years following their trials.

Anna Clark argues that defendants convicted on sexual misconduct charges in early modern Europe were treated in much the same way and uses the term "twilight moments" to describe "those sexual activities or desires which people are not supposed to engage in, but they do." Clark adds that sexual misconduct trial defendants "may not have been burnt at the stake or exiled ... but their neighbors gossiped about them or shunned them as not quite right, as promiscuous, odd, mysterious, or weird. However, after public repentance they could be returned to the fold."[37] The highly theatrical nature of the early modern court room made sexual misconduct trials ideal locations for carefully orchestrated public repentances.[38] Female defendants were particularly judged on their willingness to follow a prescribed ritual in which they named their sexual partners, identified where and when they became pregnant (preferably while making clear that they had been offered marriage and had only had intercourse on one occasion), and then confessed their hearty regrets for their actions. We cannot know why Proctor did not marry and Sessions and Osgood did; however, it is worth noting that while Proctor refused to name the man who fathered her child, both Sessions and Osgood did so.

---

[36] See Nathaniel Hawthorne, *The Scarlet Letter* (New York: Barnes and Noble Classics, 2003). Hester Prynne remains colonial New England's best known committer of sexual misconduct, despite the fact that her punishment and post-conviction experiences were highly atypical.

[37] Anna Clark, *Desire: A History of European Sexuality*, 6. David Konig also notes that the early modern courtroom "made a positive contribution to local stability by facilitating an offender's reintegration into society." Konig, *Law and Society in Puritan Massachusetts: Essex County, 1629–1692* (Chapel Hill: University of North Carolina Press, 1979), 124.

[38] See A.G. Roeber, *Faithful Magistrates and Republican Lawyers: Creators of Virginia Legal Culture, 1680–1810* (Chapel Hill: The University of North Carolina Press, 1981) and Robert Blair St George, "Massacred Language: Courtroom Performance in Eighteenth-Century Boston," in *Possible Pasts, Becoming Colonial in Early America*, Robert Blair St George, ed. (Ithaca: Cornell University Press, 2000), 327–56.

Limitations of the Documentary Record

Any study of seventeenth- and eighteenth-century court records must take into consideration their limitations as well as their benefits. While they are crowded, densely vivid pictures of colonial life, they also provide only blurred periscopes to the past. For every conviction, the question always remains: how many other colonists were equally guilty, just more fortunate? Then there is the matter of surviving information. While I had 1,843 sexual misconduct charges from my three jurisdictions, only 199 of these charges had any form of documentation beyond a bare listing of conviction and punishment.[39] Furthermore, while some of these cases provide full depositions, others only offer summary descriptions in the court record books. Survival rates for 300-year-old documents are never good, particularly when they typically exist on small, crumbling bits of paper. In addition to the normal wear and tear of absentminded stewardship, there is no telling how much selective editing occurred. Some editing may have been for political reasons, some for more personal ones, be it protecting an ancestor's good name or treasuring a document with a family member's signature. Regardless of circumstances, there is no way of tracking these alterations from a distance of 300 years.

It seems more likely that detailed documentation never existed as producing formal legal documentation on paper was an expensive business. Early modern defendants were required to pay for all court costs, including obtaining depositions and the labor of the jury, regardless of whether or not they were acquitted. Consequently, a well-documented bastardy or paternity trial was an expensive luxury rather than a necessity. If conviction was certain, there was no need to add to court fees by paying for deponents to further prove the point. Thus, colonists who paid for fully documented trials gambled that either truth or deponents willing to perjure themselves would save their honor and their purses. In addition, criminal accusations were traditionally followed by a confession before the local justice of the peace. When possible, this was done before a justice with whom the defendant shared some familial or social connection.

The trial records rarely note these familial connections, suggesting they were originally composed in much the same way as cookery books in the early modern period, namely the assumption that cooks were so familiar with the method under discussion that there was no reason to write it down.[40] Likewise,

---

[39] See Appendix C for more information on the Preservation and Publication of Colonial New England Legal Sources and Appendix D for a list of all Colonial Court Systems in Massachusetts, Maine, and Rhode Island.

[40] See Maggie Black, *A Taste of History: 10,000 Years of Food in Britain* (London: British Museum Press, 1993) and Keith Stavely and Kathleen Fitzgerald, *America's Founding Food: The*

justices deciding trials and the clerks documenting them saw no reason to record information familiar to all concerned. Local experience and oral and written legal traditions flowed freely from one to the other and intertwined without comment.[41] Nevertheless, this information is crucial for understanding the workings of colonial court decisions. An acquitted defendant whose family and friends provided the depositions suggests a defendant who may not have been wholly innocent but whom the justices decided, for whatever reasons, to acquit.

Like all court trials, sexual misconduct trials did not take place in a vacuum. They were equally shaped by their participants, justices, litigants, witnesses, and juries alike. Modern historians fill in these gaps with the traditional sources for social history: probates, tax lists, vital records, town histories, and surviving family papers. Genealogies are another invaluable source when deciphering colonial New England's tangled interfamilial relationships, though they come with blind spots of their own. Usually written by family members, most New England genealogies were created in the midst of the colonial revival of the late nineteenth and early twentieth centuries. In the effort to glorify their families, their authors range from coy hints to sweeping deletions of unpleasant facts and the only genealogists who mention their ancestors' presence in sexual misconduct trials published their work relatively recently.[42] Nevertheless, the genealogies and the court records remain closely linked, with one informing the other. The genealogists mined the court records for information about their ancestors but their writing now fills the gaps between the court transcripts.

Additional Source Material

Understanding when and how New England's political and legal leaders diverged from the laws used in England to govern sexual misconduct required some point of reference and I used three legal treatises to help with this process: Michael Dalton's *The Countrey Justice*, Edward Coke's *The Institutes of the Lawes of England*, and *The Lawes Resolutions of Womens Rights*.[43] English legal writer

Story of New England Cooking (Chapel Hill: University of North Carolina Press, 2004).

[41] See Kamensky, *Governing the Tongue* for further discussion of the intersections of verbal and written speech in colonial New England.

[42] See Byron Bucke, *Isaac. Buck of Scituate, Plymouth Colony, and Some of his Descendants, Generations 1–5* (Hightstown: B. Buck, 1998).

[43] Holly Brewer also used these three treatises to examine changing domestic laws in the North American colonies. See Brewer, "The Transformation of Domestic Law," *The Cambridge History of Law in America*, 288–323.

Michael Dalton was born in Cambridgeshire in 1564 and studied at Trinity College at the University of Cambridge in the 1580s, though the exact nature of his legal career is unclear. He probably had a chamber at Lincoln's Inn, one of London's four Inns of Court, without formally becoming a member of the organization. Dalton published the first edition of his *The Countrey Justice, Containing the Practice of the Justices of the Peace out of their Sessions, Gathered for the better helpe of such Justices of Peace as have not been much conversant in the studie of the Lawes of this Realme*, hereafter *The Countrey Justice*, in 1618. He then oversaw two more editions in 1619 and 1630 before his death in 1648, as well as publishing another legal treatise titled *Officium Vicecomitum, or the Office and Authoritie of Sheriffs* in 1623.[44]

Barbara Shapiro describes *The Countrey Justice* as "the most influential and widely distributed handbook of the seventeenth century in both England and the American colonies" and similar statements appear in nearly every other legal history of early modern England and its colonies.[45] Colonial leaders in both Massachusetts and Rhode Island ordered copies of *The Countrey Justice* when preparing to write or rewrite their legal codes in the late 1640s and copies most likely existed in Maine as well. Another benefit of using *The Countrey Justice* was its many editions. Law evolved in both the colonies and in England during the seventeenth and eighteenth centuries and the later editions document changes in the ways in which sexual misconduct was being tried in the English common law courts.[46]

---

44 James McMullen Rigg, "Michael Dalton," *Dictionary of National Biography*, Volume 13 (London: Smith, Elder & Co. 1885–1900).

45 Barbara Shapiro, *"Beyond Reasonable Doubt" and "Probable Cause": Historical Perspectives on the Anglo-American Law of Evidence* (Berkeley: University of California Press, 1991), 131. For further documentation on the use of Michael Dalton's *The Countrey Justice* in Massachusetts, the Province of Maine, and Rhode Island, see Smith and Barnes, *The English Legal System*, Herbert A. Johnson, *Imported Eighteenth-Century Law Treatises in American Libraries, 1700–1799* (Knoxville: University of Tennessee Press, 1978), Konig, *Law and Society in Puritan Massachusetts*, Eckert, *The Gentleman of the Profession*, Edgar J. McManus, *Law and Liberty in Early New England: Criminal Justice and Due Process, 1620–1692* (Amherst: University of Massachusetts Press, 1993), Patrick T. Conley, *Liberty and Justice: A History of Law and Lawyers in Rhode Island, 1636–1998* (East Providence: Rhode Island Publications Society, 1998), Bilder, *The Transatlantic Constitution*, Hugh Amory, "Printing and Bookselling in New England, 1638–1713," in *A History of the Book in America,* Volume I, Hugh Amory and David D. Hall, eds (Chapel Hill: University of Carolina Press, 2007) and Thomas Garden Barnes, *Shaping the Common Law: From Glanvill to Hale, 1688* (Redwood City: Stanford University Press, 2008).

46 See Michael Dalton, *The Countrey Justice, Conteyning the practise of the Justices of the Peace out of their Sessions, Gathered for the better helpe of such Justices of Peace as have not beene much conversant in the studie of the Lawes of this Realme* (Clark: The Lawbook Exchange, Ltd, 2004. Original edition, London: Societie of Stationers, 1618), Dalton, *The Countrey Justice* (New York:

Edward Coke was born in 1552 and became one of England's foremost justices and legal writers for much of the sixteenth and seventeenth centuries.[47] Coke's *The Institutes of the Lawes of England*, a four-volume collection of legal treatises, was published between 1628 and 1644. The first volume, *The First Part of the Institutes of the Laws of England, or, a Commentary upon Littleton*, was among the law books ordered by Massachusetts leaders in 1647 when they were preparing to write their second legal code, *The Book of the General Lawes and Liberties concerning the Inhabitants of the Massachusetts*, hereafter *The Lawes and Liberties*. Roger Williams's early years as Coke's protégé and clerk in England also suggest that Coke's ideas profoundly influenced Rhode Island's *Proceedings of the First General Assembly of 'The Incorporation of Providence Plantations' and The Code of Laws*, hereafter *The Code of Laws* in 1648. It does, however, seem unlikely that Edward Coke's writings were consulted when creating sexual misconduct laws in New England as Coke's *Third Institutes*, the volume of the Institutes addressing criminal law, was more concerned with felonies than misdemeanors, which is how most early modern sexual misconduct charges were classified.[48]

The third source considered for comparing law in England and law in New England was *The Lawes Resolutions of Womens Rights, or, The Lawes Provision for Woemen: a Methodicall Collection of Such Statutes and Customes, with the Cases, Opinions, Arguments, and Points of Learning in the Law, as doe properly concerne Women*, hereafter *The Lawes Resolutions*, which was first published in 1632.[49] T.E., the author of *The Lawes Resolutions of Womens Rights*, intended his text to guide women from their initial societal positions as unmarried girls to marriage and finally widowhood.[50] His advice focused particularly on the ways in which English property law affected women, though he does comment on sexual crime and sexual misconduct. Quoting St Paul, T.E. points out that "to avoid fornication every man have his owne wife, and every woman her own husband." T.E. later describes forced sexual intercourse as "a hideous hatefull kinde of whoredome in him which committeth it, when a woman is enforced violently to sustaine the furie of brutish concupiscence," though he distinguishes

The Legal Classics Library, Division of Gryphon Editions. Original edition, London: Company of Stationers, 1655) and Dalton, *The Countrey Justice* (Provo: Repressed Publishing Company, 2012. Original edition: London: Printed by Henry Lintot, 1746).

47 See Allen D. Boyer, *Sir Edward Coke and the Elizabethan Age* (Stanford: Stanford University Press, 2003).

48 Barnes, *Shaping the Common Law*, 147–8.

49 T.E., *The Lawes Resolutions of Womens Rights*.

50 Holly Brewer speculates that T.E. was "probably Thomas Edgar, a member of the Inns of Court ... in 1649, his views were radical, suggestive of both his religious impulses and political principles [as a Puritan]." Brewer, "The Transformation of Domestic Law," 309.

between the act of ravishment, forced sexual intercourse in which the woman was allowed to remain in her home, and the act of rape as forced sexual intercourse in which the woman was abducted.[51] *The Lawes Resolutions* was intended as more of an advice manual than a law book and I found it more useful for providing historical context than direct legal comparisons.[52]

Structure and Organization

Chapters 1 and 2 both provide historical context for the sexual misconduct trials discussed throughout this study. Massachusetts Bay, the Province of Maine, and Rhode Island were all established in the 1620s and 1630s and Chapter 2 provides their respective histories from founding to the mid-eighteenth century, including the creation of legal codes in both Massachusetts Bay and Rhode Island Colonies and the sexual misconduct laws laid out in both these legal codes. Chapter 2 provides background information on the establishment of the English common law, ecclesiastical, chancery, and prerogative courts as well as a history of sexual misconduct prosecution from the 1570s to the mid-eighteenth century. It concludes by examining the impact of the Scientific Revolution and the Enlightenment on the legal process in England and in New England.

While most sexual misconduct laws created in New England came directly from English law and custom, both the New England colonies and the other English colonies in North America created additional laws to address the possibility of interracial sexual contact. Chapter 3 considers these laws as well as the wider connotations and complications posed by conducting English style sexual misconduct trials in North America.

The most common types of sexual misconduct trials conducted in both England and in New England were fornication before marriage, bastardy, and paternity charges. Chapters 4, 5 and 6 consider these trials from three perspectives, each documenting a specific change which occurred over time and between the three jurisdictions. The New England colonies all initially focused on the moral implications of sexual intercourse outside the marriage bed and their first legal codes specify fornication charges without mentioning financial support for illegitimate children, a consideration which had been part of English common law since 1574. Chapter 4 documents how rising numbers

51 T.E., *The Lawes Resolutions of Womens Rights*, 376.

52 Mary Sarah Bilder notes that "the sections on women [in the Rhode Island legal code created in 1648] resemble sections in [the] *Lawes Resolutions*." Bilder, *The Transatlantic Constitution*, 53.

of illegitimate children in the late seventeenth century led to bastardy and paternity trials which charged women for the moral crime of illicit sex while expecting men convicted on paternity charges to provide financial support for their children in all three jurisdictions.

Massachusetts, Maine, and Rhode Island initially had very different ideas about the roles that justices and attorneys should play in their court rooms. Massachusetts created laws barring paid legal counsel in the court room but Maine and Rhode Island both encouraged defendants to seek out attorneys when preparing their legal defenses. Chapter 5 examines how sexual misconduct trials in Massachusetts were transformed by the admission of attorneys in the early eighteenth century, while also looking at the legal defenses launched by attorneys in both Maine and Rhode Island.

The Anglo-American world changed in the eighteenth century as political and legal leaders and ordinary colonists alike increasingly came to value privacy and individualism over the communally driven nature of the traditional sexual misconduct trial. Chapter 6 examines the transition from sexual misconduct prosecutions in the public court room to the privacy of a justice's chambers and from the public humiliation of a whipping in the town square to a quietly paid fine, while also considering the increasing impact that both gender and class had on the sexual misconduct trial process.

The evolving prosecution of sexual misconduct in Massachusetts, Maine, and Rhode Island opens a window onto shifting priorities and values in the New England colonies throughout the colonial period. If the early sexual misconduct trials highlight initial colonial differences, the mid-eighteenth-century trials demonstrate convergences among the English colonies, including a growing understanding of racial and gender differences, a new emphasis on the economic dimensions of illicit sex, the rise of a professional class of attorneys, and a greater interest in both privacy and individualism. These changes occurred throughout the Anglo-American world and were the result of parliamentary and royal directives and colonial leaders' decisions alike. While these influences can be traced throughout New England's sexual misconduct trials, the voices of ordinary colonists pleading their cases and commenting on their neighbors should also be considered an important part of this much wider process.

Chapter 1

Founding Law in Massachusetts Bay, Maine and Rhode Island

Similar to other early modern European colonization efforts, successful colonization in New England came from years of trial and error. The English colony at Plymouth in 1620 was followed with other permanent settlements in Massachusetts, Maine, and Rhode Island by the early 1630s. Legal systems reflecting each colony's own distinct needs, interests, and relationship with English law emerged soon after the initial settlement period.[1] First and foremost, law was used to support the challenges of creating English societies in unfamiliar landscapes, though this desire was not always shared by all colonists. On a wider scale, colonial leaders wanted law to convey their visions for their own particular colonies. Some North American colonies were founded solely for financial gain, while others came into existence for religious and political reasons as well as economic ones. These intentions profoundly shaped individual colonies' relationships with England and with English law, and this chapter examines the shifting nature of those relationships.

Early Settlement in Massachusetts Bay Colony

The roots for English settlement in Massachusetts Bay Colony dated back to the 1550s when Protestants fleeing persecution during Mary Tudor's reign settled in Geneva, Switzerland. Their interactions with John Calvin in Geneva led to the creation of the British Puritan, Separatist, and Presbyterian churches. King Charles I responded to growing numbers of Parliament members who identified themselves as Puritans by dissolving Parliament in 1626 and permanently in 1629. By that time, Separatist colonists had already established Plymouth Colony in North America and a group of Puritans were establishing plans for

[1] See Appendix C for more information on the Preservation and Publication of Colonial New England Legal Sources and Appendix D for a list of all Colonial Court Systems in Massachusetts, Maine, and Rhode Island.

a neighboring colony. Concerned about the legality of conflicting land claims given to North American settlements in the 1620s, John Winthrop and other Puritan leaders negotiated for a charter for their colony, which was granted by Charles I on March 4, 1629. Unlike most colonial charters, the Massachusetts Bay charter did not require that the annual stockholder meeting reviewing all legal and political decisions made by colony leaders be held in England, which gave Massachusetts an unusual degree of autonomy.[2]

A total of 700 men, women, and children sailed to North America on 11 ships in April of 1630. Their numbers were soon swelled by the 20,000 more colonists who moved to southern New England in the population movement known as the Great Migration. These were largely successful years for Massachusetts as the colony rapidly outdistanced earlier Plymouth Colony and remained more powerful than newly formed colonies in Connecticut and Rhode Island. Colony political and religious leaders emphasized the importance of family, community, and covenant and Massachusetts colonists largely agreed with this emphasis.

Creating a Legal System in Massachusetts

Massachusetts was the first New England colony to establish a formal legal system, with the colony's "Greate and Generall Court" organized in Boston within weeks of arriving in North America in the summer of 1630.[3] Colony leaders decided in 1634 that each town could send two deputies to serve on the General Court. The colony was further divided in 1635 into Suffolk, Middlesex, and Essex counties in order to provide a more localized legal system.[4] The county courts were authorized to address most charges, including sexual misconduct, public drunkenness, avoiding church on Sunday, and theft. Appeals and crimes with the possibility of capital punishment, such as murder, treason, rape, incest, and adultery, were tried in Boston. A 1644 decision divided the General Court in two

2 Scott Douglas Gerber, *A Distinct Judicial Power: The Origins of an Independent Judiciary, 1606–1787* (New York: Oxford University Press, 2011), 74.

3 Plymouth Colony's governor and Assistants were authorized to address legal issues on a case by case basis as they arose during the first 13 years of the colony's existence and Plymouth did not create a formal court system until 1633. See D.C. Parnes, *Plymouth and the Common Law, 1620–1775* (Kingston: Pilgrim Publishers, 1971). For Massachusetts Bay, see George Lee Haskins, *Law and Authority in Early Massachusetts, A Study in Tradition and Design* (New York: MacMillan Company, 1960) and William Nelson, *The Common Law in Colonial America: The Chesapeake and New England, 1607–1660*, Volume 1 (New York: Oxford University Press, 2008).

4 Political organization in the six New England states remains organized around the individual states and their towns, with the state and the counties providing court systems.

houses, with the Governor and his Assistants serving in one house and deputies from the towns serving in the other. While the Court of Assistants had the final say on judicial matters, all proposed laws had to be approved by both houses.

Early English settlement in Essex County centered on Salem where the deep harbor made fishing a natural choice for most settlers, though it may have hinted to some of the trade networks that would later connect the town with the rest of the world. The first villages beyond Salem followed the shore line north to Newbury. As the coastal towns burst at the seams, they were followed by inland settlements whose inhabitants cleared trees and planted fields while pushing ever westward. The first Essex County court met in Salem in 1636, with additional sessions added five years later in Ipswich. The court followed the seasons in its migrations around the county, meeting in Salem in the winter and summer and in Ipswich in the spring and fall. Defendants were allowed to delay trial to attend court at the nearest geographic session if they could prove that travel posed an undue hardship and this permission was usually granted.

Creating a Massachusetts Legal Code

Massachusetts Bay Colony functioned without a concrete legal code during the 1630s. Crimes were handled on a case by case basis and justices endeavored to create punishments suitable to both the offense and the situation. Colonists began demanding a formal legal code with clearly stated consequences for clearly stated crimes in the mid-1630s. Governor John Winthrop argued against the creation of a legal code for a variety of reasons. The wording of the Massachusetts Bay Charter had given the colony more leeway than other English colonies but Winthrop worried their charter might be revoked if Charles I objected to any laws created by the colony. As long as Massachusetts laws remained unwritten, Charles I could only receive easily refuted word-of-mouth reports on the colony's legal system. By contrast, a published legal code would provide easy documentation for a king interested in the doings of a Puritan colony.[5] Winthrop also believed a legal code would actually lead to harsher punishments for defendants as justices would be required to make rulings based on the law rather than the immediate circumstances surrounding a particular case. While this may have been the case, John Philip Reid argues that ordinary colonists believed that being "under the rule-of-law of harsh or unfair

[5] Edgar J. McManus, *Law and Liberty in Early New England: Criminal Justice and Due Process, 1620–1692* (Amherst: University of Massachusetts Press, 1993), 6.

sanctions was preferable to rulelessness."[6] Their concerns about "rulelessness" most likely stemmed from wider apprehensions about the growing use of the Star Chamber home in England, though it may also reflect concerns about the power possessed by their own leaders.

John Winthrop was eventually overruled and minister John Cotton created Massachusetts' first attempt at legal codification in 1636. Titled either "a modell of the Judiciall lawes of Moses" or "a model of Moses his judicials," Cotton's legal code was based almost entirely on Moses's rules for the Israelites. It was swiftly rejected by Massachusetts leaders as being too rigid and too brief, though elements of Cotton's ideas do appear in later Massachusetts legal codes. Two years later, minister Nathaniel Ward proposed a second legal code which was circulated to Massachusetts towns for comment, revised by the General Court and provisionally adopted in 1641 as *The Body of Liberties*, although it only ever existed in manuscript form.[7]

The Body of Liberties was determined to be incomplete and insufficient and additional revisions and expansions began in the mid-1640s. Massachusetts leaders ordered two copies each of Michael Dalton's *The Countrey Justice*, Sir Edward Coke's *Commentary upon Littleton*, Coke's *Reports*, a book titled the *Book of Entries*, which was either Coke's *Entries* or William Rastell's *Collection of Entries*, and a book titled *New Terms*, which was probably a popular law dictionary written by Rastell. These efforts produced the 1648 legal code titled *The Book of the General Lawes and Liberties concerning the Inhabitants of the Massachusetts*, which was officially authorized by the General Court on March 14, 1648. Eager to get word of their accomplishments in the hands of anxious colonists, colony leaders arranged for 600 copies to be printed on the colony's press in Cambridge, 50 of which were given to magistrates and deputies and the remaining copies sold at Hezekiah Usher's bookshop in Boston at three shillings per copy.[8] Variations on *The Laws and Liberties* continued to be used in the colony until 1692.[9]

---

6 John Philip Reid, *Rule of Law: The Jurisprudence of Liberty in the Seventeenth and Eighteenth Centuries* (DeKalb: Northern Illinois University Press, 2004), 50.

7 Richard Dunn, "Introduction," in *The Laws and Liberties of Massachusetts, Reprinted from the Copy of the 1648 edition in the Henry E. Huntington Library* (San Marino: The Henry E. Huntington Library and Art Gallery, 1998), vi.

8 Dunn, "Introduction," v. While most legal scholars find the *Body of Liberties* little more than a bill of rights and find *The Laws and Liberties* the more important text, Thomas Barnes argues that the *Body of Liberties* "was a structured, rational, moderate, and compelling articulation of human rights. It was truly a code, Ward the great codifier." Thomas Barnes, "Law and Liberty (and Order) in Early Massachusetts," in Joseph Smith and Thomas Barnes, *The English Legal System: Carryover to the Colonies* (Los Angeles: University of California Press, 1975).

9 Daniel Coquilette refers to the initial period between 1620 and 1648 as the "Early period," while the years between 1649 and 1691 were the Intercharter period and the years

The Laws and Liberties was influenced by the Bible but Edgar J. McManus argues that it was "much more than just a Puritan restatement of Scripture. Care was taken to safeguard and improve upon rights guaranteed by English law."[10] Bradley Chapin estimates that approximately 38.8 percent of all the laws found in *The Laws and Liberties* came from the Bible, while 41.2 percent came from English law and the remaining 20 percent reflected immediate legal needs which had presented themselves on the ground in North America.[11] A core element of *The Laws and Liberties* was the decision to tie suffrage to sex, economic class, *and* religion and only white freemen who were fully vested members in the Puritan Church were allowed to vote.

The most likely English source for the criminal laws in *The Laws and Liberties* was Michael Dalton's *The Countrey Justice* as it was the only law book ordered from England to address criminal law at any length. The books ordered to help with writing *The Laws and Liberties* did not include Edward Coke's *Third Institutes*, which focuses on criminal law, and the legal dictionaries would have provided terminology rather than statutes.[12] Thomas Barnes notes that "Michael Dalton ... took a new lease on life in New England. In a word, he was part of the reception of the common law."[13] Dalton's influence can also be seen in the organization of *The Laws and Liberties*, which, like *The Countrey Justice*, is arranged in alphabetical order and includes copies of necessary legal forms such as warrants and recognizances at the back to aid justices without formal legal training. Another influence from Dalton was the emphasis on the Justice of the Peace as first responders to legal infractions. David Konig argues that Puritans recognized "the role of the justice of the peace, for it, above all other legal institutions ... demonstrated a power and a flexibility lacking in the others."[14] Similar to the English justices whom *The Countrey Justice* was intended for, most Massachusetts men who became justices had little formal training in

from 1692 to 1760 were the "Second Charter Period," a demarcation recognizing the changes in Massachusetts law occurring between these three periods. See Coquilette, "Introduction," in *Law in Colonial Massachusetts, 1630–1800*, Daniel Coquilette, ed. (Boston: The Colonial Society of Massachusetts, distributed by the University Press of Virginia, 1984), xxiii.

10 McManus, *Law and Liberty in Early New England*, 11.

11 Bradley Chapin, *Criminal Justice in Colonial America, 1606–1660* (Athens: University of Georgia Press, 1983), 5.

12 See Thomas Garden Barnes, *Shaping the Common Law: From Glanvill to Hale, 1688* (Redwood City: Stanford University Press, 2008) for more information about Coke's *Third Institutes*.

13 Barnes, *Shaping the Common Law*, 7.

14 David Konig, *Law and Society in Puritan Massachusetts: Essex County, 1629–1692* (Chapel Hill: University of North Carolina Press, 1979), 5.

the law. Instead, they acquired their positions through their socio-economic connections, brushed up on their legal reading, and relied heavily on both their own instincts and knowledge of the communities around them.[15]

Sexual Misconduct Law in Massachusetts

Where *The Countrey Justice*, *The Body of Liberties*, and *The Laws and Liberties* truly differ is on the topic of sexual misconduct. Punishments for rape, sodomy, and bestiality consistently appear in all three law books. There are no fornication laws in *The Countrey Justice*, which probably reflects the fact that fornication was traditionally tried in England's ecclesiastical courts, though this briefly changed in the 1650s. By contrast, all editions of *The Countrey Justice* specify the penalties for anyone who conceived children out of wedlock. *The Body of Liberties* does not mention fornication, *The Laws and Liberties* states that "if any man shall commit fornication with any single woman, they shall be punished either by enjoyning to Marriage, or Fine, or corporall punishment, or all or any of these as the Judges in the courts of Assistants shall appoint most agreeable to the word of God."[16] There are, however, no laws regarding the support of illegitimate children to be found anywhere in either *The Body of Liberties* or the original edition of *The Laws and Liberties*, which suggests that bastard children simply did not pose the same problems in Massachusetts in 1648 that they did in mid-seventeenth-century England.

The colony's initial success evaporated in the 1660s as Massachusetts Bay increasingly saw itself as a colony besieged by "drought, crop blights, cold, and catastrophes."[17] Growing warfare with Native Americans destabilized Massachusetts society, as did the pressures created by a growing population and shrinking land stocks, not to mention rising numbers of illegitimate children who needed to be fed and clothed. These concerns resulted in a 1668 addition to *The Lawes and Liberties* stipulating how couples who conceived children out

---

15 George Haskins, "Lay Judges: Magistrates and Justices in Early Massachusetts," in *Law in Colonial Massachusetts, 1630–1800*, 39–56. Cynthia Herrup also notes that rural seventeenth-century justices in England functioned in much the same way: "Local standing, not legal expertise, qualified men as justices. The charge was the maintenance of quiet rather than simply the punishment of criminals." Herrup, *The Common Peace: Participation and the Criminal Law in Seventeenth-Century England* (Cambridge: Cambridge University Press, 1987), 43.

16 *The Laws and Liberties of Massachusetts*, 23.

17 Joseph Conforti, *Saints and Strangers: New England in British North America* (Baltimore: The John Hopkins University Press, 2006), 101.

of wedlock would be identified, punished, and required to pay child support.[18] Another challenge facing Massachusetts was growing control from England as the Stuarts both returned to the English throne and stabilized their power in the years following the English Civil War. In time, these elements fused together to create a colony perhaps better equipped to handle the challenges posed by a rapidly maturing society than the community-oriented colony created in Massachusetts Bay's early years, though most Puritan leaders saw their immediate future as profoundly bleak in the last decades of the seventeenth century.

Political Change in Massachusetts

The first English colonies were either chartered colonies like Massachusetts, with a charter authorizing their right to largely govern themselves, or proprietorships like Maine, where a single proprietor had the right to govern his colony as he saw fit. Both types of colonies benefited equally from the benign neglect which characterized English colonization for much of the seventeenth century. However, Charles II and James II both wanted their North American colonies under direct crown rule in the late seventeenth century. They hoped to bring down the costs of colonial administration by governing them as groups rather than as individual colonies and they also wanted better trade regulation to counter Dutch trade interests. Most English colonies had significant trade networks with each other and with other European countries by the mid-seventeenth century and these activities were curtailed by the introduction of the Navigation Acts in the 1660s, which were protested across Massachusetts. Charles II retaliated in 1684 by annulling Massachusetts Bay's charter and the charter remained non-existent when James II became king in 1685.[19]

James II promptly dissolved the individual colonies of Massachusetts Bay, Plymouth, Connecticut, New Hampshire, and Rhode Island and renamed them the Dominion of New England in 1686 (New York and East and West Jersey colonies were added to the Dominion two years later). The plan was to use the Dominion to increase trade regulations, reform land title practices, coordinate

---

18 "Several Laws and Orders Made at the General Court, Held at Boston in New England, October 14, 1668," in *The Colonial Laws of Massachusetts, Reprinted from the Edition of 1660, With the Supplements to 1672, Containing Also, The Body of Liberties of 1641*, William Whitmore, ed. (Boston: Rockwell & Churchill City Printers, 1889), 55.

19 See Daniel Richter, *Before the Revolution: America's Ancient Pasts* (Cambridge: Harvard University Press, 2011) and Owen Stanwood, *The Empire Reformed: English America in the Age of the Glorious Revolution* (Philadelphia: University of Pennsylvania Press, 2011).

defense systems, and expand religious freedom by mandating the acceptance of the Anglican Church in Puritan colonies. Massachusetts-born Joseph Dudley was initially chosen as the Dominion's leader but he was quickly replaced by crown appointee Edmund Andros, who also wanted to reform the Massachusetts court system.[20] Andros made himself and his council the ultimate judicial power in the colony, while also creating a lower court system which included Inferior Courts of Common Pleas and Quarter Sessions, a Chancery court, and a Probate court. There was discussion of creating an Admiralty court, but this did not happen during the years of the Dominion of New England. Finally, Andros created the first court appointed attorneys in Massachusetts, a major legal transition for a colony who had openly opposed the introduction of paid legal counsel for much of the seventeenth century.[21]

The short-lived Dominion of New England was extremely unpopular in New England and Edmund Andros was arrested in Boston in 1689 when news of the Glorious Revolution reached North America. The newly crowned William and Mary issued a second charter in 1691 which combined Massachusetts Bay and Plymouth Colonies into a single royal colony known as the "Province of Massachusetts Bay in New England." The new charter returned Massachusetts' individual political identity but also brought further changes to the colony. For the first time in Massachusetts history, religion was removed from the standards used to decide voting eligibility, which rendered almost three-quarters of the adult white male population eligible to vote rather than the 20 percent eligible under the first charter. The positions of Governor, Lieutenant Governor, and judges were transformed into crown-appointed officials, while the colony legislature remained a locally elected body who chose the members of the Governor's Council. Over time, greater emphasis was placed on Massachusetts Bay as a commercial entity than a socio-religious experiment, though it should be remembered that even the most godly of colonies had to turn a profit to survive in the seventeenth century.

Legal Changes in Massachusetts

Another element of the new charter was the creation of a Superior Court of Judicature with appellate jurisdiction over all other courts in the colony.[22] Similar

---

20 See Viola Florence Barnes, *The Dominion of New England: a Study in British Colonial Policy* (New York: F. Ungar Publishing Company, 1960).

21 See Richard Scott Eckert, *The Gentleman of the Profession: The Emergence of Lawyers in Massachusetts, 1630–1810* (New York: Garland Publishing, Inc., 1991).

22 Gerber, *A Distinct Judicial Power*, 78–9.

to the court system during the Dominion of New England years, the county courts were divided in two with a Court of Common Pleas for civil cases and a Court of General Sessions for criminal cases. The new court system established in 1692 also added a third Essex County court in Newbury to the ones previously established in Salem and Ipswich. Similar to its earlier patterns, the Essex court continued to follow the seasons in its migrations around the county, meeting in Salem in winter and summer, Ipswich in the spring and Newbury in the fall. A new legal code titled *The Acts and Resolves, Public and Private, of the Province of the Massachusetts Bay* was created in 1692 and published by printers Benjamin Harris in 1692 and Michael Perry in 1699.[23] While many laws changed with the new code, the wording for the law addressing fornication and bastardy was unchanged from the 1668 amendment to *The Lawes and Liberties*.[24]

There are decided similarities between the court system created by the Dominion of New England and the court system created under the second Massachusetts Bay charter. John Murrin notes that "the General Court adopted practically the entire court system of the hated Dominion ... in a very real sense, the ghost of Sir Edmund Andros triumphed where the man himself had failed."[25] This development most likely reflects the growing interests of the English crown and the waning power of the Puritan Church as a political institution by the end of the seventeenth century as it was no longer possible for Puritan dissenters to maintain their own separate legal code. However, the acceptance of the new political, legal, and social order also reflected the interests and desires of Massachusetts Bay residents at the turn of the eighteenth century, including the rise of laws pertaining to illegitimate children, and this will be explored in greater depth in future chapters.

Early Settlement in the Province of Maine

The founding of Massachusetts Bay Colony is easily traced. The *Arbella* and the other ships carrying the Puritan colonists arrived on a given day in the summer of 1630. There is no fixed starting point for the Province of Maine, though European interests in the region date back to the sixteenth century and possibly

---

23 Eckert, *The Gentleman of the Profession*, 69–73.

24 See *The Acts and Resolves, Public and Private, of the Province of the Massachusetts Bay* (Boston: Wright and Potter, Printers to the State, 1869), 52.

25 John Murrin, "The Legal Transformation: The Bench and Bar of Eighteenth-Century Massachusetts," in *Colonial America: Essays in Politics and Social Development*, Stanley N. Katz and John M. Murrin, eds (New York: Alfred A. Knopf, 1983), 95.

earlier. Early descriptions of the Maine coast often read like modern-day tourism brochures. Italian explorer Giovanni Verrazano's 1534 log depicted the islands of Penobscot Bay as "lying all near the land, being small and pleasant to the view, high, and having many turnings and windings between them, making many fair harbors and channels."[26] Such accounts soon caught the attention of potential colony backers in England. Threatened by Spanish wealth from the Caribbean, Mesoamerica and South America, English politicians and merchants wanted their own chance at colonization in the Americas.

The 1602 voyage of the *Archangell* under Captain George Weymouth brought naturalist James Rosier along to describe and track the voyage. Like Giovanni Verrazano before him, Rosier was enchanted with the Maine coast.[27] Plans for English settlement in Maine first took hold with the creation of a colony in 1607 at the mouth of the Kennebec River, under the direction of George Popham and Raleigh Gilbert. Unfortunately, settlement in Maine proved more than they had bargained for. After a frigid winter, largely failed efforts to trade with the Abenaki, Popham's death in Maine, and the death of Gilbert's brother in England, the Popham colonists decided to abandon the colony and sail home to England.[28]

The experiences of the early Maine explorers and the failed Popham settlement set the stage for the challenges that would shape Maine colonization for generations. All too often, the reality of Maine belied its image. On paper or from the deck of a ship in the summer months, Maine looked ideal for early settlement. It had the deep rivers, thick furs, and tall pines necessary for trade, not to mention ample fish stocks. As Maine was located at the same latitude as Spain, the English assumed the climate would be warmer than England's, not realizing that the more northerly British Isles were warmed by the Gulf Stream.

These same gaps between image and reality were heightened in 1621 when Ferdinando Gorges was granted a royal charter for lands in Maine by Charles I. Gorges was given virtual control in North America, including the right to grant smaller land holdings and the right to "make, ordaine, and establish all Manner of Orders, Laws, Directions, Instructions, Forms, and Cermonies of

---

26 Giovanni Verrazano's log, in Samuel Eliot Morison, *The European Discovery of America, the Northern Voyages* (New York: Oxford University Press, 1971), 310.

27 David C. Morey, *The Voyage of Archangell: James Rosier's Account of the Waymouth Voyage of 1605, a True Relation* (Gardner: Tilbury House Publishers, 2005).

28 Douglas Walthew Rice, *The Life and Achievements of Sir John Popham, 1531–1607: Leading to the Establishment of the First English Colony in New England* (Madison: Fairleigh Dickinson University Press, 2005).

Government and Magistracy."[29] Gorges dreamed of a medieval fiefdom, where his family ruled supreme over the colonists farming their lands. Yet the first permanent Maine settlements emerged from the seasonal fishing camps dotting the coast in the early seventeenth century. Men with little to lose in the way of family or faith came to fish through the summers and sail home before the winter gales. Money could be had but so could a swift death from a sudden wave. Many of these fisherman decided that wintering over in Maine was safer than the trans-Atlantic passage and settlements like the one established on Damariscove Island in the early 1600s were born, a bit rough on the edges but alive. Not surprisingly, many of these colonists disregarded Gorges's feudal ambitions.

Perhaps looking for more malleable subjects, Ferdinando Gorges actively recruited new settlers for Maine in the 1630s. He gave William Bradford and the Plymouth colony land on both sides of the Kennebec River as well as the exclusive right to trade on the river in 1630. Settlers from Plymouth were an active presence in the Kennebec region by the 1640s, forming the New Plymouth Colony. An extensive fishing station established on Richmond Island by merchants Robert Trelawny and Moses Goodyear in the early 1630s was functioning as a quasi-independent entity by the mid-1630s when John Winter, Trelawny's agent, drove George Cleeve and Richard Tucker from the area. Gorges then granted lands between Cape Porpoise and the Kennebec River to Cleeve and to Alexander Rigby in the late 1630s. Their holdings gradually expanded to become a semi-dependent province called Lygonia by the early 1640s.[30] In addition, Gorges encouraged other colonists to join the settlements established around by Maine colonists Richard Vines and Edward Godfrey along the Piscataqua and Saco Rivers. Most of the Gorges's new colonists came from the West Country of England, the Midlands, and the area around London. All of these colonists brought a wide range of religions with them, adding Anglican, Antinomian, and Quaker beliefs to the more orthodox Separatist and Puritan faiths present in southern New England.[31]

---

[29] "The Charter of New England of 1620," in *The Federal and State Constitutions, Colonial Charters, and Other Organic Laws of the United States*, Volume 1, Benjamin Perley Poore, ed. (Washington, DC: US Government Printing Office, 1878), 921–31.

[30] Hannah Farber, "The Rise and Fall of the Province of Lygonia, 1643–1658," *The New England Quarterly* 82, no. 3 (2009): 490–513.

[31] See Emerson Baker, *American Beginnings: Exploration, Culture and Cartography in the Land of Norumbega* (Lincoln: University of Nebraska Press, 1995), John G. Reid, *Acadia, Maine, and New Scotland: Marginal Colonies in the Seventeenth Century* (Toronto: University of Toronto Press, 1981), and Edwin Churchill, "Too Great the Challenge: The Birth and Death of Falmouth, ME, 1624–1676" (PhD diss., University of Maine, 1979).

Another Maine colony emerged on the Pemaquid Peninsula sometime after 1610. Initially a seasonal fishing camp, Pemaquid gradually became a trading colony, trading goods with the French settlements to the east, the English settlements to the west, the various Native American tribal groups living along the Maine coast, and ports in Europe. William Willis writes that Pemaquid "had paved streets, was defended by one of the best forts on the coast (which did them no good), and was surrounded by a respectable and busy population."[32] The colony was subject to frequent attacks during the wars fought in the late seventeenth and eighteenth centuries but thrived nevertheless, supporting anywhere from 300 to 400 settlers.

Concerned that his colony was getting out of hand, Ferdinando Gorges sent his cousin Thomas Gorges to be the Deputy Governor for the Province of Maine in 1640, with firm instructions to establish both a unified government and a unified legal system. Gorges envisioned the settlement of Agamenticus becoming a cathedral city, like the English towns of York or Canterbury, and drew plans for a great cathedral, state buildings, and other such structures. Charles I declared Gorgeana the first incorporated English city in America in 1642. In the end, these plans came to nothing, ended by the realities of English settlement in Maine, rising Puritan power during the English Civil War, and Gorges's death in 1647, which left the Province of Maine without a charter.

Following news of Ferdinando Gorges's death, the southern Maine settlements declared themselves an independent region and elected Edward Godfrey as Governor. With Gorges dead and Oliver Cromwell on the rise in England, Massachusetts Bay Colony hoped to benefit from Maine's furs, fish, and rivers. With Cromwell and Parliament's permission, Massachusetts officials redrew the boundaries of their colony to include New Hampshire and southern Maine in 1650. Charles II's restoration to the English throne in 1660 led to the return of the Province of Maine to Gorges's grandson, Ferdinando Gorges II, in the early 1660s. Unlike his grandfather, Gorges II was uninterested in North American settlement and sold the Provinces of Maine and Lygonia to Massachusetts in the mid-1670s. Massachusetts then reorganized the region as York County, the northernmost Massachusetts County.[33] New Plymouth Colony on the Kennebec remained part of Plymouth Colony until 1692 when

[32] Willis, William, *A History of the Law, the Courts, and the Lawyers of Maine, From its First Colonization to the Early Part of the Present Century* (Portland: Bailey & Noyes Press, 1863), 33.

[33] See Reid, *Acadia, Maine, and New Scotland*, Charles Clark, *The Eastern Frontier, The Settlement of Northern New England, 1610–1763* (Hanover: University Press of New England, 1983) and Jenny Hale Pulsipher, *Subjects unto the Same King: Indians, English, and the Contest for Authority in Colonial New England* (Philadelphia: University of Pennsylvania Press, 2005).

all of Plymouth became part of Massachusetts as part of the second charter. Pemaquid Colony gradually came under Massachusetts control, though it was not considered part of York County. Plymouth Colony attempted to remain an independent colony during negotiations for a new Massachusetts charter in 1692 but there is no evidence that Maine colonists made any effort at this time to break away from Massachusetts, though New Hampshire was able to become permanently independent.

Creating Legal Systems in Maine

Maine's multiple colonies all handled legal infractions differently and made their decisions based on the needs and the political status of the individual colony in question. The initial fishing camps addressed crimes as they occurred, usually by a rough form of justice meted out by camp leaders or the group as a whole.[34] New Plymouth colonists on the Kennebec River were governed under Plymouth law and any crimes they committed were tried in the Plymouth Colony court system.[35] George Cleeve "instituted a Lygonian circuit court [in 1640 which] rotated sessions among the towns of Casco, Black Point and Saco."[36] In addition, he created Commissioners, a Provost Marshall, and other officers to oversee legal proceedings in the colony. Very little is known about law in Pemaquid Colony owing to ongoing attacks from both French colonists and Native Americans, but William Willis argued that "there was need of laws [in Pemaquid Colony], and an efficient administration of them."[37] Recent archeological excavations in Pemaquid found a building believed to be used as a jail which reinforces the argument that Pemaquid Colony had some form of a legal system.

The first attempt to create a formal legal system for the Province of Maine occurred in the late 1630s when Ferdinando Gorges's charter to the colony was renewed by Charles I. The first court held in Maine was the New Somersetshire Province Court in 1636. Gorges sent the colony his first Commission in

---

[34] Clark, *The Eastern Frontier* and Edwin Churchill, "English Beachheads in Seventeenth-Century Maine," in *Maine, The Pine Tree State from Prehistory to Present*, Richard Judd, ed. (Orono: University of Maine Press, 1995), 51–75.

[35] For an example of a New Plymouth Colony crime tried in the Plymouth Colony court system, see the Plymouth Colony General Court trial for Mary Atkins and Thomas Atkins in 1668, in *Records of the Colony of New Plymouth, in New England*, Volumes 3–4, Nathaniel B. Shurtleff, ed. (Boston: W. White Press, 1855–61), 197.

[36] Farber, "The Rise and Fall of the Province of Lygonia," 506.

[37] Willis, *A History of the Law, the Courts, and the Lawyers of Maine*, 30.

1639, which named Thomas Josselin, Richard Vines, Francis Champernone, Henry Josselin, Richard Bonithton, William Hooke, and Edward Godfrey as "Counselors for the due execution of Justice in such manner & forme as by my ordinaunces herunto subscribed is directed" and ordered them to create a General Court for the Province of Maine, with a clerk to keep records.[38]

These efforts were reinforced in 1640 when Thomas Gorges arrived with his instructions to create laws for the colony. He was 22 years old and had just completed two years at the Inns of Court in London. Neal Allen describes Gorges as a "sensitive, thoughtful young man who was certainly concerned not merely with the technicalities of current English practice."[39] Gorges sent multiple letters home to Ferdinando Gorges and his other family members, which provide a vivid picture of the various challenges facing the region. Most Maine colonists had no interest in living in Ferdinando Gorges's envisioned feudal empire and Thomas Gorges's arrival had not reassured them: "it angered John Winter, who referred to 'the boy, Gorges.' It troubled Richard Vines, who had been in Maine so long ... even Edward Godfrey, more trusted by young Gorges than others of the council, could be stubbornly opposed."[40] After three years of struggling with warring factions, Gorges booked himself passage home and went to fight for the Puritan cause during the English Civil War, never to return to Maine.

Thomas Gorges's letters do, however, make clear that he took the task of creating laws for the Province of Maine seriously. Shortly after arriving in Maine, he wrote to his father that "I wish I could had my law books ... for I studdy law and have more and more need to use it then I ever had," a desire reinforced by two later requests for his errant family members to hurry up and send his books.[41] Gorges wrote to Ferdinando Gorges on September 19, 1642 to say that "we sent you our Laws. You may please to add as you see cause & inform wherin we are to amend."[42] Unfortunately, no copy of these laws survives so it is impossible to know what they specifically entailed and whether they were ever implemented, though excerpts from his letters provide some clues regarding his intentions.

---

38 Ferdinando Gorges, "First Commission," in *Province and Court Records of Maine*, Volume 1, Charles Thornton Libby, ed. (Lewiston: Penmor Lithographers, 1991), 30.

39 Neal Allen, "Law and Authority to the Eastward: Maine Courts, Magistrates and Lawyers, 1690–1730," in *Law in Colonial Massachusetts, 1630–1800*, 278.

40 Thomas Gorges, *The Letters of Thomas Gorges, Deputy Governor of the Province of Maine, 1640–1643*, Robert Moody, ed. (Portland: Maine Historical Society, 1978), ix.

41 Gorges, *The Letters of Thomas Gorges*, 22, 23, and 45. No record of what books Thomas owned or whether they ever arrived currently exists.

42 Gorges, *The Letters of Thomas Gorges*, 121.

Thomas Gorges wrote to Richard Bernard on August 21, 1641, that "The Governours of the Bay goe according to the Judiciall Laws of Moses. I would desire your opinion on it, for it neerly concerns me. 'Tis very doubtful to me that we are in all points held to them." Gorges appears unfamiliar with *The Bodies of Liberty* which largely abandoned Mosaic codes and would have been in the process of being created when these letters written. His letter to Bernard on October 9, 1640 included the statement that "for the civill we steared as neere as we could to the course of Ingland."[43] Another letter to Ferdinando Gorges in June of 1642 suggests his familiarity with conditions on the ground in Maine: "We shall not be able to keep our Courts soe often as you speake of, for ... ther will be noe possibilities of travelinge at those times of year, for you must looke uppon us as prisoners from the end of 9ber till the beginning of Aprille, the snow beinge soe deep."[44] Ferdinando Gorges's interest in founding an Anglican cathedral in Georgeana suggests he may also have wanted an ecclesiastical court system, but none of Gorges's letters mention this possibility. Suffrage appears to have been granted to free white men who were property owners. All in all, the Gorges's letters suggest an early Maine legal code rooted in English law but with allowances for local needs.

Ultimately, the Gorges family began a tradition of absentee landlords and local justices which remained in place long past the early seventeenth century. The men who oversaw Maine's courts in the later colonial period were similar to the justices found in Massachusetts, colonists who came to prominence due to their socio-economic positions and whose knowledge of the law was acquired via secondhand sources. They were nearly all from the Wheelwright, Preble, Pepperrell, Frost, Plaisted, and Hammond families who dominated Maine's political and legal systems for decades serving as justices, sheriffs, and clerks.[45] Maine would not regain its political independence until the early 1820s but the records demonstrate that they maintained their domination over Maine's legal system long after the region was absorbed into Massachusetts. Daniel Coquilette describes the colonial Maine legal system as a "remarkably efficient, practical, and surprisingly legalistic," and this efficiency may have led to Massachusetts' decision to leave well enough alone when it came to the running of Maine's courts.[46]

---

[43] Gorges, *The Letters of Thomas Gorges*, 17 and 36.

[44] Gorges, *The Letters of Thomas Gorges*, 114.

[45] See *Maine Province and Court Records*, Volumes. 1–6, Charles Thornton Libby, Robert Moody, and Neal Allen, eds (Portland: Maine Historical Society, 1928–75) for a comprehensive discussion of the judicial activities of the Wheelwright, Preble, Frost, Pepperell, and Hammond families over an 82-year period.

[46] Coquilette, "Introduction," *Law in Colonial Massachusetts, 1630–1800*, xliv.

Sexual Misconduct Law in Maine

Ferdinando Gorges's First and Second Commissions both instructed Maine's Counselors to try colonists for "rapes ... adultryes, incests [and] fornications" and to "inflict such paynes and punishmentes upon any person or persons duly convicted ... as by his Majesties lawes and statutes here in his Majesties realm."[47] The order to try colonists on fornication charges in the colony court rather than an ecclesiastical court probably reflected the lack of such a court system rather than a colonial effort to streamline the judicial process into a single court system. Illegitimate children are not mentioned in the Commissions but the court records make clear that couples who conceived children out of wedlock would be expected to financially support them.

Early Settlement in Rhode Island

The colony of Rhode Island also had multiple beginnings, starting with the settlement created by Roger Williams in 1635. Prior to coming to North America, Williams studied at the University of Cambridge and spent time in Smithfield, a community on the outskirts of London known for its dynamic reformist preachers. Once in North America, he became a minister in Salem, Massachusetts, where his sermons questioning Puritan religion, political rule, and the treatment of Native Americans led to his expulsion from the colony late in the fall of 1635. Williams then spent the winter with a Wampanoag community on the eastern side of Narragansett Bay. In the spring, he purchased land from the Narragansett tribe for a settlement he called Providence. Shortly afterwards, he was joined by his wife, children, and some of his followers. Later religious dissidents from Massachusetts Bay, Anne Hutchison, William Coddington, and John Clarke, founded Portsmouth on the north end of Acquidneck Island in 1638. Coddington, Clarke, and their followers then broke away from Portsmouth to found Newport in 1639. Following several years of wrangling with Massachusetts Bay Colony, Plymouth Colony, and the existing Rhode Island towns, Samuel Gorton founded Warwick in 1643. These settlers shared a geographic location but lacked a common political identity, which left them vulnerable to the imperial ambitions of both Massachusetts Bay and Connecticut.

---

[47] Gorges, Ferdinando, "First Commission" and "Second Commission," in *Province and Court Records of Maine*, Volume 1, 33–8.

The initial stages of founding colonies in North America were usually dangerous and cold and colonists needed some larger goal to surmount the misery. Massachusetts Bay, Connecticut, and Plymouth Colonies had their own variety of religious freedom and the hope of reforming English society. The Province of Maine had fish, timber, and furs. All colonies had land, which was increasingly scarce home in England. Roger Williams's vision was as much political as it was religious. Where John Winthrop famously wanted a "city on a hill," Williams dreamed of a "livelie experiment" in human relations, a phrase used by Charles II to describe the colony's emphasis on religious toleration and (relative) democracy.[48]

Recognizing that unification was their best chance of survival, Roger Williams used his "livelie experiment" to yoke together the largely unwilling Rhode Island towns in the early 1640s and to apply for official recognition from England's parliamentary government. The 1644 patent united Rhode Island's towns as the Colony of Rhode Island and Providence Plantations. Unlike Massachusetts Bay, suffrage in Rhode Island did not require church membership. After moving to the colony and acquiring enough land, white male Protestant heads of household could apply for voting rights from their towns, a process that generally took anywhere from three to 10 years.[49] Once they had been accepted, white male Rhode Islanders voted for political leaders who then created laws for the colony. The colony also promised religious toleration and a community of Jews settled in Newport in 1656 and were followed by Quakers in 1657 fleeing persecution in New Netherland Colony.[50] Over time, the colony also became home to Baptists, Anglicans, and Methodists.

The restoration of Charles II to the English throne in 1660 posed new challenges for Rhode Island. Concerned about the legality of their patent, the colony sent John Clarke to England to renegotiate. Charles II then granted an official charter to the Colony of Rhode Island and Providence Plantations in 1663. In addition to confirming Rhode Island's commitment to religious freedom, the new charter established that the colony would be ruled by an annually elected

---

48 "The Charter Granted by His Majesty, King Charles the Second to the Colony of Rhode-Island and Providence Plantations in America," in *The Earliest Acts and Laws of the Colony of Rhode Island and Providence Plantations, 1647–1719*, John D. Cushing, ed. (Wilmington: M. Glazier Press, 1977).

49 See Rhode Island Historical Society, *The Early Records of the Town of Portsmouth* (Providence: E.L. Freeman & Sons, 1901), Sydney James, *Colonial Rhode Island: a History* (New York: Scribner, 1975), and Bruce Daniels, *Dissent and Conformity on Narragansett Bay, The Colonial Rhode Island Town* (Middletown: Wesleyan University Press, 1983).

50 See James, *Colonial Rhode Island*.

Governor, Deputy Governor, and General Assembly. The General Assembly consisted of 10 Assistants and 10 Deputies, with representatives from all Rhode Island towns, who met twice a year with the Governor.

Creating a Rhode Island Legal Code

A major challenge facing Roger Williams and the other Rhode Island political leaders in the late 1630s was the issue of laws for the new colony. The individual Rhode Island towns already had their own legal systems for addressing criminal acts, thereby rendering the "town covenants [a] crazy quilt of mutually antithetical political and religious views."[51] The 1644 Rhode Island patent had granted the colony the right to create its own body of laws and so a decision was made in 1647 to create a colony-wide code. It was also agreed that since none of the four towns could claim precedence over the others, court sessions in Rhode Island would move from town to town. This decision remained in place until 1663 when the court moved to Newport, the largest and most financially stable town in the colony. Over time, the process of creating a legal code provided much of the necessary mortar to hold together the colony's divergent visions and political leaders from all four towns were involved with its creation.

Bradley Chapin estimates that 86.2 percent of all Rhode Island laws created in the *Proceedings of the First General Assembly of 'The Incorporation of Providence Plantations' and The Code of Laws adopted by that Assembly* were based on English law, the highest ratio in New England. Another 12.9 percent were created in Rhode Island and only .9 percent came from Biblical codes.[52] The construction and organization of the Rhode Island legal code appears most closely modeled on Edward Coke's *The Institutes of the Laws of England.* Like the *Institutes,* Rhode Island's legal code listed and defined criminal activity, outlined penalties, and provided a short history of the law. Unlike both Michael Dalton's *The Countrey Justice* and *The Laws and Liberties of Massachusetts,* the Rhode Island legal code is not arranged in alphabetical order. Prior to studying religion at Cambridge University, Roger Williams had worked as a stenographer for Coke, a man whose reputation rested on his constant defense of English common law against challenges from both royal and ecclesiastical interests. Williams's final year with Coke was spent taking notes as Coke helped draft the

[51] G.B. Worden, "The Rhode Island Civil Code of 1647," in *Saints and Revolutionaries: Essays on Early American History,* David D. Hall, John M. Murrin, and Thad W. Tate, eds (New York: W.W. Norton, 1984), 141.

[52] Chapin, *Criminal Justice in Colonial America,* 5.

1628 *Petition of Right*, providing Williams with an immediate familiarity with Coke's understanding of the workings of English common law.[53] However, some of the Rhode Island criminal laws do appear to have been drawn from Michael Dalton's *The Countrey Justice*. Mary Sarah Bilder also notes that "the sections on women resemble sections in [The] *Lawes Resolutions* [of Womens Rights: Or the Lawes Provision for Woemen]."[54] Rhode Island's legal code existed only in manuscript form until the eighteenth century, which may reflect the lack of a printing press in Rhode Island until the 1720s.[55]

An immediate similarity between English and Rhode Island legal systems was the active presence of attorneys in Rhode Island. Unlike the Puritans in Massachusetts and Connecticut, Rhode Island's leaders believed that legal counsel was an important part of the judicial process. In addition, Rhode Island colonists were encouraged to request trial by jury for most crimes and the court records make clear that many Rhode Island colonists took full advantage of both options. Trial by jury was legal in other New England colonies but was only used for serious charges such as murder, rape, or adultery.

The decision to base Rhode Island law on English common law was a wise tactic from a political standpoint as it helped the colony maintain its connections with the English government. Remaining independent of neighboring New England colonies was contingent on Rhode Island's ability to appeal to English authority. An active demonstration of adherence to English law was an important tool in a complicated world of negotiated colonial charters and patents. There was, however, one way in which Massachusetts' legal system in the seventeenth century bore a closer resemblance to legal practices in England than was the custom in Rhode Island. After the initial settlement years, both Massachusetts Bay and the Province of Maine created separate political and judicial positions, though many men served as political leaders after being justices or vice versa. By contrast, similar to Plymouth Colony, Rhode Island's Governor and Assistants served as justices in the colony's court system for much of the seventeenth century. Having Rhode Island and Plymouth's political leaders double as justices may have been a practical decision for these smaller colonies. Rhode Island may also not have had enough men with any form of legal training to provide justices *and* attorneys in the seventeenth century. Like their counterparts in other New England jurisdictions, these men took their responsibilities seriously and gained their training by serving "in official

53 Bilder, *The Transatlantic Constitution*, 33–6.

54 Bilder, *The Transatlantic Constitution*, 53.

55 Lawrence Wroth, *The Colonial Printer* (Portland: Southworth-Anthoensen Press, 1938, Second Edition), 224.

positions that gave them access to the colony's repositories of statues. To learn the laws of England, English law books- bought and borrowed- remained an essential resource."[56]

Sexual Misconduct Law in Rhode Island

The *Proceedings of the First General Assembly of 'The Incorporation of Providence Plantations'* include a variety of laws regarding sexual misconduct. Similar to both *The Countrey Justice* and the *Laws and Liberties*, sodomy was defined as "a vile Affection men given up thereto leave the Naturall use of women & burn in their lust one Towards Another." Bestiality or buggery was defined as "a most Filthy lying with A beast as wth a woman & is Abomination & Confusion." Rape was defined as "when a man through his wild & unbridled affection eth wth & Forceth A Woman against her will like unto him."[57] All three of these crimes received capital punishment "without remedy," though Rhode Island justices decided in 1671 to whip a Native American accused of rape, based on his perceived inability to understand his actions, rather than put him to death, a decision suggesting indigenous legal influences, rather than English.[58] The law for adultery only spelled out punishment for men, describing the act as embracing "a vile Affection whereby men doe turne aside from ye naturall use of there own wives & do Turn in their Lusts Towards Strange Flesh" and it was recommended that justices "follow ye Laws of England" when punishing such men.

Unlike both *The Countrey Justice* and the *Laws and Liberties*, Rhode Island law spelled out that the "takeing away Deflowering or Contracting in marriage A maid under Sixteen Yeares of Age Against the will of or Unknown to the Father and Mother of the maid is a kind of Stealing." The punishment for this crime was either five years imprisonment or "Sattisfaction to her Parents," which presumably meant either marriage or providing a dowry substantial enough to attract other marital partners. Fornication trials were prosecuted in the Rhode Island courts in the mid- to late seventeenth century, though there was no specific law against engaging in sexual intercourse outside of marriage until 1719. The most striking departure from English law in Rhode Island was the total absence

[56] Bilder, *The Transatlantic Constitution*, 30.

[57] *The Earliest Acts and Laws of the Colony of Rhode Island and Providence Plantations*, 64.

[58] See the Rhode Island General Court of Trials, June 15, 1671 for Quashcome, in Jane Fiske, *Rhode Island General Court of Trials, 1671–1704*, Jane Fiske, ed. (Boxford: Fiske Press, 1998), 13.

of bastardy laws anywhere in the colonial Rhode Island legal code, though both bastardy and paternity trials were conducted in the colony. Taken together, these laws suggest that Rhode Island followed neither its colonial neighbors nor English law when it came to the prosecution of sexual misconduct.

Conclusion

The year 1650 marked an important legal watershed in all three colonies. Both Massachusetts Bay and Rhode Island had just created legal codes in a time period when legal codification was rarely utilized in England and Europe. Lawrence Friedman speculates that "codification is natural in a colony. A new settlement cannot sit back and wait for the slow evolution of its legal system ... any fresh start demands codification."[59] While Massachusetts created its legal code to satisfy the demands of wary settlers, Rhode Island hoped that its code would unify its diverse towns and even more diverse colonists. Both colonies also used their legal codes to demonstrate their particular relationship with England as Massachusetts deliberately balanced source material from English law, the Bible and local needs in North America, while Rhode Island relied more on English common law and local needs when crafting their own legal systems. If legal codification marked a major step forward towards the creation of individual identities for both Massachusetts and Rhode Island, Maine experienced a very different transition as 1650 marked the first shift towards Massachusetts Bay's eventual takeover of the region, which would, in turn, shift Maine away from the closer relationship with English law intended by Thomas Gorges in the early 1640s. Nevertheless, the Maine court records suggest that, over time, Maine maintained a legal identity distinct from Massachusetts, one that would eventually help Maine to become an independent state in the early 1820s.

[59] Lawrence, M. Friedman, *A History of American Law* (New York: Touchstone, 2005, Third Edition), 50.

Chapter 2
Evolving Law in England and its Influence on New England

England underwent multiple political and social transitions in the early modern period, some unique to the British Isles, others common to Europe as a whole. British monarchs shifted from the Tudors to the Stuarts, experimented with a very different political system in the mid-seventeenth century, came back to the Stuarts, and moved on to the Hanoverians. Expanding colonial interests gradually led to the recreation of the small island kingdom as the British Empire at the turn of the eighteenth century. Growing populations and shrinking land stocks brought thousands more people to urban areas for the first time, while the early stages of the Industrial Revolution changed both material production and the lives of its workers. Both the Scientific Revolution and the Enlightenment transformed the ways in which many people understood the world around them. Over time, these transitions gradually shaped and changed English law, only to then be accepted or rejected in the laws created by the various British North American colonies.

Medieval and Early Modern English Legal Systems

Law in medieval and early modern England was conducted in multiple court systems, each possessing its own specific participants and practices.[1] Minor crimes, such as assault or slander, were labeled misdemeanors and were addressed at the local level, generally feudal or manorial courts in the medieval period and county courts in the early modern period, when the manorial lords were replaced by justices from the landed gentry class. Growing numbers of cities in

---

1 See Martin Ingram, *Church Courts, Sex and Marriage in England, 1570–1640* (Cambridge: Cambridge University Press, 1982), J.A. Sharpe, *Crime in Early Modern England, 1550–1750* (New York: Longman Group Limited, 1984), J.M. Beattie, *Crime and the Courts in England, 1660–1800* (Princeton: Princeton University Press, 1986), Harold J. Berman, *Law and Revolution II: The Impact of the Protestant Reformations on the Western Legal Tradition* (Cambridge: The Belknap Press of Harvard University Press, 2003), and Thomas Garden Barnes, *Shaping the Common Law: From Glanvill to Hale, 1688* (Redwood City: Stanford University Press, 2008).

the fifteenth century led to the creation of urban and mercantile courts which became ever more important in the sixteenth century. Major violent crimes, such as murder, rape, arson, and robbery, were considered felonies and were addressed by royal justices, whether at standing courts in London or at circuit courts in the outlying counties. For the most part, these courts operated within the traditions of English common law.

Ecclesiastical courts were established in the medieval period and "ranked in importance with the various systems of secular criminal justice—[as well as being] far more sophisticated."[2] Their laws were rooted in the canon law of the Roman Catholic Church and had complete jurisdiction over clerics, which included university students. They also could try non-clerics for nonviolent crimes such as heresy, sacrilege, sorcery, and various forms of sexual misconduct, though rape was generally tried in the secular courts as it was considered a felony rather than a moral failing.

The medieval ecclesiastical courts were disrupted but not wholly replaced by Henry VIII when he created the Anglican Church and created or expanded various royal prerogative courts including the Star Chamber, the High Commission, the Privy Council, the High Court of Admiralty, the Court of Requests, and the High Court of Chancery. The Star Chamber supplemented both the common law and chancery courts and was originally intended to enforce laws against English subjects considered too powerful to be convicted in the ordinary courts. It met in private and all decisions were made without indictments or witnesses. Abuses of the Star Chamber's power by both the Tudor and the Stuart monarchs led to its dissolution in 1641. The chancery courts were rooted in equity rather than law and, consequently, rulings in criminal trials at these courts differed from criminal trials held in the common law courts. The chancery courts also addressed nonviolent crimes such as bribery, extortion, forgery, and perjury, which were not originally covered by the common law courts. The rising power of the chancery courts in the late sixteenth century led to resistance and much of Sir Edward Coke's career was spent arguing for the importance and centrality of English common law rather than chancery law.[3] These efforts took hold in the seventeenth century and laws covering nonviolent crimes became part of English common law and common law courts in 1640.[4]

---

[2] Berman, *Law and Revolution II*, 308.

[3] See Allen D. Boyer, *Sir Edward Coke and the Elizabethan Age* (Stanford: Stanford University Press, 2003) and Barnes, *Shaping the Common Law*.

[4] Harold J. Berman writes that this process occurred "only after the triumph of the common law courts over their rivals ... not, as is often supposed, because previously English legal theory and English legal institutions were not sufficiently sophisticated, but because previously these

North American Adaptations to Early Modern English Legal Systems

The English colonies founded in the seventeenth century all established single, unified court systems, rather than the diversified English legal system.[5] David Konig's observation that "this relative simplicity enabled the Massachusetts courts to make a powerful contribution to social stability" is equally applicable to the courts created in the Chesapeake and mid-Atlantic colonies.[6] For the most part, the law created and practiced in the colonial courts was based on English common law and even heavily Anglican colonies like Virginia did not create ecclesiastical courts. Individual colonists could, however, make appeals to the English chancery and admiralty courts, which demonstrates a thorough colonial knowledge of the complex workings of legal systems home in England.[7]

Changes in the English Legal Systems

The English Civil War in the early 1640s brought political, religious, and legal changes in its wake. Just as the Protestant Reformation had emphasized the use of vernacular languages in church services, judicial courts were now held only in English, rather than the Latin or French which had lingered in some courts. The Restoration returned Charles II to the throne in 1660, but Parliament retained its power throughout the seventeenth and eighteenth centuries. Another important influence during this period was the growing numbers of

---

branches and elements of criminal law were within the province of other types of English courts." Berman, *Law and Revolution II*, 311.

5 See Julius Goebel, Jr and T. Raymond Naughton, *Law Enforcement in Colonial New York: A Study in Criminal Procedure* (Montclair: Patterson Smith, 1970), Douglas Greenberg, *Crime and Law Enforcement in the Colony of New York, 1691–1776* (Ithaca: Cornell University Press, 1974), A.G. Roeber. *Faithful Magistrates and Republican Lawyers: Creators of Virginia Legal Culture, 1680–1810* (Chapel Hill: The University of North Carolina Press, 1981), Edgar J. McManus, *Law and Liberty in Early New England: Criminal Justice and Due Process, 1620–1692* (Amherst: University of Massachusetts Press, 1993), Jack D. Marietta and G.S. Rowe, *Troubled Experiment: Crime and Justice in Pennsylvania, 1682–1800* (Philadelphia: University of Pennsylvania Press, 2006), William Nelson, *The Common Law in Colonial America: The Chesapeake and New England*, Volume 1 (New York: Oxford University Press, 2008), and *The Common Law in Colonial America: The Middle Colonies and the Carolinas, 1660–1730*, Volume 2 (New York: Oxford University Press, 2013).

6 David Konig, *Law and Society in Puritan Massachusetts: Essex County, 1629–1692* (Chapel Hill: University of North Carolina Press, 1979), 115.

7 Mary Sarah Bilder, *The Transatlantic Constitution, Colonial Legal Culture and the Empire* (Cambridge: Harvard University Press, 2004), 73–90.

landed gentry and wealthy merchants. Statutes were increasingly devised within the body of English common law to protect both their property and financial interests. Anxiety regarding the rising numbers of landless, poor members of English society appears throughout these laws, particularly when addressing responsibility for their welfare and moral behavior, an issue that will be more fully addressed in a future paragraph.

Other changes in the English legal systems between the medieval and early modern periods include the use of trial by jury, rather than by combat or ordeal, and an ongoing discussion on how to punish convicted criminals. Trial by jury was first used only in civil trials but it appeared in criminal trials by the fourteenth century.[8] Jurors were originally expected to serve as "men who of their own knowledge or from knowledge immediately available from the neighborhood, [who] might swear to the guilt or innocence of the accused." By the mid-fifteenth century, they were "beginning to hear evidence that was produced in court, though jurors still continued to obtain facts by their own inquiry," until they were forbidden to do so in the eighteenth century.[9] The overall assumption until the late eighteenth century was not that the defendant "was innocent until the case against him was proved beyond a reasonable doubt, but that if he *were* innocent he ought to be able to demonstrate it for the jury."[10] Jurors could be instructed by a justice, but were expected to make their own independent decisions about a case.

Trial by jury was used for capital offenses, which covered a great deal of territory as any crime defined as a felony could result in execution.[11] These included, but were not limited to, treason, murder, robbery, burglary, larceny, rape, housebreaking, horse-theft, homicide, and counterfeiting coins. While many defendants were able to escape death by pleading "benefit of clergy," which was tied to literacy rather than actually proving that the defendant was a member of a clerical order, thousands of convicts were put to death, generally by hanging. The first major transition away from capital punishment for all but the most extreme crimes began in the mid-seventeenth century when convicts were offered transportation to North America rather than execution, a practice which dwindled in the mid-eighteenth century but was then replaced with transportation to Australia. Prisons or jails were only used in the early modern

8 See Leonard W. Levy, *The Palladium of Justice: Origins of Trial by Jury* (Chicago: Ivan R. Dee, 1999) and J.R. Pole, *Contract and Consent, Representation and the Jury in Anglo-American Legal History* (Charlottesville: University of Virginia Press, 2010).

9 Levy, *The Palladium of Justice*, 22.

10 Beattie, *Crime and the Courts in England*, 341.

11 Beattie, *Crime and the Courts in England*, 452–73.

period for holding defendants prior to trial and, if convicted, punishment, though they emerged as a systematic punishment system in the early nineteenth century.

Trial by jury was allowed in all of the English colonies and punishments in the English colonies were generally more lenient than they were in England. The death penalty was almost never imposed in the colonies, though this probably says more about the need for colonial labor than any concern for the welfare of convicted criminals. Another difference between England and the colonies was their respective uses of jails or prisons. English defendants were held in prison until the time of their trial. Most colonial communities had jails, or at least an available semi-secure space, but these were only used for holding potential defendants deemed flight risks before their initial statements and surety, or bail, were taken.[12] Holding convicted defendants in prison was not used as a punishment in either England or its colonies. Similar to England, the punishments used in the English colonies evolved over time, and this will be addressed in a future chapter.

The Evolution of Sexual Misconduct Prosecution in Early Modern England

The question of where and how sexual intercourse outside of marriage should be regulated was hotly debated among political, religious, and legal leaders in early modern England. These debates are usually linked to the political rise of the Puritans in the mid-seventeenth century but laws passed in the late sixteenth century suggest this particular debate began long before the Puritans came to political power.[13] Medieval couples accused of intercourse before marriage or conceiving a child out of wedlock were tried in the English ecclesiastical courts, while rape, if prosecuted at all, was tried in the secular courts. The primary issue at stake during these trials was sexual immorality. Financial support for illegitimate children was not part of the trial process.

Medieval children born out of wedlock to wealthy parents were generally supported by their relatives, while children born to poor parents relied primarily on monasteries or their local communities for their support. A 1553 law passed in London defined "the Fatherless Poor Man's Child" as one of nine categories of poverty deserving financial support. It was generally understood "that destitute

---

12 See Adam Jay Hirsch, *The Rise of the Penitentiary: Prisons and Punishment in Early America* (New Haven: Yale University Press, 1992).

13 Keith Thomas, "The Puritans and Adultery: The Act of 1650 Reconsidered," in *Puritans and Revolutionaries: Essays in Seventeenth-Century History*, Donald Pennington and Keith Thomas, eds (Oxford: Oxford University Press, 1978), 257–82.

children, legitimate and illegitimate, should be looked after by the community- that is, fed, reared and trained for some kind of work- all at public expense."[14] However, public opinion on this issue changed as rising population levels and shrinking need for agricultural labor made the matter of financial support for poor residents an increasingly pressing one for English towns. Statutes passed throughout the 1560s and 1570s allowed towns to raise poor rates, create almshouses which doubled as workhouses, and pay for Guardians and Collectors for the Poor to manage their unfortunate charges.[15] Impoverished residents could still look to their communities for financial support but the process was rapidly becoming more bureaucratic. Parliament then passed a law in 1574 which granted "justices of the peace the authority to condemn mothers and reputed fathers of chargeable bastards to gaol if they refused to maintain their children."[16] The primary emphasis in these trials was economic rather than moral and parents who could support their illegitimate children were generally not put on trial.

The logistical difficulties posed by conducting such trials plays out in the multiple editions of Michael Dalton's *The Countrey Justice*, which was first published in 1618. The first edition devoted 10 paragraphs to instructing justices in best practices for identifying men and women who had conceived children out of wedlock and conducting their eventual court trials and punishments. Thirty-seven years later, the 1655 edition featured a total of 14 paragraphs on the topic and the 1746 edition had 18 paragraphs. The additional paragraphs in the later editions provide examples of loopholes to be avoided when convicting defendants and cautionary tales for justices who did not follow Dalton's advice and found themselves in legal difficulties of their own. Both the 1655 and 1746 editions unequivocally state that "such corporall punishment ... is not to be untill after that the woman is delivered of her childe." They then note that a pregnant woman had been whipped at the Bridewell prison in London before giving birth and had subsequently miscarried her child. The justices who ordered her whipped were then "in the Star Chamber fined to the Queene at a great summe, and were further ordered to pay a summe of money to the said woman."[17] The ever increasing number of exceptions and cautions to the original law published in the later

14 Jenny Teichman, *Illegitimacy: An Examination of Bastardy* (Ithaca: Cornell University Press, 1982), 61.

15 See Helen Berry and Elizabeth Foyster, *The Family in Early Modern England* (New York: Cambridge University Press, 2007).

16 Mark Jackson, *New-Born Child Murder, Women, Illegitimacy and the Courts in Eighteenth-century England* (New York: Manchester University Press, 1996), 30.

17 Dalton, *The Countrey Justice* (New York: The Legal Classics Library, Division of Gryphon Editions. Original edition, London: Company of Stationers, 1655), 41.

editions suggests that many defendants not only resisted their sentencing but also possessed sufficient knowledge of the workings of the judicial system to employ a wide range of legal technicalities while doing so. Laura Gowing observes that "this familiarity with legal concepts and rules mean[s] that the words we hear in court were less estranged from popular culture than we might expect."[18] English colonists in North America display a similar adeptness while negotiating similar situations, which again suggests that most residents of the Anglo-American world were intimately familiar with the workings of the legal systems around them.

The moral issues posed by extramarital sex entered the secular legal system with the passing of a law in Parliament intended to "suppress the detestable sins of incest, adultery, and fornication" in 1650.[19] The law specified that any English subject who had "carnal knowledge of the body" of any family member was guilty of incest and would "suffer death as in case of Felony, without benefit of Clergy." Married women who were "carnally known by any man (other them her Husband) (except in Case of Ravishment)" and the men with whom they had sexual intercourse were also subject to the same punishment. However, married men who had sexual intercourse with unmarried women, men who did not know their sexual partners were married, and women whose husbands had been gone for at least three years were not considered adulterers. Men who had "carnal knowledge of the body of any Virgin, unmarried Woman or Widow" and their resulting partners were ordered to be "committed to the common Gaol, without Bail or Mainprize, there to continue for the space of three Moneths." Men and women convicted "for being a common Bawd" or for "wittingly keeping a common Brothel or Bawdy-house" were to be whipped and set in the pillory "and there marked with a hot Iron in the forehead with the Letter B and afterwards committed to Prison or the House of Correction, there to work for his or her living for the space of three years" for their first offense. Second offenses were deemed felonies, with the resulting capital punishment. All trials for these crimes were to be conducted by the "Justices of Assize in their respective Circuits, and the Justices of Peace in every County, at their usual and General Sessions," which were both secular, common law English courts.

---

18 Laura Gowing, *Common Bodies: Women, Touch and Power in Seventeenth-Century England* (New Haven: Yale University Press, 2003), 13.

19 For the complete text of the 1650 law, see "May 1650: An Act for suppressing the detestable sins of Incest, Adultery and Fornication.," *Acts and Ordinances of the Interregnum, 1642–1660* (1911), 387–9. URL: http://www.british-history.ac.uk/report.aspx?compid=56399 Date accessed: July 7, 2014. For discussion of the law, see Thomas, "The Puritans and Adultery," Bernard Capp, "Republican Reformation: Family, Community and the State in Interregnum Middlesex, 1649–1660," published in Berry and Foster, eds, *The Family in Early Modern England.*

The 1650 law was harsher than anything that had been created earlier, or would be created in the future, though a substantial gap existed between what the law specified and what actually occurred in English courts in the 1650s. Court records for every single English jurisdiction from this period have not been scrutinized but Keith Thomas writes that "trials for incest were understandably rare, but even for the commoner offence of adultery only four death sentences could be found."[20] There is evidence that fornication trials were conducted but these also appear to have been fairly rare. Given these gaps, the inevitable question emerges regarding why the law was created in the first place, particularly since it was repealed in 1660 and never replaced. Thomas speculates that the "importance of the 1650 act was primarily symbolic. It was a public assertion of offences to be abominated" in a Protestant society which emphasized the nuclear family and worried that both adultery and incest could fundamentally destroy that same family unit.[21]

While most people in England thought capital punishment for adultery was an unnecessary extreme, many were concerned about the economic repercussions posed by sexual intercourse outside of marriage in a time period before reliable birth control.[22] If laws intended to discourage couples from having children out of wedlock resulted in fewer children in need of support, then most communities were willing to embrace the resulting inquiries into their members' private lives. Farmerz Dabhoiwala writes that "sexual policing was not merely some top-down, external imposition ... it was brought to life by popular participation, and broad concurrence with its principles, a system of grassroots self-regulation, of communities policing themselves."[23] Laura Gowing's research also documents similar patterns, particularly among women who were closely tied with assessing sexual misconduct among their neighbors.[24]

This communal willingness was further reinforced in the late seventeenth century by the creation of various Societies for the Reformation of Manners. These organizations were reasonably successful in their early years and Bernard Capp argues that any perceived societal and legal disconnects between the 1650 law and the Societies was probably because their creators "judged it unwise to acknowledge

---

[20] Thomas, "The Puritans and Adultery," 258.

[21] Thomas, "The Puritans and Adultery," 280. Also see Lawrence Stone, *The Family, sex and Marriage in England, 1500–1800* (New York: Harper and Row Publishers, 1977).

[22] See Ingram, *Church Courts, Sex and Marriage in England*, Anthony Fletcher, *Gender, Sex and Subordination in England, 1550–1800* (New Haven: Yale University Press, 1995) and Capp, "Republican reformation: Family, community and the state in Interregnum Middlesex."

[23] Faramerz Dabhoiwala, *The Origins of Sex: A History of the First Sexual Revolution* (Oxford: Oxford University Press, 2012), 22.

[24] See Gowing, *Common Bodies*.

the[se] parallels."[25] Nevertheless, despite grassroots support in many communities, the Societies largely disappeared by the 1720s and 1730s. Money was a major problem as most Society organizers lacked the funds to carry through with the legal prosecution of brothel owners who took full advantage of the growing number of attorneys available to them. Another challenge was the growing disappearance of laws regulating sexual misconduct from all the English legal systems. The exception to this rule remained laws affecting couples who conceived children out of wedlock and were unable to financially support them. By contrast, wealthy couples who conceived illegitimate children and then married or made private arrangements for the support of their children stood an excellent chance of flying under the radar, particularly after the 1650 law was repealed. Sexual misconduct was rapidly becoming something committed by the lower classes, rather than an act which all members of English society could expect to be held liable.

Sexual Misconduct Laws in England and in New England

There are multiple parallels between the sexual misconduct laws created in England and in the English colonies in the seventeenth and eighteenth centuries. The Puritan colonies of Massachusetts Bay and Connecticut created adultery and incest laws similar to the English ones established in 1650 and, likewise, put very few people to death for these crimes. While not all English colonies were concerned by the moral issues posed by couples who had sexual intercourse outside the marriage bed, they were concerned about the economic challenges posed by illegitimate children and these concerns will be addressed in future chapters. Another similarity was the growing belief that sexual misconduct was only committed by the lower classes.[26] All of these transitions took place within wider Anglo-American societal conversations about what it meant to have a private life and a public life, as well as a growing emphasis on the individual rather than the community in society.

---

[25] Capp, "Republican reformation: Family, community and the state in Interregnum Middlesex," 66.

[26] See Cornelia Hughes Dayton, *Women Before the Bar: Gender, Law and Society in Connecticut, 1639–1789* (Chapel Hill: University of North Carolina Press, 1995), Kathleen Brown, *Good Wives, Nasty Wenches, and Anxious Patriarchs: Gender, Race, and Power in Colonial Virginia* (Chapel Hill: University of North Carolina Press, 1996), and Clare Lyons, *Sex among the Rabble: An Intimate History of Gender & Power in the Age of Revolution, Philadelphia, 1730–1830* (Chapel Hill: University of North Carolina Press, 2006) for more discussion of this evolution in Connecticut, Virginia and Pennsylvania, respectively.

Linguistic Transitions in English Sexual Misconduct Trials

An important, and generally overlooked, parallel between legal systems in England and its colonies was the evolving language used in early modern sexual misconduct trials. Sixteenth-century English defendants were often charged with a crime classified as incontinency during their trials but the term almost completely disappears from the court records in the seventeenth century.[27] A sequence of closely detailed trials from the Province of Maine provides insight into how the term was used and why it may have appealed to sixteenth-century English justices but not to seventeenth or eighteenth-century justices. In addition, these trials also speak to shifting experiences for men and women placed on trial for sexual misconduct in the early modern Anglo-American world.

The first of the Maine incontinency trials occurred on March 25, 1636 when John Bonithon was convicted by the New Somersetshire Province Court for committing incontinency with his father's servant, Ane.[28] He was ordered to pay a fine of 40 shillings and Ane had to pay 20 shillings. The trial concluded by ordering Bonithon to keep the child, a boy named William. The presence of a child makes clear that the judges defined incontinency as sexual intercourse for John Bonithon and Ane but the other incontinency trials are less clear cut.

Minister George Burdett was convicted on September 8, 1640 for being "infamous for incontinency, a publisher and broacher of divers dangerous speeches the better to seduce that weake sex of women to his incontinent practices."[29] Attracting ministers to the fledgling colony was a major challenge in colonial Maine. Good ministers tended to settle in southern New England where the congregations were ardent and the winters easier; northern New England generally attracted ministers whose past actions gave them few other options. Burdett was no exception. Originally educated at the University of Cambridge, he abandoned his wife and child in England to come to Salem, Massachusetts, in the early 1630s. A few years later, Burdett moved to New Hampshire and finally to Maine where

---

[27] The first written reference to this term occurred in 1485 when Parliament passed a law enjoining the British people to "Avoutrie fornicacion inceste or eny other flesshely incontinency." Other popular terms from this period included light or uncivil carriage, lascivious behavior, and too much familiarity, though incontinency was the most popular charge

[28] I have chosen to include trials from the period from 1636 to 1649 in this chapter as they are crucial for understanding the linguistic evolution which took place in Maine's sexual misconduct trials in the mid- to late seventeenth century. See the Commissioners trial for Ane and John Bonithon in 1636, in *Maine Province and Court Records*, Volume I., Charles Thornton Libby, ed. (Lewiston: Penmore Lithographers, 1991), 1.

[29] All quotes from the Province of Maine General Court trials for Mary Puddington, Ruth Gouch and George Burdett trial in 1640, in *Maine Province and Court Records*, Volume 1, 73–5.

his style of preaching initially impressed Thomas Gorges, who wrote that "he reads & expounds a chapter, then singes, then preacheth some, concludes with a prayer."[30] Following the indictment, Gorges quickly ceased to be impressed by Burdett's preaching and his letters document a growing sense of frustration with Burdett.

The first person on trial in connection with George Burdett was Mary, the wife of George Puddington, who was charged with frequenting Burdett's company after being warned not to see him. She was ordered to make a public confession to atone for her "disobedience and light carriage." Burdett was ordered to pay 10 pounds sterling to the King and 10 pounds to George Puddington. Next, the court tried Burdett for "deflowring Ruth the wife of John Gouch" and fined him 20 more pounds. Finally, Ruth Gouch was convicted on adultery charges. She was ordered to stand "in a white sheete publiquely ... six weeks after she is delivered of Child." There was no mention of Burdett paying a fine to Gouch's husband. George Puddington and John Gouch had very different reactions to the trial. Puddington forgave his wife but Gouch wrote his wife out of his will.[31] A total of four separate crimes emerge from these trials, each with its own attendant punishment. George Burdett was on trial for "incontinent practices," in particular with Mary Puddington and in general with the women of the colony. Puddington was not pregnant and was accused only of light carriage, suggesting questionable behavior but not necessarily intercourse. By contrast, "deflowring Ruth Gouch" was a specific charge, as was her charge that she had committed "adulterie with Mr. George Burdett." Not surprisingly, both of these crimes carried heavier penalties than Mary Puddington's charges.

Thomas Gorges's letters provide a rare window onto Burdett's activities as references to the Burdett trial appear in 10 different letters to five different correspondents between July of 1640 and September of 1641. According to the Maine court records, Burdett was initially charged with the "publish[ing] and broach[ing] of divers dangerous speeches the better to seduce that weake sex of women." Writing to Ferdinando Gorges on September 22, 1640, Gorges explained that the jury required Burdett pay 10 pounds to George Puddington because Burdett had "detain[ed] his wife against her will, & with high looks & lofty words ke[pt] the man in slavish fear that he durst claime the power of a husband over his wife" and that he had "perswad[ed her] by scripture to satisfy his insatiable lust," a true misuse of his role as minister.[32] Both Gorges and the

30 Thomas Gorges, *The Letters of Thomas Gorges, Deputy Governor of the Province of Maine, 1640–1643*, Robert E. Moody, ed. (Portland: Maine Historical Society, 1978), 3.

31 See Sybil Noyes, Charles Thornton Libby, and Walter C. Davis, *Genealogical Dictionary of Maine and New Hampshire* (Portland: Anthoensen Press, 1928–39).

32 Gorges, *The Letters of Thomas Gorges*, 11.

court records also suggest that other women received similar insinuations from Burdett, though these women remain unidentified. Burdett eventually left the Province of Maine, headed, as Gorges darkly remarked with the tone of a man willing to believe anything negative about his subject, to "Ingland by the way of Spayn. Tis thought he will turn priest. He is amply fitted for such an Imployment."[33] There is no evidence to indicate whether or not Burdett did, indeed, "turn priest;" regardless, he did not return to Maine.

A third trial used the term incontinency to describe entirely different circumstances. Robert Collens of York was accused of forcing "Jane Bond, the sayd wife of Nicholas Bond to incontency" on July 2, 1650 while her husband was away.[34] His trial was conducted using a jury, referred to in the records as the "Jury of life and death." If Collens was convicted on rape charges, hanging was likely. Trial statements were given by Jane Bond, her son (by an earlier marriage) Henry Simpson, and five neighbors. York was the second oldest town in Maine, with 350 to 400 residents in 1650, making it unsurprising that the Bond family had neighbors close enough to know when something was wrong.[35] The court found Collens "guiltie of the ackt of Incontinencie, not guilty of the forsement." He was ordered to pay 10 pounds, five to the "cuntrey," five to Nicholas Bond and to receive 39 lashings.

Robert Collens was not convicted of "forsement" but the severity of his punishment suggests the jury defined incontinency in his case as something resembling rape. He was the first colonist to receive a whipping for a sexual crime in the Province of Maine and 39 lashes was the harshest penalty assigned in the records. On average, convicted offenders received 10 to 15 lashes. The only other defendants receiving the maximum were convicted on adultery charges. Perhaps most importantly, Jane Bond received no punishment, which strongly indicates Collens's guilt in the eyes of the jury, especially when compared to the Burdett/Gouch trial. Only women who could prove rape could avoid sexual misconduct charges. Nevertheless, the jury still avoided the most severe punishment available to them. Richard Godbeer writes that "New England courts refused to convict individuals ... unless the evidence satisfied fully the standards of proof ... in a capital case, this meant either confession or at least two independent witnesses."[36] Collens had pleaded not guilty so there could be no confession. Jane Bond

---

[33] Gorges, *The Letters of Thomas Gorges*, 50.

[34] All quotes from the Province of Maine General Court trial for Jane Bond and Robert Collens in 1650, in *Maine Province and Court Records*, Volume 1, 140–43.

[35] See Geo B. Varney, *History of York, Maine* (Boston: B. Russell, 1886).

[36] Richard Godbeer, *Sexual Revolution in Early America* (Baltimore: The Johns Hopkins University Press, 2004), 102.

was also unable to produce two witnesses. While her son testified to Collens's presence in the bedchamber, neighbors could only report hearing a "great noyes" at the Bond house. Without a confession or two witnesses, convicting Collens for the "ackt of Incontinencie" was the best sentencing option available.[37]

The Province of Maine continued to convict defendants on incontinency charges until the late 1660s. George Garland worked as a tenant farmer for the Jordan family on the Nonesuch River in the town of Scarborough in the 1660s. Only about 10 years old in the late 1660s, Scarborough was one of the more northerly of the Maine settlements, with approximately 75 households scattered on outlying farms.[38] Despite the isolation provided by the town's location and household arrangements, trial records suggest that most Scarborough inhabitants were well aware of each others' activities. The York County Court of Associates charged Garland on July 18, 1668 with incontinency and living together with Sarah Mills. For good measure, the justices also questioned whether Garland was still married to a woman in England. Mills was a recent widow trying to scrape together a living in the Black Point section of Scarborough, which adjoined the Nonesuch River. The couple was ordered to choose between paying five pounds each or having 10 lashes each. As they could not pay the fine, they were whipped. The court also ordered the couple to obey an "act of separation."[39] This particular term appears frequently in the seventeenth-century Maine court records, with the last "act of separation" sworn in 1685. Couples usually posted a bond, ranging from anywhere between five and 50 pounds, and promised not to see each other again. If they were found together, the bond money was forfeited and they were placed on trial.

George Garland and Sarah Mills were again presented for living together out of wedlock on September 15, 1668. The charge was based on a complaint made by Andrew Auger, who lived on Prout's Neck in Scarborough. Despite the presentment, there is no record of the trial taking place and the matter appears to have been dropped, probably because the couple married at this time. George Garland's name appeared again four years later in the records for the September 10, 1672 meeting of the Court of Associates for York County. This time, he was

---

37 Sharon Block's research on rape trials from "all of mainland British North American and the later states and territories of the new United States" documents similar patterns in other trials, including efforts to reduce the actual charge in an effort to avoid capital punishment for convicted defendants. Block, *Rape & Sexual Power in Early America* (Chapel Hill: University of North Carolina Press, 2006), 5.

38 See Geo B. Varney, *History of Scarborough, Maine, From A Gazetteer of the State of Maine* (Boston: B.B. Russell Press, 1886).

39 All quotes from York County Court trial for Sarah Mills and George Garland in 1668, in *Maine Province and Court Records*, Volume 2, Charles Thornton Libby, ed. (Portland: Southworth Press), 169.

accused of publicly announcing his intentions to marry Lucretia Hitchcocke of West Saco. Widowed since the death of her husband Richard Hitchcocke in 1668, Hitchcocke inherited enough of her husband's property to support her and their young children, presumably rendering her financially more attractive than Sarah Mills. The court objected to Garland's intentions, believing that "hee hath lately owned him selfe to bee the husband of another woman called Saraih Mills."[40] Garland and Hitchcocke were ordered to separate, with the threat of being sent to Boston for trial if they were found together.

George Garland and Lucretia Hitchcocke returned to court on April 1, 1673 and the justices again ordered them to separate and to post bonds for good behavior, Garland for 50 pounds, Hitchcocke for an unspecified amount. That summer, they returned to court on July 1 where Garland was accused of "Incorageableness in frequenting of the Company of Widow Hitchcocke to all advise & restraynt, Lucretia Hitchcocke was accused of fornication, the second such charge levied in York County."[41]

The first fornication charge was against George and Sarah Gray on July 2, 1672. Following their conviction of fornication before marriage, they were ordered to pay three pounds and officers' fees or receive 10 lashes each. Other fornication trials from the same period carried similar punishments. The following year, Hitchcocke was ordered to pay 10 pounds, or receive 20 lashes, while Garland received 39 lashes and to pay a bond of 50 pounds to the County Treasurer on promise of his future good behavior. In addition, both had to pay court fees and the severity of their punishments suggests the justices' growing frustration with the couple's repeated sexual offenses.

The Garland/Mills/Hitchcocke trials neatly encapsulate the linguistic transition which took place in English sexual misconduct trials between the sixteenth and seventeenth centuries. Martin Ingram's research on sexual misconduct trials in England documents that the early charges "often included explanatory details ... [while] later the charges tended to become less colourful [and more] routine."[42] Depending on justices' legal needs, incontinency as a legal term could suggest intercourse, adultery, flirtation, potential bigamy, or borderline rape and the resulting punishments could be set accordingly. The vagueness of the term, however, became a liability over time. Rising population

---

40 All quotes from the York County Court trials for Lucretia Hitchcocke and George Garland in 1672, in *Maine Province and Court Records*, Volume 2, 461–2.

41 All quotes from the York County Court trials for Lucretia Hitchcocke and George Garland in 1673, in *Maine Province and Court Records*, Volume 2, 268.

42 Martin Ingram, *Church Courts, Sex and Marriage in England, 1570–1640* (Cambridge: Cambridge University Press, 1987), 223.

numbers meant that justices were trying more cases than they could handle. They also made it less likely that the guilty couple's neighbors knew enough to provide the information necessary for deciding between levels of sexual activity. Using the more formulaic fornication charge required little in the way of evidence or deliberation, while easily producing convictions that could stand as warnings to the couple's neighbors. In time, the courts would eventually go so far as to remove sexual misconduct trials completely from the court room, initially for the middle and upper classes and eventually for all members of society.

While all English-speaking court rooms experienced this transition between the colorful, descriptive sexual misconduct trials and the more clinical fornication trials, the timing and the pace at which these transitions occurred varied from place to place. English court rooms completed their gradual transition between the incontinency and fornication trials by the end of the sixteenth century. Justices in both Massachusetts and Rhode Island used the terms incontinency and fornication interchangeably throughout the first half of the seventeenth century and fornication did not fully replace the more descriptive terms until the early 1660s.[43] By contrast, the incontinency trials for Garland and Mills in the 1660s and the fornication trials for Garland and Hitchcocke in the mid-1670s demonstrate that Maine justices made their own linguistic transition almost overnight. Massachusetts Bay colony completed its takeover of the Province of Maine in the mid-1670s which suggests a transition made for political reasons rather than judicial ones.

The Scientific Revolution's Influence on Sexual Misconduct Trials and Women's Experiences

The impetus for using fornication rather than incontinency as a legal term stemmed from the practical needs of the court room but its creation also documents wider conversations between the various seventeenth-century professions. Barbara Shapiro writes that "the formulations of some legal doctrines were shaped by developments in religion and epistemology ... one theme, then, is the interaction between legal conceptualization and other intellectual traditions."[44] Scientists were

---

43 For more information on this process, including both Plymouth and New Hampshire colonies, see my dissertation, "At the Magistrate's Discretion: Sexual Crime and New England Law, 1636–1718" (PhD diss., University of Maine, 2008). See Appendix A for a complete list of Alternate Sexual Misconduct Charges found in colonial New England court records.

44 Barbara Shapiro, *"Beyond Reasonable Doubt" and "Probable Cause": Historical Perspectives on the Anglo-American Law of Evidence* (Berkeley: University of California Press, 1991), xiii. See

developing language for classifying their findings about the natural worlds and legal professionals often borrowed their terminology when classifying their own efforts to regulate the human world. Fornication was a charge rooted in the biological act of sexual intercourse, with none of the messiness necessitated by having to decide exactly which forms of sexual contact the defendant had experienced. Convicting sexual crime defendants on fornication charges meant more efficient trials and the universal Anglo-American transition towards fornication trials by the 1670s demonstrates that this was a popular decision among justices.

These transitions increasingly had wider ramifications for the ordinary lives of both men and women in the Anglo-American world. Trade professionalization alongside the emerging Industrial Revolution in the eighteenth century meant, of course, that economic production would now be conducted outside the home and away from the women who lived in those homes. But linguistic changes like the transition between the incontinency and fornication trials also had their own particular implications for early modern English women placed on trial for sexual misconduct. The new system meant that all sexual acts described as fornication were judged as the same crime. Under the older system of trying defendants for incontinency, Mary Puddington and Ruth Gouch's crimes could be judged as separate acts, thus allowing Puddington to receive a less stringent sentence than Gouch. The incontinency trials were intentionally humiliating, but they allowed time for defendants' actions to be considered on an individual basis. Mary Puddington may well have regarded the public terms of her court hearing as worth the bargain.

Further Influences of the Scientific Revolution on Sexual Misconduct Trials

The Scientific Revolution also contributed to the growing availability of printed texts and documents in the Anglo-American world. The first printing press in England is generally thought to have been introduced by William Caxton in the early 1470s.[45] The use of printing presses in England continued to expand in the sixteenth century and the Stationers Company, a formalized guild for members of the printing profession, which included printers, book-binders, type-

also *Probability and certainty in seventeenth-century England: a study of the relationships between natural science, religion, history, law, and literature* (Princeton: Princeton University Press, 1983) and *A Culture of Fact: England, 1550–1720* (Ithaca: Cornell University Press, 2003).

[45] See Lotte Hellinga, *William Caxton and Early Printing in England* (London: British Library, 2010).

founders, and book sellers, was created in 1557.[46] Deborah Harkness argues that the English Scientific Revolution was as much about the ways in which ordinary people created and used technology as the experiments conducted by scientists in Oxford and London. These interactions played out in the connections between the growing expansion of English print culture and growing knowledge within and without the court room.[47] The ability to easily produce printed forms such as warrants and recognizances meant that sheriffs and attorneys no longer had to employ clerks to laboriously hand copy said documents, which helped growing efforts to streamline the legal process.

Printing Presses in New England

Printing presses were gradually imported to North America, though they were more common in New England than in the other English colonies. Wealthy British minister Joseph Glover solicited donations in both England and the Netherlands to support bringing a press to Massachusetts in the late 1630s. Glover's press arrived in 1638 along with printer Stephen Day whom he had hired to run it, although Glover died on the voyage to North America. Glover's press was eventually established in the home of Henry Dunster, the first president of Harvard, whom Glover's widow married shortly after her arrival in Massachusetts.[48] The second press was brought by Marmaduke Johnson in 1660, though he moved it to Boston in 1674. The following year, John Foster founded another press in Boston and others followed in the early eighteenth century. The first document known to have been printed in Massachusetts was the Freeman's Oath of 1639, which contained "propositions to which each man in the Massachusetts colony must give his assent as a condition of citizenship."[49] Most other documents published in this early period were either political or religious in nature.

Like their counterparts in England, Massachusetts presses also printed "recognizances, subpoenas, deeds, or letters of attorney, whose virtue lies in what Benjamin Franklin called their 'correctness,'" a transition which Hugh Amory

46 See Frederick W. Hamilton, *A Brief History of Printing in England* (Chicago: United Typothetae of America, 1918).

47 Deborah Harkness, *The Jewel House: Elizabethan London and the Scientific Revolution* (New Haven: Yale University Press, 2008).

48 See George Emery Littlefield, *Early Boston Booksellers, 1642–1711* (Burt Franklin: New York, 1969).

49 Lawrence C. Wroth, *The Colonial Printer* (Portland: Southworth-Anthoensen Press, 1938), 224.

dates to the late 1680s.[50] Initially, the production of such documents posed the occasional challenge to Massachusetts presses since demand sometimes outstretched the amount of paper they had on hand. Nevertheless, they forged on, printing warrants and subpoenas on all sizes and qualities of paper. These challenges eased in the late 1720s with the founding of the first paper mill in Milton, Massachusetts.[51] Lawrence Wroth notes that the printing of such documents was "by no means a hardship to the printer; on the contrary, there is evidence that he regarded the profits from the sale of this staple as the 'velvet' of his business."[52] They also provided both colony and county governments with a more efficient means of processing the growing numbers of early eighteenth-century colonists either on trial for criminal charges or taking each other to trial on civil charges.

Massachusetts printers also "published law books or books related to the law [rendering them] the most active legal printers in the colonies."[53] *The Laws and Libertyes* was first published by Matthew Day in Cambridge in 1648 and further supplements were printed throughout the seventeenth century. In addition, presses in Massachusetts published law books for Plymouth, Connecticut, and New Hampshire colonies and probably also printed legal documents for both Maine and Rhode Island. However, even after the founding of the paper mills in the 1720s, the Massachusetts presses continued to use imported paper for law books. An indifferent scrap of locally made paper was acceptable for use as a warrant or recognizance; the colony's laws needed the greater authority provided by smooth, uniformly made paper from Europe.[54]

Preprinted Documents in Massachusetts

An early example of the presence of both preprinted legal documents and paid legal counsel in Massachusetts is a lengthy preprinted court document dated January 1, 1728 which allowed any colonist using it to authorize the person of their choice "to be my True, Sufficient, and Lawful Attorney, for me and in

---

50 Hugh Amory, "Printing and Bookselling in New England, 1638–1713," in *The Colonial Book: A History of the Book in America*, Volume I, Hugh Amory and David D. Hall, eds (Chapel Hill: University of Carolina Press, 2007), 111.

51 See Amory, "Printing and Book-Selling in New England" and Wroth, *The Colonial Printer*.

52 Wroth, *The Colonial Printer*, 224.

53 Morris Cohen, "Legal Literature in Colonial Massachusetts," in *Law in Colonial Massachusetts, 1630–1800*, Daniel Coquilette, ed. (Boston: The Colonial Society of Massachusetts, distributed by the University Press of Virginia, 1984), 247.

54 Wroth, *The Colonial Printer*, 123.

my Name and Stead, and to my Use, to Ask, Demand, Levy, Require, Recover and Receive of and from all and every person ... all and singular Sum and Sums of Money, Debts, Goods, Ware Merchandise, Effects and Things."[55] The first surviving use of a preprinted form in a sexual misconduct trial in Essex County dates to 1727.[56] The form is a recognizance for Ephraim Eaton, who was charged with "the crime of fornication committed by him with Sarah Hutchins Daughter of Samuel Hutchins of Salisbury." The printed section labeled the document as a recognizance form and was divided into two parts. The preprinted text in the upper section provided spaces for the court clerk to fill in the calendar date and the appropriate "Year of the Reign of Our Sovereign Lord George," the names of the defendant and his or surety and the Justice of the Peace they had appeared before, and the amount of money pledged as recognizance. The preprinted text in the lower section provided spaces for the court clerk to fill in the date for the defendant's court hearing and the crime which he or she was being charged with. Finally, there was space for the signature of the Justice of the Peace, in this case, William Bradbury.[57]

Another commonly used preprinted form used in sexual misconduct trials was the form requiring the appearances of various persons in court. Unlike the recognizance form, warrants were divided into three sections. The top section had space for the clerk to fill out the name or names of the defendants and their crime. The middle section provided space for the clerk to fill in the date of the court hearing. The lower section provided room for the clerk to fill in the names of any witnesses. If the female defendant was pregnant, as was often the case, the midwife and the women who had attended the birth were called as witnesses. Finally, the document was dated and signed, usually by a court clerk rather than a Justice of the Peace.[58]

An entirely handwritten arrest warrant from Marblehead in 1719 demonstrates an interest in creating more efficient methods for processing multiple defendants prior to 1727. The warrant charged Sarah Wescot, Grace Davis, and Mary Johnson

55 Preprinted warrant signed by John King declaring Edward Shoue to be his attorney, Essex County Court of General Sessions, File Papers Box 12, Judicial Archives, Massachusetts State Archives, Boston.

56 Preprinted forms from earlier in the eighteenth century related to other types of charges also exist in the surviving Essex County court records. At this point, it is difficult to know whether it took court officials longer to use preprinted forms for sexual misconduct trials or whether there just are no surviving forms from these trials.

57 All quotes from the Essex County Court of General Sessions trial for Ephraim Eaton in 1727, File Papers Box 9. Judicial Archives, Massachusetts State Archives, Boston.

58 All quotes from the Essex County Court of General Sessions trial for Isaac and Mary Hall in 1735, File Papers Box 12. Judicial Archives, Massachusetts State Archives, Boston.

alias Baker with fornication and ordered all three of them to appear in court in Salem in February of 1719. It also ordered Mrs Austin, Midwife, Mrs Lyndsey, Midwife, and the Widow James to appear in court as witnesses, presumably to their respective clients' births.[59] Differences in both the handwriting and the ink color make clear that most of the warrant was created in advance by one person and the names, charges, and dates were filled in later by someone else. As the handwriting in the warrant itself is particularly clear, this suggests a clerk with good handwriting was hired to create warrants and other legal forms in advance. This practice was more efficient than creating individual warrants on the spot as needed but it still required paying clerks to spend hours filling out forms. Essex County sheriffs and justices adapted very quickly to the relative ease of preprinted forms as 1733 was the last year in which handwritten legal forms consistently appear and preprinted legal forms dominate the Essex County court records by the end of the 1730s.

Preprinted Documents in Maine

Preprinted documents were also used for civil trials in Maine before they were used for criminal trials. The earliest surviving preprinted document in the Maine court records was used in 1724 when a colonist was put on trial for debt. The first surviving preprinted document from a sexual misconduct trial in Maine dates to 1734, some seven years after the first equivalent document from Essex County. This particular form guaranteed that Charles Stuard would provide surety that his wife, Mary Stuard, would appear in court to answer for the charge of fornication before marriage, which she then did a few months later.[60] Preprinted legal documents dominated Maine's sexual misconduct trials by the end of the 1730s. A key difference between Maine and Essex County was how these individual jurisdictions used their preprinted legal documents. There are several preprinted warrants in the Essex County records in which a single document was used to call multiple defendants and witnesses from the same town for multiple trials. By contrast, preprinted documents in Maine were used only for single trials and only for calling specific legal roles within those same trials, as separate forms were created for calling defendants and witnesses.

---

[59] All quotes from the Essex County Court of General Sessions trials for Sarah Wescot, Grace Davis and Mary Johnson in 1719, File Papers Box 6. Judicial Archives, Massachusetts State Archives, Boston.

[60] All trial quotes are from the York County Court of General Sessions trial for Charles and Mary Stuard in 1733, York County Court of Common Pleas & General Sessions File Papers, Box 63. Maine State Archives, Augusta.

Two examples of the Maine form used for calling witnesses come from a bastardy and paternity trial in 1739. The document provided space for the court clerk to write in the names of "Elinor Sayer, the wife of David Sayer & Jn. Barry Cordwainer, Both of Scarborough" to tell them in the printed part of the document that they were required "To give Evidence of what you know relating to an Action then and there to be Heard and Tryed." The next part of the form provided space for the clerk to write in the names of "Mary Macgown, Complainant" and "Abraham Tyler, Respondant." The form finished by warning Sayer and Barry to "Hereof Fail not, as you will Answer your Default under the Pains and Penalty in the Law" and provided further space for the document to be dated on March 7, 1739.[61] The second document for the same trial was issued to "Susanna Brown, the wife of Andrew Brown and Sarah Hagire, the wife of Fergus Hagire and Deborah Pickerring, Spinster," all of whom lived in Scarborough as well. Warrants for Macgown and Tyler did not survive but they were probably also called to court and expected to make arrangements for surety to be sworn to guarantee their appearances in court.

At first glance, the York County judicial system appears possessed with a wild disregard for paper conservation. The first printing press did not reach Maine until 1785, which meant that all of these preprinted documents had to be imported from Massachusetts.[62] However, the decision to invest in both single trial warrants and separate warrants for defendants and witnesses probably reflected reality on the ground in Maine. Most Essex County towns were densely populated enough that sheriffs routinely needed to call multiple defendants and their witnesses from the same town or the same section of town for the same court session and so could use a single warrant for all of them, though one question left unanswered by the court records is how a single warrant for multiple trials actually worked. Possible explanations are that the warrant was published in a public place in the town, read aloud in church, or taken from house to house, and that the individual colonists were instructed to write down the particulars of their court summons. Maine was thinly populated enough in the 1730s that a single warrant for multiple trials was unfeasible as two colonists from the same town were rarely charged with sexual misconduct for the same court session and, even if two defendants from the same town were charged, the odds of them living near each other were unlikely. The warrants requesting witnesses for the Macgown/Tyler trial bear this last theory out as two warrants

---

61 All trial quotes are from the York County Court of General Sessions trial for Mary Macgown in 1739, York County Court of Common Pleas & General Sessions File Papers, Box 78. Maine State Archives, Augusta.

62 Wroth, *The Colonial Printer*, 27.

were issued for five witnesses, all of whom lived in Scarborough, and, presumably, the first warrant was issued for two witnesses who lived near one another and the second was for three witnesses who lived in another part of the town.

Single use warrants served a practical purpose for Maine sheriffs trying to cover a wider space than their Essex County counterparts. Investing in so many different legal forms also reflects Maine justices' continued desire for visibility both in the eyes of their colonists and in the eyes of Massachusetts Bay. The piles of documents headed north to Maine and outward to individual colonists provided a vivid reminder in the eighteenth century that York County officials were as capable of modernizing their judicial practices as they had proven themselves capable of adapting the legal language used in the sexual misconduct trials in the seventeenth century. Maine's first paper mills were established in the 1730s, just as the use of preprinted documents was taking off in Maine, and perhaps York County officials were able to trade paper for printing their legal forms.

Preprinted Documents in Rhode Island

Lawrence Wroth argues that the first printing press in Rhode Island was James Franklin's in 1727 as Franklin published a book titled *John Hammett's Vindication and Relation: Giving an Account of his separating from the Baptists, and joining the Quakers* in Newport, Rhode Island, that year. The following year Franklin advertised that he had "Bonds, Bills, Power of Attorney, Paper by the Ream" available for sale, indicating that he also provided preprinted legal documents.[63] The earliest preprinted legal document in the Rhode Island court records is a warrant for the arrest of George Thomas dated on January 25, 1725. This either means that Rhode Island, like Maine, published their legal documents in Massachusetts or that the Franklin press was started before *John Hammett's Vindication and Relation* was published in 1727. Given the two-year time gap between the arrest warrant and the first book published by James Franklin in Rhode Island and the ongoing antipathy between Rhode Island and Massachusetts, I would argue the Franklin press was started in 1725 and earned money to print its first book by printing legal and financial documents.[64]

---

[63] Wroth, *The Colonial Printer*, 224. For his part, Isaiah Thomas dates the founding of the Franklin press to 1732. Thomas, *The History of Printing in America, with a Biography of Printers & an Account of Newspapers* (New York: Weathervane Books, 1970), 315.

[64] See the Newport County Supreme Court trial for George Thomas in 1725, Newport County Supreme Court File Papers, Rhode Island Judicial Archives, Pawtucket.

Conclusion

The process of being tried on sexual misconduct charges underwent multiple transitions in early modern England. Sixteenth- and early seventeenth-century defendants were tried in ecclesiastical courts on moral grounds and the economic challenges potentially posed by the conception of illegitimate children were not considered in the court room. The 1574 statute requiring that men and women who could not financially support their illegitimate children be prosecuted in secular courts brought economic issues to the forefront for the first time. The 1650 law requiring that adultery, incest, and fornication be tried in the secular courts was a short-lived experiment, though the late seventeenth-century Societies for the Reformation of Manners can be seen as its legitimately conceived descendants. Economic and class issues became ever more important in the eighteenth century as sexual misconduct laws came to affect only the lower classes. Justices prosecuting sexual misconduct in Massachusetts, Maine, and Rhode Island followed similar paths to their English counterparts, albeit at different times and sometimes for different reasons. The colonial experience would, however, add racial issues to the already existing moral and economic dilemmas posed by extramarital sex and, in time, this created the first real break between law in England and law in its North American colonies.

Chapter 3

"Exposing our children, to be bred ignorantly like Indians": Frontier Peripheries and Cross-Cultural Sexual Contact

Early modern Europeans often used highly sexualized linguistic and visual images in their efforts to define the Americas.[1] John Smith's encounter with Pocahontas is one of several contact narratives focused on exchanges between white men and Native American women. A late sixteenth-century engraving created by Jan van der Straet portrayed America as a woman dressed in feathers waiting for Europe to discover and claim her, an image further substantiated by longstanding European beliefs regarding the male and female genders.[2] Medieval and early modern women were often portrayed as naturally lustful, unrestrained, and fecund, and thus in need of male guidance and restraint.[3] Such portrayals played easily into the ongoing rhetoric of conquest and colonization, which suggested that the Americas had much to offer in the way of raw goods and open spaces, but needed to be carefully shaped by European style law and order in order to become both prosperous and profitable.

The process of shaping the Americas took a wide variety of forms in the different European colonies. Once settlement was established, English colonists were expected to remain within their own cultural groups and limit their

---

1 Richard Goodbeer, *Sexual Revolution in Early America* (Baltimore: The Johns Hopkins University Press, 2002), 3–6 and 154–89.

2 Louis Montrose, "The Work of Gender in the Discourse of Discovery," *Representations* 33 (1991), 57.

3 See Anthony Fletcher, *Gender, Sex and Subordination in England, 1500–1800* (New Haven: Yale University Press, 1995), Kathleen Brown, *Good Wives, Nasty Wenches, and Anxious Patriarchs: Gender, Race, and Power in Colonial Virginia* (Chapel Hill: University of North Carolina Press, 1996), Mary Beth Norton, "Communal Definitions of Gendered Identity in Seventeenth –Century English America," in *Through a Glass Darkly: Reflections on Personal Identity in Early America*, Ronald Hoffman, Mechal Sobel, and Fredricka Teute, eds (Chapel Hill: University of North California Press, 1997), and Faramerz Dabhoiwala, *The Origins of Sex: A History of the First Sexual Revolution* (Oxford: Oxford University Press, 2012) for a variety of discussions on early modern definitions of gender and gender differences.

contact with Native Americans to mercantile exchanges and political alliances, though this did not always happen. Attacks on settlements on both sides often led to captivity in northern New England or Canada for English colonists, while Native Americans taken captive by the English came to labor in their households. In addition, the mid- to late seventeenth century saw rising numbers of Africans sent as slaves to colonies up and down the eastern seaboard, who added another reminder of different cultural systems beyond the borders of the English colonies. Colonial leaders were not allowed to create laws "contrary or repugnant to the laws of England."[4] They were, however, allowed to create new laws to address situations which had neither precedent nor parallel in English law.[5] Over time, the presence of both Native and African-Americans, whether as political entities outside the English colonies or as servants or slaves within the colonies, were used to justify the creation of new laws addressing interracial sexual contact, whether consensual or nonconsensual.

Regional and Peripheral Implications of Cross-cultural Sexual Contact

Most comprehensive studies on interracial sexual contact in the English colonies have focused on individual colonies or cities in the southern and mid-Atlantic colonies, with the equivalent research in New England focused more on individual cases.[6] These studies all contribute greatly to discussions on the ways in which English colonists in North America understood both racial identity and sexual contact between races in a period when both of these things were rapidly

---

4 Mary Sarah Bilder, *The Transatlantic Constitution: Colonial Legal Culture and the Empire* (Cambridge: Harvard University Press, 2004), 3.

5 See Bradley Chapin, *Criminal Justice in Colonial America, 1606–1660* (Athens: University of Georgia Press, 1983) which provides a breakdown for the source material for the laws created in Virginia, Plymouth, Massachusetts Bay, Maryland, Rhode Island, Connecticut, and New Haven colonies in the first half of the seventeenth century.

6 See Brown, *Good Wives, Nasty Wenches, and Anxious Patriarchs*, Kirsten Fischer, *Suspect Relations: Sex, Race and Resistance in North Carolina* (Ithaca: Cornell University Press, 2002), and Clare Lyons, *Sex among the Rabble: An Intimate History of Gender & Power in the Age of Revolution, Philadelphia, 1730–1830* (Chapel Hill: University of North Carolina Press, 2006) for studies on the southern and mid-Atlantic colonies. For New England, see John Wood Sweet, *Bodies Politic: Negotiating Race in the American North, 1730–1830* (Philadelphia: University of Pennsylvania Press, 2006), Elaine Forman Crane, *Witches, Wife Beaters, & Whores: Common Law and Common Folk* (Ithaca: Cornell University Press, 2011), and M. Michelle Jarrett Morris, *Under Household Government: Sex and Family in Puritan Massachusetts* (Cambridge: Harvard University Press, 2013).

evolving. Nevertheless, colonial and regional differences were not the only factors which shaped contact experiences between English colonists and non-whites in North America. Interracial sexual contact was also affected by whether those same colonists lived in the center or the periphery of their particular colonies and regions and this distinction appears throughout the construction and the prosecution of laws governing interracial sex in English North America.[7]

The Puritan colonies of Massachusetts and Connecticut are commonly regarded as New England's cultural and political center, with the northern New England colonies of Maine and New Hampshire as the periphery and Rhode Island somewhere in-between.[8] Interracial sex in northern New England generally occurred outside the legal jurisdictions of the English colonies. By contrast, interracial sex in southern New England took place within colonial jurisdictions which meant that it could be addressed by laws and court trials. This paradox created a lingering unease about events occurring just beyond their borders which hovers around Maine's sexual misconduct trials, regardless of the racial identity of the defendants.[9] Colonial leaders worried that the political fluidity created by the settlement process would encourage settlers to break away from the English colonies in search of the North American wilderness and its less restrained inhabitants. Maine's position on the edge of English settlement made the region a concern long after the southern New England colonies were believed safely tamed and managed, their non-white inhabitants under English law and English rule.

Colonial Warfare in Maine

English efforts to maintain a cultural separation between colonists and Native Americans were further challenged by the long series of colonial wars at the turn of the eighteenth century, beginning in 1675 with King Philip's War, a conflict between the Wampanoag and their English neighbors in Plymouth Colony. The war came to Maine in the summer of 1676 just as it was winding

---

7 See Amy Turner Bushnell and Jack P. Greene, "Peripheries, Centers, and the Construction of Early Modern American Empires," in *Negotiated Empires: Centers and Peripheries in the Americas, 1500–1820*, Christine Daniels and Michael V. Kennedy, eds (New York: Routledge Press, 2002), 1–14 for further discussion of the use of peripheries and centers when considering the expansion of colonial political and social structures.

8 Joseph Conforti, *Saints and Strangers: New England in British North America* (Baltimore: The John Hopkins University Press, 2006), 67–97.

9 This chapter will also draw on sexual misconduct trials from Plymouth Colony as there are some applicable trials.

down in southern New England. An uneasy peace was declared in Maine with the Treaty of Casco in 1678 which lasted until the outbreaks of King William's War in 1689 and Queen Anne's War in 1702. The ensuing tensions dragged on through the 1740s with King George's War, not to mention multiple smaller and more localized conflicts. Maine was particularly affected by these wars and decades of conflict nearly proved disastrous for the Maine settlements. New Plymouth Colony was almost destroyed, as were the eastern towns in York County, including Wells, Scarborough, and Falmouth.[10] Over time, the years of warfare took their toll on Maine in a variety of ways. The York County Court of General Sessions records document that Mathew and Elizabeth Young were charged and convicted on April 1, 1697 for fornication before marriage. The couple was ordered to pay court fees of nine shillings each and to receive nine lashes each or pay 25 shillings each in fines. The Youngs then humbly petitioned the court to reduce their fine by 10 shillings each. They could not afford the full fine but they did not want to be whipped. Over half of all defendants convicted on sexual misconduct charges paid reduced fines between 1697 and 1714. None of the records say why the court agreed to the reduced fines. However, the disappearance of this practice from the court records the year after the Treaty of Portsmouth concluded Queen Anne's War in 1713 suggests that the decision was linked to these conflicts. York County was desperate for money at the turn of the eighteenth century. With the waves of attacks continuing to sweep over Maine, surviving militia members needed to be on constant alert, with a ready stream of guns and ammunition at hand. Hundreds of colonists were also taken captive from Maine settlements by Native American or French forces and needed to be ransomed back from their captors and their surviving family members often looked to York County for financial assistance with these efforts.[11] All in all, these attacks were an expensive business indeed for an already cash poor region. By contrast, while Essex County was affected by both King Philip's War and King William's War, there is no evidence that Essex County justices ever reduced fines to persuade colonists to pay in currency rather than receiving the less expensive whippings. Nor is there evidence that Rhode Island justices ever reduced fines during King Philip's War.

---

[10] See Jenny Hale Pulsipher, *Subjects unto the Same King: Indians, English and the Contest for Authority in Colonial New England* (Philadelphia: University of Pennsylvania Press, 2005) and Julie Wheelwright, *Esther, The Remarkable True Story of Esther Wheelwright: Puritan Child, Native Daughter, Mother Superior* (Toronto: HarperCollins Publishers Ltd, 2011).

[11] See Emma Lewis Coleman, *New England Captives Carried to Canada Between 1677 and 1760 During the French and Indian Wars* (Portland: Southworth Press, 1925) for further discussion on the financial resources committed to ransoming back Maine captives.

Maine Colonists and Native American Captivity

Maine colonists taken as captives to Canada also posed other challenges for the region. While the trial record for the York County Court of General Sessions on October 1, 1695 documents the presence of new clerk and registrar John Newman, the record fails to explain why York County needed a new clerk. Neal Allen writes that Joseph Hammond, the prior clerk, had been captured by an Abenaki raiding party the previous summer while hunting for a lost cow. Newman had been serving unofficially in the position since July and the justices probably waited until they received word that Hammond had been taken to Quebec before officially replacing him. Likewise, Hammond's return to English society did not warrant discussion in the court records. The only indication of his presence is a change in the handwriting of the court transcripts. Hammond continued to hold his position until 1700 when he was succeeded by his son. Maine had only been part of Massachusetts Bay Colony for a short time in the 1690s and a court system in a region where the clerk could be captured by Native Americans while hunting for a lost cow could have invited closer investigation from Massachusetts.

Even more problematic than a briefly missing court clerk for most English communities were returning long-term captives, whose perspectives were assumed to encompass the worldviews of their captors as well as their English families and neighbors.[12] Life was uncertain enough already without the threat of the social destabilization such colonists might now be capable of provoking. These concerns took center stage when newly returned captive Elisha Ingersoll was tried on October 1, 1695 for adultery with Dorothy, wife of Robert Saterly, in a trial notable more for the events which did not occur than the ones that did.[13]

At first glance, the Saterly/Ingersoll trial was a typical sexual misconduct trial from the turn of the eighteenth century. Five of the deponents repeated colonist Elizabeth Crecy's statement that she had seen "unsivell acksons ... between Elisha Ingersoll and doryty Satarly" in late May of 1695. Other deponents provided Ingersoll with alibis for the period described by Crecy. The Ingersoll family was prosperous and Ingersoll's father John had run a mill in Falmouth

---

[12] See John Gyles, "Memoirs of Odd Adventures, Strange Deliverances, Etc. in the Captivity of John Gyles," in *Puritans among the Indians: Accounts of Captivity and Redemption, 1676–1724*, Alden T. Vaughan and Edward W. Clark, eds (Cambridge: Harvard University Press, 1981) for an example of a returned captive who remained balanced between European and Native American societies for the rest of his life.

[13] Elisha was, most likely, a phonetic spelling of Elijah.

before purchasing a farm in Kittery in 1690.[14] The Saterlys were far poorer and Ingersoll's sister Mary testified that Dorothy was hired to help card wool in the Ingersoll household, a low- status job usually performed by orphaned teenagers.[15] While doing this work, Mary verified that "I was never out of her compeney nether day nor neights except it was to stepe out for a boucket of water or the like." This pattern of an initial accusation and a series of alibis appears throughout colonial New England sexual misconduct trials, and further examples of such trials will be discussed in the next two chapters.

With the initial depositions out of the way, the Ingersoll/Saterly trial proceeded to head in a very different direction. Deponent John Andorson stated that he "came out of captivity with Elisha Engresell [around May 25, 1695] & kept company with him on tell: wee bouth came to pescatweay [around May 29]." The exact date of Ingersoll's initial capture is unknown but he was captured as a boy and returned to English society around the age of 20. Like Mary Ingersoll, Andorson was trying to provide Ingersoll with an alibi by suggesting that there was not enough time for him to have committed adultery with Dorothy Saterly, but his reminder that Ingersoll was a newly returned captive may, albeit unwittingly, have added fuel to the prosecution's fire. Deponent Thomas Starbord testified next that Elizabeth Crecy had seen Ingersoll lying on a bed in the middle of the day and had "axt Him whether he was not a shamed to sleep that time of day." Most English colonists thought all Native Americans lived immoral lives and the sight of a young man lounging on a bed in broad daylight may have reminded Ingersoll's neighbors of these beliefs.[16] Such a young man would, no doubt, have thought nothing about making sexual advances to the married Dorothy Saterly and Starbord's testimony adds that Crecy had also seen "dot upon hir Back and hir coats up and She saw hir thights and His Breeches down."

At this point, however, the trial broke down entirely. The problem with the evidence against Elisha Ingersoll was that it was based solely on hearsay. None of the deponents had actually seen Ingersoll and Dorothy Saterly together.

---

14 Sybil Noyes, Charles Thornton Libby, and Walter C. Davis, *Genealogical Dictionary of Maine and New Hampshire* (Portland: Anthoensen Press, 1928), 368.

15 All quotes from the York County General Sessions of the Peace trial for Elisha Ingersoll in 1695, in *Province and Court Records of Maine*, Volume 4, Neal Allen, ed. (Portland: Anthoensen Press, 1958), 46–7. See Marla Miller, *The Needle's Eye, Women and Work in the Age of Revolution* (Amherst: University of Massachusetts Press, 2006) for further discussion of women's hired work in the colonial period.

16 See Ann Marie Plain, *Colonial Intimacies, Indian Marriage in Early New England* (Ithaca: Cornell University Press, 2000).

Instead, they were all reporting what Elizabeth Crecy said she had seen. Neal Allen speculates that Ingersoll's position as a young man held captive by Native Americans for his entire adolescence made his neighbors more willing to believe Crecy's accusations than they might have been otherwise.[17] One after another, they all cited her stories as truth. The justices eventually declared Elisha Ingersoll not guilty based on lack of evidence. Elizabeth Crecy never testified in person and her role in the trial remains a mystery. Allen notes that "a warrant [was] issued by William Pepperell, dated 22 July 1695, ordering the sheriff to hold her in jail for her *refusal* to find sureties for her appearance in court."[18] There are no surviving statements from either Ingersoll or Saterly and Saterly was never charged. Like rape, adultery required both witnesses and confessions to be prosecuted. The justices finished the trial by ordering Ingersoll to pay court fees of 11 shillings and sixpence. Requiring acquitted defendants to pay court fees was customary in the colonial period, since it provided an indirect form of punishment. Had the defendant's behavior not warranted the suggestion that he or she might be guilty, a court appearance would not have been necessary. Regardless of whether he was guilty of adultery, Ingersoll was held liable for his potential acculturation among the Abenaki. His neighbors did not so much fear his actual actions as the potential ripple effects on their community caused by a young man who seemingly had lost all comprehension of European sexual mores. Arguably, Ingersoll was also put on trial because his Native American captors could not be tried for exposing him to their (in the minds of the English colonists) lax morals and dangerous ways.

The Province of Maine as Cultural Frontier

Elisha Ingersoll's position as a returned Native American captive was given center stage during his adultery trial. It also points to another component common to many of colonial Maine's sexual misconduct trials. Even before the colonial wars began, most southern New England colonists believed Maine colonists to be little different from their Native American neighbors when it came to sexual morals. Commissioners sent by Charles II in 1668 were reputed to have said that Maine colonists were without "any Government amongst them ... some heere

17 Neal Allen writes that "it is a conjecture only, but one that seems to be borne out by the evidence here, that he had been to some extent weaned from English ways. Allen, "Introduction," *Province and Court Records of Maine*, Volume 4, xxxix.

18 Allen, *Province and Court Records of Maine*, Volume 4, 46.

are of opinion, That as many men may share in a woman, as they do in a boat."[19] Cotton Mather's seven-volume *Magnalia Christi Americana or the Ecclesiastical History of New England* provided a wide array of commentary on the subject when it was published in 1702. The first volume tells the story of a frustrated Massachusetts minister told by a member of his congregation that "Sir, you ... think you are preaching to the people at the Bay; our main end was to catch fish."[20] A later comment on Maine's disorderliness came from the captivity narrative of Hannah Swarton, which was recorded in volume six. Swarton was taken captive from Casco, Maine, during King William's War in 1690 and was held captive in New France for over five years. According to Mather, Swarton deeply regretted "leaving the publick worship and ordinances of God ... to remove to the north part of *Casco Bay* ... thereby exposing our children, to be bred ignorantly like *Indians*" and saw her captivity as punishment for leaving Massachusetts for the wilds of Maine.[21] Modern historians have also questioned whether colonial Maine's reputation for sexual immorality was deserved. Charles Clark's 1970 assessment of Maine largely agreed with contemporary portrayals of the colony from outside observers. Edwin Churchill countered Clark by arguing that any negative colonial descriptions of Maine were simply political propaganda but Clark still observed in 1983 that while Churchill made some good points, he "only did limited damage, as I see it, to the overall argument developed in [*The Eastern Frontier*]."[22]

The behavior of colonist Thomas Reed suggests Reed was equally familiar with Maine's reputation as a place where sexual immorality would be tolerated. Like the Reverend George Burdett in the previous chapter, Reed abandoned a wife and child to move to Maine where he began a sexual relationship with

---

19 "Copy of a Narrative of the Commissioners from England, about New England," *The Hutchison Papers*, Volume II (Albany: Printed for the Prince Society by Joel Munsell), 153.

20 Cotton Mather, *Magnalia Christi Americana or the Ecclesiastical History of New England*, Volume I (Hartford: Silas Andrus and Son, 1853), 62.

21 Mather, *Magnalia Christi Americana*, Volume 6, 307. Mather originally used Swarton's story as a sermon and published it in *Magnalia Christi Americana* under the title "A Narrative of Hannah Swarton, containing Wonderful Passages, relating to her Captivity and her Deliverance." While Swarton's account is written in the first person, the tone suggests Mather as ghost-writer. Another work by Mather with similar themes is Mather, *The Fisher-mans Calling A Brief Essay, to Serve the Great Interests of Religion among our Fisher-men* (Boston: T. Green, 1712).

22 Edwin Churchill, "Too Great the Challenge: The Birth and Death of Falmouth, Maine,1624–1676" (PhD diss., University of Maine, 1979) and "A Most Ordinary Lot of Men: The Fishermen at Richmond Island, Maine, in the Early Seventeenth Century," *The New England Quarterly* 57, no. 2 (1981): 184–204 and Charles Clark, *The Eastern Frontier: The Settlement of Northern New England, 1610–1763* (Hanover: University Press of New England, 1983), xv.

a woman named Elizabeth Brookes, which led to his being charged with fornication on October 1, 1717. The first deponents, Samuel Donner and Joseph Sayward, document the presences of both Thomas Reed and Elizabeth Brookes in York County.[23] Both acknowledge Brookes's pregnancy and assume that Reed and Brookes were married. However, the third deponent, Samuel Littlefield, describes growing suspicions among Reed and Brookes's neighbors, namely that "Mistress Stover desired him to Enquire about Thomas Reeds wife whether She were living ... when I was at Braintry I saw his wife and She sent a Letter by me." This same deposition raises additional questions about just who fathered Brookes's child, noting that Reed had said that "Brookes was with Child & Laid it to him but he was afraid it was by a Negro," a point that will be further discussed later in this chapter. The final deposition was a letter from Reed's wife, Sarah, pleading with Thomas to come home to her. If she was aware of Elizabeth Brookes's presence in her husband's life, she makes no mention of it. The letter closes with the remark that "my mother and all [*illeg.*] disir kind Love to you."

The use of Sarah Reed's letter as court deposition changed the trial from a simple bastardy and paternity trial to one with much greater implications. In addition to impregnating a single woman in Maine, Reed had deserted his loving wife and family and left them without any means of financial support. With Sarah Reed's existence verified, the court ruled that the initial crime of fornication and bastardy was "aggravated by Sundry Notorious Circumstances." They ordered Reed to receive 25 lashes, pay court fees of 26 shillings and be jailed until posting a bond for his good behavior. He was not given a choice between being whipped or paying an additional fine, which suggests his crime was less fornication and bastardy than adultery. While a less harsh punishment for adultery than the hanging or 39 lashes recommended in some seventeenth-century cases, 25 lashes "severely laid on his Naked back," was still quite stark for the period. Similar to the Saterly/Ingersoll trial, Thomas Reed was not the only entity on trial on 1717. Maine and its reputation were also on trial in the minds of the York County justices. They needed to make it abundantly clear that Maine was not a safe haven for men who abandoned their wives and children in other colonies, lest other colonists decide to follow suit.

Contemporary observers and some modern scholars alike have seen colonial Maine's position on the periphery of both English and Puritan North America as fixing it permanently in the early exploration period when sexual practices

---

[23] All quotes are from the York County Court of General Sessions trial for Thomas Reed in 1717, in *Province and Court Records of Maine*, Volume 5, Neal Allen, ed. (Portland: Anthoensen Press, 1964), 201.

were more fluid in the minds of many colonists. The colonial wars added to this impression with their continual disruptions of Maine society, whether kidnapping court clerks or exposing Maine residents to the practices of their Native American neighbors. Nevertheless, the court records demonstrate Thomas Reed's and George Burdett's belief that Maine was a place where extramarital sex would be tolerated was swiftly corrected when they were tried, convicted, and punished in short order. Edwin Churchill notes that the early Maine judicial system as "surprisingly vital ... [with] a remarkable resiliency and adaptability while retaining [its] basic functions and vigor."[24] Dating back to the colony's origins in the early seventeenth century, Maine authorities had always made it abundantly clear to their colonists that there would be laws regarding all forms of misconduct, including sexual, and breaking those laws would result in court trials, convictions, and punishments. The fact that they were so vehement on this point highlights their uneasiness about both their reputation and the potentially dangerous acculturating effects of their neighbors to the north and east.

Growing Political Control in Southern New England

The ongoing uneasiness present throughout the Maine court records stands in sharp contrast to southern New England's growing political confidence at the turn of the eighteenth century when it came to Native American sovereignty. Yasuhide Kawashima has identified three stages of acculturation between Native Americans and English colonists, Extraterritoriality, Legal Coexistence, and Legal Imperialism.[25] Maine and New Hampshire spent much of the colonial period between Extraterritoriality and Legal Coexistence, which Kawashima defines, respectively, as almost no knowledge of each other and two co-existing cultural groups. Not coincidentally, there were no Native Americans placed on trial for sexual misconduct in Maine before 1750.[26] But the close of King Philip's War in 1676 had brought all hopes of Native American sovereignty in southern

[24] Edwin Churchill, "English Beachheads in Seventeenth-Century Maine," in *Maine, The Pine Tree State from Prehistory to Present*, Richard Judd, ed. (Orono: University of Maine Press, 1995), 33.

[25] See Yasuhide Kawashima, *Puritan Justice and the Indian: White Man's Law in Massachusetts, 1630–1763* (Middletown: Wesleyan University Press, 1986).

[26] There was a Native American woman named Patience Boston who lived on Casco Bay in the 1730s, though she was originally from Massachusetts and had been sold to the Bailey family. She was convicted and hanged for murder in 1735 and left behind an illegitimate child who was granted child support by York County. Boston was not prosecuted for conceiving an illegitimate child, most likely because she was already facing capital punishment for murder. Daniel E.

New England to a close and Kawashima describes the period after 1676 in southern New England as Legal Imperialism, which he defines as total legal domination of one group by another. Members of the Wampanoag, Narragansett, Mahican, and other tribal groups remained in southern New England but they either lived on the outskirts of English society or were embedded in English towns as servants or slaves.[27]

Native Americans and Sexual Misconduct Trials in Essex County

Massachusetts Bay, Plymouth, and Rhode Island colonies did not create specific laws addressing sexual intercourse between white colonists and Native Americans but a handful of sexual misconduct trials involving white colonists and Native Americans were tried in the Essex County, Plymouth, and Rhode Island courts and these trials reinforce the subtle differences which existed between the colonies of Massachusetts, Plymouth, and Rhode Island. The two Essex County trials involving white colonists and Native Americans were both bastardy and paternity trials and both featured Native Americans living in English households as servants following Massachusetts Bay's victory during King Philip's War. By contrast, the sexual misconduct trials from both Plymouth and Rhode Island colonies demonstrate that Native Americans living alongside these colonies were able to maintain a stronger sense of tribal identity than their Massachusetts Bay counterparts.

The Salem court put a woman described as "An, Samuel Gardiner's Indian Servant" on trial for bastardy in 1680. No further information regarding her tribal identity or how she came to work as a servant in Gardiner's household is available but the timing of the trial in 1680 again suggests that she became a servant in the period immediately following King Philip's War. An confirmed her pregnancy and named neighbor William Raine as the father of her child, a charge promptly denied by Raine. In lieu of a confession from Raine, the court turned instead to four deponents who included midwife Mary Woodberry. Early modern European legal practices required midwives to repeatedly ask their unmarried clients for the name of their partner during labor. Given An's status as a Native American who had probably only lived in an English household for a few years, it is uncertain whether she knew about the ritual of naming a father

Williams, *Pillars of Salt, Monuments of Grace: New England Crime Literature and the Origins of American Popular Culture, 1674–1860* (Boston: University of Massachusetts Press, 2006), 71–9.

27 See Daniel Mandell, *King Philip's War: Colonial Expansion, Native Resistance, and the End of Indian Sovereignty* (Baltimore: The Johns Hopkins University Press, 2010).

during childbirth before her pregnancy. Another uncertainty is whether she came from a tribal group who traced descent through the mother's line or the father's line, thereby potentially adding another level of cultural disconnection to her experience of birth in an English household. What is clear is that she followed the rules of her new society to the letter. Mary Woodberry's deposition firmly states that An "Answered William Raine [when asked] & held to the same the whole time of her travail unto her delivery."[28] Women who named fathers at their births were required to constantly name the same man while their midwives reminded them that they would answer at the Day of Judgment for lying and, again, it is uncertain whether An believed this last point as it is unknown whether she had converted to Christianity. It does, however, appear that Woodberry believed her testimony.

Mary Woodberry's testimony was accompanied by an array of deponents claiming to have seen An and William Raine together at all hours of day and night. Adding weight to the case against Raine was the fact that these deponents came from a range of both social classes and races, making collusion unlikely in the eyes of the court justices. Neighbor Mary Smith described watching An and Raine together while she was visiting Samuel Gardner's wife. Deliverance Towne, a servant in the Gardner household, described seeing "William Raine in Company with An ... at severall times about ten or eleven A Clock at night." Finally, a member of the Gardner household described as "Arrow, Negro" testified that he had seen "Raine in Company with An ... at severall times about ten or eleven A Clock at night also the said William Raine asked me [whether] our An were with child before I heard any others speak of it." It is unclear what Arrow meant by referring to An as "our An," although it seems a simple reference to someone he viewed as a member of the household in which he lived as there is no apparent evidence that the child was Arrow's. The child was probably carefully scrutinized at the birth to determine the father's race and the fact that this scrutiny is not mentioned suggests that the child's skin color backed up An's birth testimony. Likewise, had there been any chance that the child was Arrow and An's, William Raine would have mentioned it as part of his defense. Instead, he appears to have hoped that the court would take his testimony as a white man over testimony given by a Native American woman.

The justices convicted An on bastardy charges and ruled that she could choose between a whipping or paying a fine of 20 shillings monthly, an unusually steep financial punishment for a period in which convicted female defendants

[28] All quotes from the Essex County Quarterly Court Trial for An and William Raine in 1680, File Papers, Box 2. Judicial Archives, Massachusetts State Archives, Boston, Massachusetts.

were usually charged a flat fee of 50 shillings. William Raine was convicted on paternity charges and ordered to pay the court 70 shillings in costs as well as three shillings weekly to Samuel Gardner for the child's upkeep. An was most likely whipped since she would have been unable to pay the fine as a servant.

Essex County resident Sarah Pillsbury was placed on trial for bastardy in 1705 and the court records indicate some doubt as to whether her child was fathered by English colonist John Allen or by a man identified as Wiltshire, Richard Dole's Indian. The depositions document the following exchange between Pillsbury and the justices: "How many times had Willsheere to doe with you *Twice* When was it *When the Cherry trees was just out of the blossom*."[29] However, midwife Mary Lowell also testified that Pillsbury said during her labor that the child's father was "John Allens and said if I should lay it to Any Body else I should damne my owne soule." Unable to decide whether the child had been fathered by Allen or Wilshire, the justices acquitted both men and left Pillsbury to support her child as best she could. It is unclear whether the decision to follow English custom and acquit Wiltshire alongside Allen because Pillsbury did not know who had fathered her child was done to spare Wiltshire or his master, who would have been responsible for any penalties assigned to his servant.

Native Americans and Sexual Misconduct Trials in Plymouth Colony

The political alliance formed between Plymouth Colony and the Wampanoag tribe in 1621 created an extended contact period between the two groups for much of the seventeenth century. However necessary from a political and economic standpoint, the alliance also posed ongoing challenges for both groups. While it was generally understood that actions within the Wampanoag community and the English community would be handled as separate affairs, cross-cultural crimes were handled within the Plymouth legal system. This method did not, however, address preexisting cultural and legal differences between the two groups. Crimes committed within Wampanoag society were addressed within families and emphasized some form of privately agreed upon retribution. Crimes committed within Plymouth colony or involving Plymouth colonists used the court system to reach a conclusion, emphasizing punishment administered before the community as a whole.

[29] All quotes from the Essex County Court of General Sessions trial for Sarah Pillsbury, John Allen and Wilshire in 1705, File Papers, Box 3, Judicial Archives, Massachusetts State Archives, Boston, Massachusetts. I have italicized Pillsbury's responses as the original document is unpunctuated.

Ten sexual misconduct trials involving white colonists and Native Americans were conducted in Plymouth Colony between 1636 and 1689, with none thereafter. These trials were equally divided, with five trials for white men and Native American women and five trials for white women and Native American men. Sam, "the Indian, soe called," was tried on October 31, 1682 for raping Sarah Freeman of Eastham, described in the records as "an English gerle." Freeman was the approximately 11-year-old daughter of John and Sarah Merrick Freeman. Both the Freeman and Merrick families were comfortably off, although Sarah Merrick Freeman's father initially arrived in Plymouth Colony as an indentured servant in the 1630s.[30] Sam was probably a Christian Indian living on the outskirts of Eastham. Similar to other colonial court systems faced with a law requiring capital punishment for rape, the Plymouth court justices also sought to avoid such a ruling. The court eventually ruled that since "hee was but an Indian, and therfore in an incapisity to know the horibleness of the wickednes of the abominable act," his punishment would consist of a severe whipping and banishment from Plymouth Colony.[31]

Two other Plymouth trials involving white colonists and Native Americans grappled with the very different issue of adultery. A Native American man raping a white girl was comprehensible to the seventeenth-century English mind. White women choosing sexual relations with Native American men over their own husbands was not. The first of these trials occurred in 1639 when Mary, wife of Robert Mendame of Duxbury, was accused of "using dallyance divers tymes" with Tinsin, described in the records as "an Indian."[32] Both their punishments were severe. Mendame was ordered to be whipped behind a cart tail through the town streets and to wear a badge upon her left sleeve. Tinsin was ordered to be whipped with a halter about his neck. Some 50 years later, Hannah, wife of William Tubbs, also of Duxbury, was put on trial for committing adultery with James Brown, identified in the records as "an Indian." Tubbs was ordered to be whipped 30 times and to pay a fine of five pounds. There is no mention in the records of Brown's punishment. Jennifer Aultman suggests that Mendame received the harsher punishment because "the Court felt she should

---

30 Eugene Aubrey Stratton, *Plymouth Colony: Its History and People, 1620–1691* (Salt Lake City: Ancestry Publishing, 1986), 327.

31 All quotes from the Plymouth Colony General Court trial for Sam the Indian in 1682, in *Records of the colony of New Plymouth, in New England*, Volume 6, Nathaniel B. Shurtleff, ed. (Boston: William White Press, 1855), 98.

32 All quotes from the Plymouth Colony Court of General Sessions trial for Mary Mendame and Tinsin in 1639, in *Records of the colony of New Plymouth, in New England*, Volume 1, Nathaniel B. Shurtleff, ed. (Boston: William White Press, 1855), 132.

have 'known better'" as an adult English woman raised in a community which distrusted adultery and interracial sex equally.[33] Tinsin and James Brown were deemed incapable of comprehending adultery and resisting temptation from their white lovers. In turn, the Plymouth justices had declared Sam incapable of understanding his rape of Sarah Freeman because he was a Native American. It is, however, clear that the Plymouth officials read Sam's actions as rape as Freeman was not punished for fornication.

Native Americans and Sexual Misconduct Trials in Rhode Island

The colony of Rhode Island was also on good terms with its Narragansett neighbors, though the nearly inevitable cultural collisions occurred there as well. The Rhode Island Court of Tryalls conducted a similar trial in 1671 to the one held for "Sam the Indian" in Plymouth when "an Indian called by the English John by the Indians Qashcome" was tried for "offeringe very great abussis unto Martha, the wife of Edward Lay by throwing her downe in the high way and actine as if he would Ravish her."[34] The court depositions note that Qashcome testified in court that "he doth not know whither he did any such act as charged withall, and if the English doe say he did. He will not say they ly for he doth not know himself whether he did such act or not." The jury found him guilty but, similar to Sam's trial, were undecided as to whether they could put him to death for his actions. The last court record to mention Qascome notes only that he was to be "remanded againt to prisson till calld ffor" and it is unclear how, or if, they eventually punished him.

Most trials involving white colonists and Native Americans in southern New England were for consensual sex, though a few were plainly nonconsensual. The tones set by the trials range from colonial indifference to outrage to occasional bewilderment, suggesting that there was no one set response to the prospect of white colonists and Native Americans engaging in sexual intercourse in southern New England. The question of whether Native Americans should be tried differently than white colonists occasionally surfaced as justices considered their options and cast their rulings. On the whole, Native Americans tried for sexual

[33] Jennifer Aultman, "Native American Criminal Cases, 1630–1675," Plymouth Colony Archive Project, URL: http://www.histarch.uiuc.edu/plymouth/wampanoag.html Date accessed: August 26, 2007).

[34] All quotes from the Rhode Island Court of Tryalls trial for Qashcome in 1671, Newport Court Record Book, Volume A, 1671–1724, Rhode Island Judicial Archives, Pawtucket, Rhode Island.

misconduct in southern New England received treatment little different from their white counterparts. An's trial was almost identical to the other bastardy trials held in Essex County, Wilshire was acquitted alongside John Allen when the justices could not decide which man had fathered Sarah Pillsbury's child. Similar to the white men accused of rape in the New England colonies, the Plymouth and Rhode Island courts both took pains to avoid executing Sam and Qashcome. The differences and similarities between the consensual and nonconsensual trials suggest that while English leaders did not automatically assume that white women would only have sexual contact with Native American men if it was nonconsensual, they did assume that Native American men were, at some level, incapable of understanding how and why interracial extramarital sex was wrong. Ultimately, the parties held most responsible in these trials were Hannah Tubbs and Mary Mendame. Women who committed adultery were generally punished far more harshly than their partners throughout the Anglo-American world, but these women were also expected to understand the laws they were breaking, while their partners were not judged by the same expectations.

The Rise of African Slavery in the English Colonies

Another massive cultural shift occurring in the English colonies in the late seventeenth century was the development of laws legalizing African slavery.[35] Both Charles II and James II had invested heavily in the first English slave trading company, the Royal African Company and the creation of such laws supported imperial interests.[36] While the New England colonies never invested in African slaves on the same scale as the southern colonies, many New England sea captains were involved in the Triangle Trade, conveying molasses, rum, and African slaves across the Atlantic Ocean. Most African slaves who did live in New England generally did so in the port towns. There were approximately 2,000 Africans living in Massachusetts by 1715 and this number increased to 4,500 by 1750, while Rhode Island had 426 Africans living in the colony in 1708 to somewhere between 3,077 and 4,373 African residents by 1748.[37]

[35] See Anthony S. Parent, *Foul Means: The Formation of a Slave Society in Virginia, 1660–1740* (Chapel Hill: University of North Carolina Press, 2003) and Sweet, *Bodies Politic*.

[36] See David W. Galenson, *Traders, Planters, and Slaves: Market Behavior in Early English America* (Cambridge: Cambridge University Press, 1986).

[37] Richard A. Bailey, *Race and Redemption in Puritan New England* (New York: Oxford University Press, 2011), 26.

Research from the Scientific Revolution of the sixteenth and seventeenth centuries and the Enlightenment of the eighteenth was used to justify the legalization of African slavery in the English colonies. Scholars believed that different climates produced different types of people and used the writings of early European explorers around the globe as evidence that their theories were correct. Carolus Linneaus began in the 1730s to divide "humankind into varieties distinguished by both physical appearance and qualities of the mind. The European's body was 'fair, sanguine, brawny,' and his character '*gentle*, acute, inventive,' ... [while] the American was 'copper-coloured, choleric, erect,' and '*obstinate*, content, free' [and] the African was 'black, phlegmatic, relaxed,' 'crafty, indolent, negligent.'"[38] Ideas like these made it far easier for both Europeans and white Americans to obtain cheap labor by justifying both African slavery and Native American conquest as they argued that it was part of the natural world order for one race to dominate another. They also helped support growing numbers of laws throughout the English colonies which laid out specific penalties for white colonists who had sexual contact with non-whites, whether Native or African-Americans.[39]

African-Americans and Sexual Misconduct Trials in Essex County

Laws regarding sexual contact between white colonists and Africans were created in both Massachusetts and Rhode Island. An "Act for the Better Preventing of a Spurious and Mixt Issue" was added to Massachusetts' *The Acts and Resolves* in 1705. As its title suggests, the real focus of the 1705 act was the children who might result from sexual contact between mixed-race couples. John Wood Sweet notes that "slave masters ...were among the only father figures in colonial New England who could not shunt the costs of rearing a bastard child onto someone else."[40] The law spelled out specific penalties for parents of different races who conceived children out of wedlock. African-American men and their white female partners were both ordered to be "severely whip'd ... and [then] the man shall be ordered to be sold out of province ... and the woman shall be enjoyned to maintain the child (if any there be) at her own charge." White men were ordered to be "severely whip'd ... and shall also pay a fine of five pounds to their majesties, for and towards the support of the government and be enjoyn'd to maintain

---

38 Sweet, *Bodies Politic*, 272.

39 See Brown, *Good Wives, Nasty Wenches & Anxious Patriarchs* for the creation of equivalent laws in Virginia.

40 Sweet, *Bodies Politic*, 155.

the child, if any there be" while their African-American female partners were ordered to be "sold and sent out of the province."[41]

The 1705 Massachusetts law also outlawed marriage between "her majesty's English or Scottish subjects ... with any negro or molatto" and promised to punish any who did so with a 50 pound fine "one [part] thereof to her majesty for and towards the support of the government within this province and the other to him or them that shall inform and sue for the same."[42] This section of the law highlights a clear difference between Massachusetts and Virginia. White men or women who married a "negroe, mulatto, or Indian man or woman" were punished by being "banished and removed from this dominion forever."[43] Another part of the act stated that "no master shall unreasonably deny marriage to his negro with one of the same nation," though it did not spell out any resulting penalties for a master who did so.

The decision to make white women and men who had children with African-American partners responsible for both fornication charges *and* financial support for their children was deliberately intended to convey colonial lawmakers' particular unease with the subject of whites having sexual contact with Africans.[44] Nevertheless, while the 1705 Massachusetts law laid out clear strictures against mixed-race colonists who had sexual relations, the court records suggest that Essex County justices did not deem the matter pressing enough to follow the letter of the law. Maybell Evans of Beverly was convicted in the Salem court on August 14, 1719 on bastardy charges, while Grigory, "a negro belonging to Francis Norwood of Lyn," was charged with fathering her child.[45] Evans was ordered to be whipped 10 times while Grigory was given 20 lashings and there is no mention of who would provide financial support for their child, though this suggests Evans would probably be held responsible.

A warrant issued for Mehitabel Nicholls of Amesbury on April 20, 1747 noted that "Mehitabel Nichols of Amesbury Singlewoman in May last Comitted Fornication with a Negro." However, when it came time for Nichols to be charged in court, she was simply convicted on fornication and bastardy

---

41 *The Acts and Resolves*, 578.

42 *The Acts and Resolves*, 578.

43 Brown, *Good Wives, Nasty Wenches & Anxious Patriarchs*, 198.

44 Both Sharon Block's *Rape & Sexual Power in Early America* (Chapel Hill: University of North Carolina Press, 2006) and Clare Lyons's *Sex among the Rabble: An Intimate History of Gender & Power in the Age of Revolution, Philadelphia, 1730–1830* (Chapel Hill: University of North Carolina Press, 2006) also provide further discussion on growing unease with sexual contact between races.

45 All quotes from the Essex County Court of General Sessions trials for Maybell Evans and Grigory in 1719, File Papers Box 7. Judicial Archives, Massachusetts State Archives, Boston.

charges and ordered to pay a 20 shilling fine, and there is no mention of her African-American partner in the court records.[46] Finally, a Salem court record notes that while there was some question as to whether the man who fathered Ann Conner's child in 1749 was African-American, the court ruled that "there being no proof that it was with a negro It is ordered that she pay a fine of 50 shillings."[47] Similar to the Nichols trial, there is no mention of the man who fathered Conner's child in the court records.

Essex County justices' decision not to fully apply the 1705 law stands in stark contrast to decisions made by their counterparts in Virginia where Kathleen Brown notes that "white servant women bearing children by black men constituted more than 17 percent of [the bastardy] cases during the 1690s and nearly 30 percent by the 1700s" and these women were punished according to the fullest extent of Virginia's 1691 law against mixed-race sexual contact.[48] This disparity may reflect the fact that there were relatively few African-Americans lived in northern New England but whether this was the case has not yet been fully researched.[49]

African-Americans and Sexual Misconduct Trials in Maine

A similar pattern appears in the York County court where there were only three trials which mention the possibility of white women in Maine having sexual contact with African-American men in the eighteenth century and no trials involving white men and African-American women. Mary Brooking appeared in the York County Court of General Sessions on January 4, 1709 where she acknowledged that she had given birth to a child out of wedlock. The court record then notes that since she "refus[ed] to Discover the father of her Child and the said Child proveing to be Black ... She is for her said Offence Sentenced to receive Twenty Stripes on her Naked back."[50] No further effort was made to identify the father of her child, which suggests the justices knew her partner

---

46 All quotes from the Essex County Court of General Sessions trial for Mehitable Nicholls in 1748, File Papers Box 15. Judicial Archives, Massachusetts State Archives, Boston.

47 All quotes from the Essex County Court of General Sessions trial for Ann Conner in 1749, File Papers Box 15. Judicial Archives, Massachusetts State Archives, Boston.

48 Brown, *Good Wives, Nasty Wenches & Anxious Patriarchs*, 198.

49 To the best of my knowledge, no comprehensive research has been conducted to see how often the 1705 law was fully executed in Massachusetts.

50 All quotes from the York County Court of General Sessions trial for Mary Brooking in 1690, in *Maine Province and Court Records*, Volume 4, 360.

was enslaved and, therefore, unable to pay child support, which, in turn, would have made putting him on trial a waste of the court's time. Sentencing Brooking to 20 whippings and not allowing her to choose between a whipping or a fine was a harsh punishment in a time period when most convicted defendants were whipped seven to 10 times, but it is unclear whether her punishment was because she had had a child with an African-American or whether it was because she had refused to identify the father of her child, which customarily did lead to women receiving harsher punishments regardless of the race of the father's child. Sarah Clark was convicted by the York County Court of General Sessions on fornication and bastardy charges in 1744 and the court records note that since she "refused to tell who was the father of the said Child whereupon we Determined that she should pay a fine of twenty-five shillings Lawful Money or Receive ten stripes on her naked back at the Public whipping post which fine she paid."[51]

An African-American man known as "Black Will" was charged in 1712 with "being the reputed Father of a bastard child begotten on the body of Elizabeth Brooks" but as there was "no Evidence appearing Sufficient to Convict him," he was acquitted after being ordered to pay one pound and six shillings in court fees. For her part, Brooks received a court summons but she was never charged and it is unclear what happened to her child, who, as was noted earlier in this chapter, could also have been fathered by English colonist Thomas Reed.[52] Some 30 years later, Sarah Muzzeet was accused in 1746 of having an illegitimate child by an African-American man but was acquitted due to lack of evidence.[53] Again, these trials are much like the equivalent trials conducted in Essex County during the same time period where the letter of the law was also not being followed. Similar to the bastardy and paternity trials conducted for white colonists and Native Americans in the Essex County courts, the real motivation for putting men on trial was identifying the father to pay child support, and if a putative father could not pay child support, there was little point in pursuing him.

---

[51] All quotes from the York County Court of General Sessions trial for Sarah Clark in 1744. York County Court of Common Pleas & General Sessions, Box 73. Maine State Archives, Augusta.

[52] All quotes from the York County Court of General Sessions trial for Black Will in 1712, in *Maine Province and Court Records*, Volume 5, Neal Allen, ed. (Portland: Maine Historical Society, 1964), 126.

[53] All quotes from the York County Court of General Sessions April 1, 1746 trial for Sarah Muzeet. York County Court of Common Pleas & General Sessions, Box 100. Maine State Archives, Augusta. Her acquittal was summed up in a single line so there is no further evidence of the events leading to her trial.

African-Americans and Sexual Misconduct Trials in Rhode Island

Massachusetts laws addressing sexual contact between white colonists and Africans were focused almost entirely on prosecuting couples for conceiving illegitimate, mixed-race children. There were no laws addressing children conceived by mixed-race parents in Rhode Island, though it should be noted that there were also no laws addressing illegitimate children conceived by white parents in Rhode Island. The only law affecting sexual intercourse between white colonists and Africans in Rhode Island was the 1743 "An Act for the more effectual Punishment of *Negroes* that shall attempt to commit a *Rape* on any white Woman."[54] It recommended that African-American men convicted of raping white women "be branded on each Cheek with the Letter R, and shall be whipped in the most publick Manner ... and shall be sold ... to any Purchaser who will transport or carry him out of this Colony." Elaine Forman Crane notes that this legislation almost certainly resulted from the 1743 conviction of African-American slave Cuff on charges that he had assaulted Comfort Taylor and "then & there in the Prosecution of that wicked Purpose the Body of said Comfort did greatly bruise so that of her Life it was dispaired."[55] The 1743 law notes that it was written in response to "Instances of Negroes attempting to commit Rapes on white Women, and there being no particular Law subsisting too punish such Offenders," though the Cuff trial is the only one of its kind in the Rhode Island court records.

The 1743 law was also the only one of its kind in New England, which makes the colonies of Massachusetts, Connecticut, and New Hampshire the exception rather than the rule in English North America. Laws promising a wide array of punishments for African men who raped white women were passed in all of the southern and mid-Atlantic colonies by the mid-eighteenth century and Sharon Block notes that "the racialization of rape was the primary Americanization of British common law regarding rape."[56] English rape laws laid out the terms under which trials were to be conducted and the appropriate punishments but they did not make any form of racial distinctions.

---

[54] "An Act for the more effectual Punishment of *Negroes* that shall attempt to commit a *Rape* on any white Woman," in *Acts and laws, of His Majesty's colony of Rhode-Island, and Providence-Plantations, in New-England, in America* (Gale ECCO, Print Editions, 2010), 263.

[55] All quotes from the Judicature Court of Assize and General Goal Delivery trial for Cuff in 1743, Newport County Court Record Book, Volume C, Rhode Island Judicial Archives, Pawtucket, Rhode Island. See also Crane, *Witches, Wife Beaters, and Whores*, 137.

[56] Block, *Rape and Sexual Power*, 148.

Conclusion

The early eighteenth century's new reality was that English colonists were now living in close quarters with both African and Native Americans, though the nature of this proximity was determined by whether they lived in colonial peripheries or centers. Settlers in northern New England needed to worry about the dangers of Native American attacks but worried less about Native Americans living in their homes as servants after military victories. Likewise, these periphery communities were less apt to have the economic stability needed for the ownership of African-American slaves. By contrast, southern New England's growing political and economic power led to growing numbers of both Native and African-Americans living in the homes of white colonists. This familiarity made sexual contact between the different races inevitable. Nevertheless, the clear gap between the lack of laws pertaining to Native Americans who had sexual relations with whites and the growing presence of laws pertaining to African-Americans who had sexual relations with whites reflects the aspirations of southern New England's leaders. They preferred to ignore the presences of the Native Americans living in their colonies but they increasingly desired the presence of African slaves *and* worried about their behavior.

While both Massachusetts and Rhode Island created harsh legal penalties for colonists who had sexual relations with non-whites, the court records suggest that in Essex County, Maine, and Rhode Island, at least, justices rarely implemented the full penalties prescribed by law. This may simply reflect how rarely such cases crossed their benches. But it also speaks to the fact that most white colonists who had sexual relations with non-whites did so with fellow servants, rendering both parties marginal members of increasingly class-conscious colonial English society. This chapter opened with the image of North America as a Native American woman who, like other medieval and early modern women, was viewed as both lustful and unrestrained. Late eighteenth-century European society, however, increasingly classified women's natures by both race and class. Non-white and poor women remained lustful and restrained while middle- and upper-class white women were increasingly portrayed as refined and passionless, a development which also serves as a reminder that discussions of peripheries and centers can be as much cultural and personal as geographical. New England justices' decision to draw few distinctions between poor white colonists who had sex with non-whites and non-whites who had sex with other non-whites reflects this changing understanding of class identities as well as racial ones, a view further reinforced by Cotton Mather's censoring of Hannah Swarton for moving her family to Maine where her children may be "bred ignorantly like *Indians*." Middle-class Comfort Taylor's alleged rape by African slave Cuff was worthy of a new Rhode Island law in 1743; African slaves who had sex, consensual or not, with white servant women were barely noticed in New England's court rooms.

I earlier used the phrase "Alternating Anglicization" to describe the various New England colonies' shifting relationships with English law. The phrase is equally applicable to England's own relationship with laws regulating interracial sex across the wider British Empire. The only sustained disconnect between sexual misconduct laws created in the English colonies in North America and sexual misconduct laws created in England was the language specifically referencing race as a category to be considered in colonial court rooms. Perhaps ironically, these laws steered colonial legal codes away from English law, even while the colonies were becoming more politically and culturally English in a period of heightened interest in colonial activities from both Parliament and the English monarchs. The new laws were easily viewed as not "repugnant to the laws of England" because they applied to situations without precedent in either English common or ecclesiastical law. However, their true appeal to Parliament and crown alike came from their logistical support for England's growing entrance into both the African slave trade and the use of African slave labor.

In time, the colonial body of laws regulating interracial sex would be used to support the British Empire as early colonization in India led to similar quandaries over the question of what to do with children from parents of different races. Imperial leaders created the first laws curtailing sexual relations between English colonists and native Indian residents in the late 1700s, nearly a century after their North American counterparts.[57] The first colonial laws regulating interracial sex in North America may have marked a true break with England and English law but their contributions to the growing political and economic success of the British Empire in the nineteenth century raises the question of where the true peripheries and centers of that same empire lay.

---

[57] William Dalrymple, *White Mughals: Love and Betrayal in Eighteenth-Century India* (New York: Penguin Books, 2004), 39–43.

Chapter 4

"He Shall Be Liable to the Charge of Maintenance": Morals, Economics, and Illegitimate Children in New England Communities

Elizabeth Gould. Lydia Hammon. Rebeckah Saxbey. The names of the women accused of conceiving children out of wedlock in colonial New England court rooms echo throughout the record books. Mary Towne. Esther Bane. Mercy Jones. All were convicted on fornication and bastardy charges and punished. Hannah Clarke. Sarah Dore. Margaret Hall. The numbers of women convicted on such charges was on the rise in the late seventeenth century and concern about financial support for their illegitimate children was an increasing headache for colonial political and legal leaders alike.[1] The English practice of requiring that towns provide financial support for indigent residents was maintained throughout the North American colonies and New England towns were no more interested in paying for those children than their counterparts in England. Sexual misconduct laws in New England in the 1650s and early 1660s governed only moral failings, rather than the economic consequences of those same failings, and colonial leaders could look only to their town poor laws for children whose mothers could not financially support them. Over time, new laws and new institutional structures would be created in New England to

---

1 Other English colonies also had rising numbers of children conceived out of wedlock. See Cornelia Hughes Dayton, *Women Before the Bar: Gender, Law, and Society in Connecticut, 1639–1789* (Chapel Hill: University of North Carolina Press, 1995), 207–8, Julias Goebel and T. Raymond Naughton, *Law Enforcement in Colonial New York: A Study in Criminal Procedure* (Montclair: Patterson Smith, 1970), 101–2, Clare Lyons, *Sex among the Rabble: An Intimate History of Gender & Power in the Age of Revolution, Philadelphia, 1730–1830* (Chapel Hill: University of North Carolina Press, 2006), 65, Kathleen Brown, *Good Wives, Nasty Wenches, and Anxious Patriarchs: Gender, Race, and Power in Colonial Virginia* (Chapel Hill: University of North Carolina Press, 1996), 188–94, and William Nelson, *The Common Law in Colonial America: The Middle Colonies and the Carolinas, 1660–1730*, Volume 2 (New York: Oxford University Press, 2013), 81.

address these challenges which would bring the region ever closer to English practice in the early modern period.

The Morals and Economics of Illegitimate Children in New England

The moral issues posed by couples who had sexual intercourse outside of wedlock in England had been addressed by the English ecclesiastical courts since the medieval period. The economic challenges posed by the need for financial support for their children entered the English legal system in 1574 when the first law mandating that convicted fathers pay child support was passed. Jamestown, the first successful English colony in North America, was founded in 1607. Permanent English settlement arrived in New England in 1620 with the founding of the Plymouth Colony. By the time Massachusetts Bay was founded in 1630 and Rhode Island in 1636, English laws requiring financial support for illegitimate children had existed for over half a century.

However, the first legal codes created in Massachusetts, *The Body of Liberties* in 1641 and *The Laws and Liberties* in 1648, detailed punishments only for couples who engaged in sexual intercourse outside of wedlock. Rhode Island's *Proceedings of the First General Assembly of The Incorporation of Providence Plantations* included a similar law in 1647. Mid-seventeenth-century court records from both colonies document that couples who subsequently married and couples who did not marry received identical punishments. In addition, these punishments were not gender-specific and men and women alike were generally allowed to choose between being whipped or fined as punishment for their transgressions.

Rising numbers of illegitimate children in late seventeenth-century Massachusetts led to the creation of an amendment to *The Laws and Liberties* on October 14, 1668 which mandated that couples who conceived a child and did not then marry would now receive gender-specific punishments. Male defendants who were "charged by the Woman to be the Father, shee holding constant in it, (especially being put upon the real discovery of the truth of it in the time of her Travail)" were now convicted on paternity charges and "accordingly [held] liable to the charge of maintenance as aforesaid (though not to other punishment)."[2] The new law made it possible for them to enter into what were, essentially, plea bargains. Convicted fathers were responsible for paying child support but were

---

[2] "Several Laws and Orders Made at the General Court, Held at Boston in New England, October 14, 1668," in *The Colonial Laws of Massachusetts, Reprinted from the Edition of 1660, With the Supplements to 1672, Containing Also, The Body of Liberties of 1641*, William Whitmore, ed. (Boston: Rockwell & Churchill City Printers, 1889), 257.

not convicted on fornication charges, which allowed them to avoid the resulting public whipping or fine. Towns benefited from the courts' ability to extract child support, which saved them from unwanted financial burdens. For their part, unwed mothers were now prosecuted on fornication *and* bastardy charges, though their punishments remained the same choice between a whipping and a fine. This distinction demonstrates that men who conceived children out of wedlock were charged with committing economic crimes, while women who did so were charged with committing moral crimes. By contrast, men and women convicted on fornication before marriage charges continued to be tried and punished in the same way, with both halves of the couple submitting to either a whipping or a fine. Men convicted on fornication before marriage charges were assumed to have taken on financial responsibility for both their female partners and their children and so there was no point in prosecuting them on economic charges.

The 1668 decision in Massachusetts to charge men and women differently for engaging in sexual intercourse out of wedlock and to emphasize the financial repercussions of conceiving illegitimate children marks an early transition towards English law in Massachusetts, one predating the changes brought on by the Dominion of New England and the second charter by almost two decades. With 24 bastardy and paternity trials conducted in Essex County alone between 1650 and 1674 and another 87 bastardy and paternity trials between 1675 and 1700, Massachusetts lawmakers needed a way of guaranteeing support for these children.[3] The resulting 1668 law suggests they consciously looked to preexisting English laws for the support of illegitimate children because their original legal codes provided no such provisions. The decision suggests a certain pragmatism on behalf of Massachusetts leaders and Massachusetts communities. If English legal structures could address the growing social challenges of a maturing society, then English legal structures would be embraced.

Maine and Rhode Island never formally passed laws equal to the 1668 Massachusetts law but their bastardy and paternity trials demonstrate that justices in both colonies employed a similar legal process when dealing with couples convicted on bastardy and paternity charges. Maine conducted 7 bastardy and paternity trials between 1650 and 1674 and 19 bastardy and paternity trials between 1675 and 1700, while Rhode Island conducted 5 bastardy and paternity trials between 1650 and 1674 and 22 bastardy and paternity trials between 1675 and 1700. Maine never created a legal code after Ferdinando

---

3 Else Hambleton does point out that while the numbers of illegitimate children were rising in Massachusetts, overall numbers for these children remained quite small. Hambleton, *Daughters of Eve, Pregnant Brides and Unwed Mothers in Seventeenth-Century, Massachusetts* (New York: Routledge Press, 2004), xiii.

Gorges's "First Commission" and "Second Commission" in the late 1630s so the lack of a bastardy and paternity law in the colony makes sense, particularly since Massachusetts laws were first used in Maine around the same time that the 1668 bastardy and paternity law was created. Rhode Island's decision not to update its legal code to include separate punishments for men and women convicted for conceiving children out of wedlock is puzzling because Rhode Island's greater emphasis on the use of English law suggests that the colony should have been even more willing to adapt such a law. The overall ratios of parents convicted for conceiving children of wedlock in Rhode Island remained consistently lower than in Massachusetts or Maine and the colony may have decided that the matter simply did not justify passing an additional law.

The lack of specific laws outlining penalties for colonists who conceived illegitimate children in Maine and Rhode Island may also reflect their own close ties to English law. Neither colony was founded by Puritans and neither colony had a particular reason for avoiding English legal and social practices when crafting their initial legal practices or codes. Colonial leaders in both Maine and Rhode Island may simply have begun prosecuting women on fornication and bastardy charges and men on paternity charges without formally changing their legal practices because they assumed that their colonists would be familiar enough with the practice not to question it.

The Anatomy of a Colonial New England Bastardy and Paternity Trial

The nine women named in the opening paragraph of this chapter were all convicted on fornication and bastardy charges in colonial New England court rooms between 1650 and 1750.[4] Their names, convictions, and punishments, along with the names, convictions, and punishments of hundreds of other New England women, are all we know about their trials because their hearings did not result in further legal documentation. Colonial New England bastardy and paternity trials with surviving documentation nearly all turn on the question of whether or not the accused man was guilty. Doubt was difficult to weigh in the woman's favor. Regardless of how she became pregnant, the fact was displayed in her swelling body. The early modern belief that conception came about as a direct result of willingness on both parties made women even more

---

4 Elizabeth Gould, Mary Towne, and Hannah Clarke were convicted in Essex County, Lydia Hammon, Esther Bane, and Sarah Dore were convicted in Maine, Rebeckah Saxbey, Mercy Jones, and Margaret Hall were all convicted in Rhode Island.

vulnerable, particularly in rape cases.[5] A trial for a man who believed himself wrongfully accused of fathering a child raised all kinds of doubt. Lacking the certainty of DNA testing, justices relied instead on a complicated intersection of confessions, witnesses, circumstantial evidence, birth testimonies, and their own instincts, thereby making identifying putative fathers a highly collective affair in the early modern period.[6]

Men dominated the first stage of bastardy and paternity trials with heads of household whose sons were accused of fathering illegitimate children or whose daughters were pregnant out of wedlock providing the courts with either alibis for their sons or proof of honorable intentions from their daughters' suitors. Women became central in the second stage of the process, when unwed mothers were repeatedly questioned by their midwives regarding the identity of the child's father during birth, a ritual reinforced by reminders that they would answer at the Day of Judgment if they lied. Fear of dying in childbirth added a certain edge to this proceeding as a woman facing potential death within the next 24 hours was considered less likely to lie under oath. An unwed mother who named a father then had the satisfaction of a court conviction and child support for a specified amount of time; if she refused to identify the presumptive father, she faced stricter penalties in the court room, and her family remained financially responsible for her child.[7] In summary, the couple's family and neighbors served as both helpmeets and witnesses during the process from birth to trial, providing aid and documentation as the situation demanded.[8]

---

5 Sharon Block, *Rape & Sexual Power in Early America* (Chapel Hill: University of North Carolina Press, 2006), 139–41 and Anna Clark, *Desire: A History of European Sexuality* (New York: Routledge, 2008), 104. This particular belief was also used in political rhetoric during congressional elections in the United States in 2012.

6 See Merry E. Weisner, "Early Modern Midwifery: A Case Study," in *Women and Work in Preindustrial Europe*, Barbara Hanawalt, ed. (Bloomington: Indiana University Press, 1986), 94–113 and Hilary Marland, *The Art of Midwifery: Early Modern Midwives in Europe* (New York: Routledge Press, 1993) for examples of the use of this process across early modern Europe. See Abby Chandler, "From Birthing Chamber to Court Room: The Medical and Legal Communities of the Colonial Essex County Midwife," *Early Modern Women: An Interdisciplinary Journal* 10, 1 (2015) for further information about this process in Essex County.

7 Henrik Hartog notes that "the fine ultimately paid by the mother to the sessions court was less a punishment than a fee paid to invoke the power of the county to secure the support of a putative father." Hartog, "The Public Law of a County Court: Judicial Government in Eighteenth-Century Massachusetts," *The American Journal of Legal History*, Volume 20, No. 4 (1976), 303.

8 M. Michelle Jarrett Morris argues that these forms of surveillance were more apt to be conducted by family members than non-related neighbors. See Morris, *Under Household Government: Sex and Family in Puritan Massachusetts* (Cambridge: Harvard University Press, 2013), 40.

Caring for Illegitimate Children in Seventeenth-Century New England

Once couples who conceived illegitimate children had been identified and assigned their respective punishments, the next question was how and where their children would be cared for and housed. This process provides further evidence of growing parallels between laws and customs in England and in New England. For much of the sixteenth century in England and the seventeenth century in Massachusetts, Maine, and Rhode Island, poor children were "bound out," placed in other households where they labored, and, in theory at least, were taught a trade until they were of age, either 21 for boys and anywhere between 16 and 18 for girls.[9] Most children were not bound out until the age of seven or eight but the records document that the youngest children placed in such indentures were only a few months old, most likely illegitimate children whose mothers could not provide homes for them with or without financial support from their fathers. Payment for illegitimate children who were bound out came from their fathers or, in the case of legitimately conceived children whose parents could not support them, their towns. This particular system was not "invent[ed in the American colonies, rather] they inherited it. From the early 1600s until well into the 1800s, local authorities in both England and North America regarded pauper apprenticeship as an acceptable, even a desirable, way to raise the children of the poor."[10] Such apprenticeships were created on an ad hoc basis by individual towns with little or no standardization from one town to the next.

England, however, transitioned towards a more institutionalized system with the creation of an Overseers for the Poor in 1597 and an "Act for the Relief of the Poor in 1601," which eventually led to formalized poor houses where indigent residents could be housed together.[11] Massachusetts followed suit in 1692 when *The Acts and Resolves* ordered that the "freeholders and other inhabitants of each town ... choose three, five, seven or nine persons, able and

---

[9] See Ruth Herndon, *Unwelcome Americans: Living on the Margin in Early New England* (Philadelphia: University of Pennsylvania Press, 2001), Carole Shammas, *A History of Household Government in America* (Charlottesville: University of Virginia Press, 2002) and Ruth Herndon and John E. Murray, eds, *Children Bound to Labor: The Pauper Apprentice System in Early America* (Ithaca: Cornell University Press, 2009).

[10] Steve Hindle and Ruth Wallis Herndon, "Recreating Proper Families in England and North America: Pauper Apprenticeship in Transatlantic Context," in *Children Bound to Labor*, 19.

[11] Tim Hitchcock, "Paupers and Preachers: The SPCK and the Parochial Workhouse movement," in *Stilling the Grumbling Hive: The Response to Social and Economic Problems in England, 1689–1750*, Lee Davison, Tim Hitchcock, Tim Keirn and Robert Shoemaker, eds (New York: St Martin's Press, 1992), 145–66.

discreet, of good conversation ... to be selectmen or townsmen and overseers of the poor."[12] The overseers of the poor or selectmen were then instructed to "bind any poor children belonging to such town to be apprentices ... which shall be as effectual to all intents and purposes as if any such child were of full age and by indenture of covenant had bound him or her self."[13] Both Boston and Salem created Overseers of the Poor in 1692, though Boston's Overseers were a more formal organization than Salem's.

Caring for Illegitimate Children in Eighteenth-Century New England

Overseers at the turn of the eighteenth century generally provided "outdoor relief" in the form of food, housing and, sometimes, money, to colonists who could prove that they were both in need and legal residents of their respective towns. With poverty levels increasing in the eighteenth century, some towns wondered if "indoor relief" in the form of institutionalized housing would be a more efficient means of supporting their poor colonists. Boston created an almshouse in 1662 and it grew rapidly. Salem created one in 1719 and ordered all indigent members of the community to be moved to the poor house, rather than provide any kind of outdoor relief for them by 1749. Meanwhile, a 1744 law ordered all Massachusetts towns to build poor houses and outdoor relief was used less and less often.

The transition towards a more institutionalized use of Salem's Overseers of the Poor plays out in Essex County's bastardy and paternity trials. The overall numbers of children conceived out of wedlock in the early eighteenth century were continuing to grow, with 192 bastardy and paternity trials conducted between 1700 and 1724 and 180 trials between 1725 and 1750, and town leaders wanted a more efficient means of managing their care. Hannah Johnson of Andover was convicted on fornication and bastardy charges on July 12, 1743. After "Elizabeth Stevens the midwife and Susannah Fiske made oath that the said Hannah Charged the said Abraham with being the father of the said child in the time of her extremity," Abraham Dow of Roxbury was convicted on paternity charges and ordered to pay child support to the Salem Overseers of the Poor. While neither Johnson nor Dow lived in Salem, the justices probably decided that the most efficient means of raising Johnson and Dow's child was

12 *The Acts and Resolves*, 64.

13 See *The Eighteenth-Century Records of the Boston Overseers of the Poor*, Eric Nellis and Anne Decker Cecere, eds (The Colonial Society of Massachusetts, distributed by the University of Virginia Press, 2006).

to place it with the Overseers of the Poor in Salem and have it be supported by Dow until it was able to fend for itself. Likewise, the Elizabeth Dean trial cited earlier noted that John Gray, the convicted father of her illegitimate son, was ordered to pay his 15 pound bond to the "overseers of the poor of the town of Salem," rather than to Dean herself or to the town of Salem.

The creation of the Salem Overseers of the Poor in 1692 and the poor house in 1719 meant that illegitimate children born in Salem to mothers unable to provide homes for them could be financially maintained by their fathers in the poor house, rather than forcing their towns through the process of finding a household willing to accept an infant child unable to care for itself. Ruth Wallis Herndon adds that the growing need for a more institutionalized approach to caring for illegitimate children whose parents could not look after them "coincided with a number of other phenomena and can be explained by them. The population of New England grew rapidly in the eighteenth century ... with the increase of population came an increase of poor people."[14] These transitions also reflect the same growing pragmatism and need for efficiency demonstrated by Massachusetts leaders discussed earlier in this chapter.[15]

Similar to Massachusetts, Maine also rapidly expanded in the early eighteenth century. The earliest court records from the 1630s and 1640s mention defendants from the southern Maine towns of York, Kittery, and Wells. Defendants from communities surrounding modern-day Portland appear by the 1720s. English settlements filled the Kennebec River region in the 1730s when defendants from Georgetown, Arrowsic, and Montsweag began to populate the court records. Similar to England and southern New England in earlier centuries, Maine's growing population came with an increase in the numbers of children conceived out of wedlock, with 59 bastardy and paternity trials between 1700 and 1724 and 133 trials between 1725 and 1750, and the creation of an institutionalized Overseers of the Poor is also mentioned in York County's bastardy and paternity trials. The first such trial to mention payment to the Overseers occurred in 1723, some 20 years before they were mentioned in an Essex County bastardy and paternity trial. Phebe Tanner of York, Maine, was convicted on fornication and bastardy charges on October 2, 1722 and ordered to either be whipped seven times or pay a fine of 30 shillings. During her trial, Tanner "continu[ed] constant in her accusation in said Court face to face ...

14 Herndon, "'Proper' Magistrates and Masters: Binding out Poor Children in Southern New England, 1720–1820," *Children Bound to Labor*, 41.

15 Nellis and Cecere's *The Eighteenth-Century Records of the Boston Overseers of the Poor* documents equally rising numbers of indigent colonists in Boston in the 1730s and 1740s.

that Thomas Pickering was the father of her child."[16] Pickering initially denied her charges but eventually acknowledged himself as the father of Tanner's child on April 2, 1723, most likely because the community around him would have believed him guilty after Tanner's public accusation. Pickering, Thomas Phips, and Elisha Plaisted then "Acknowledge[d] them Selfes bound & Oblig'd Joyntly & Severally unto the Overseers of the poor of the Town of york in the penal Sum of sixty pounds." Pickering was also ordered to pay Tanner two shillings and six pence per week in child support, which suggests that the 60 pound bond was intended as insurance in case Tanner ever did appeal to the York Overseers for financial support.

A similar action was taken on January 1, 1734, when Hannah Cane and Thomas Spinney promised "to the Overseers of the Poor of the Town of Kittery ... the sum of One hundred pounds that they will Save the said Town harmless from the Maintenance of the Bastard Child lately born."[17] Both these amounts, 60 pounds and 100 pounds, respectively, were large sums by any standards in a colony where most people were still farming on a subsistence basis rather than a commercial one. They loom particularly large in comparison to the standard weekly child support fees of two shillings and six pence charged at that time, which add up to six pounds and five shillings per year. While few court records specify how long convicted fathers were expected to pay child support charges, the specific time frames mentioned range from one to seven years, suggesting that convicted fathers eventually paid a total of anywhere from six to 45 pounds in child support.

Hannah Cane was convicted on fornication and bastardy charges on October 22, 1733 when she was ordered to either receive 14 lashes or pay a fine of 80 shillings, an unusually steep punishment for the period when most women were ordered to receive seven lashes and pay fines ranging between 40 and 60 shillings. The harsh punishment and the requirement that Cane provide the Kittery Overseers of the Poor with the previously mentioned 100 pound bond most likely stemmed from doubts from the court justices that the father of Cane's child would be convicted and would pay child support. The court records note that "being Examd upon oath [she] saith that she is with Child by the said William Brooks." There is no evidence that Cane's midwife documented

[16] All quotes from the York County Court of General Sessions trials for Phebe Tanner and Thomas Pickering in 1722 and 1723, York County Court of Common Pleas & General Sessions Record Book, 1718–27, Volume 7, Maine State Archives, Augusta.

[17] All quotes from the York County Court of General Sessions trial for Hannah Cane in 1733, York County Court of Common Pleas & General Sessions Record Book, 1733–57, Volume 10, Maine State Archives, Augusta.

that she had named Brooks during labor and no mention of Brooks in the court records, which suggests Cane was unable to provide enough evidence to have Brooks convicted.

The Tanner/Pickering trial, the Cane trial and the other bastardy and paternity trials which mention the Overseers of the Poor suggest that York County used the Overseers slightly differently than they were used in Massachusetts and in England. Rather than providing poor houses where illegitimate children (and other impoverished members of Maine society) could be housed or someone to process child support payments, Overseers of the Poor in the individual Maine towns collected lump sum payments in advance against the day when an illegitimate child might need financial support. This approach dovetails with the handful of surviving documentary evidence about the functioning of Overseers of the Poor in Maine in the first half of the eighteenth century. Presumably, they were created following the 1692 law which ordered all Massachusetts towns to either create Overseers positions or to authorize selectmen to address issues of poverty within individual towns. Unlike Overseers of the Poor in Massachusetts and in England, they were either entirely unfunded or only partly funded by tax money. Beginning in the 1720s, colonists convicted for not attending the public worship of God, for drunkenness and for swearing were ordered "to pay a fine to the use of the poor" in the towns of Berwick, Falmouth, Kittery, Wells, and York. These were, however, the only crimes whose fines were used in this manner, which suggests that York County officials believed that colonists who made public nuisances of themselves could also provide financial support for the indigent, although this may also have been a comment on the realities of managing with a comparatively smaller tax base than existed in Massachusetts towns. All other fines levied in Maine, including fines for both bastardy and paternity convictions, were ordered to be paid "to the king," which was standard procedure throughout the English colonies.

Mandating that child support payments be sent to the Overseers of the Poor was standard practice in bastardy and paternity trials conducted in Massachusetts and Maine in the early eighteenth century. By contrast, Overseers of the Poor do not appear to have been particularly used in Rhode Island. The 1647 Rhode Island legal code stipulated that "each town shall provide carefully for the relief of the poor, to maintain the impotent, and employ the able and shall appoint an overseer for the same purpose" and later Rhode Island laws included similar language.[18] Nevertheless, bastardy and paternity trials for Rhode Island

[18] *The Earliest Acts and Laws of the Colony of Rhode Island and Providence Plantations, 1647–1719*, John D. Cushing, ed. (Wilmington: Michael Glazier Inc., 1977), 39.

continued to specify that child support payments should go to "ye Assistance or Justisses of ye town" as the conviction for William Arnold stipulated in 1703.[19] The Arnold conviction was, however, one of the last bastardy and paternity convictions in Rhode Island and the colony may have been more pro-active in their use of the Overseers of the Poor to manage homes for indigent children if they had continued to actively prosecute colonists for conceiving children out of wedlock into the eighteenth century as there were only 12 bastardy and paternity trials in Rhode Island between 1700 and 1724 and none after 1725.

Community-Driven Bastardy and Paternity Trials in Massachusetts

A wider trajectory from moral concerns to moral and economic concerns was consistent throughout colonial New England's bastardy and paternity trials. Massachusetts also developed a particular style for conducting bastardy and paternity trials at the turn of the eighteenth century, one seemingly unique both to Massachusetts and to that moment in time. These types of trials will be addressed in this chapter, while components specific to Maine and Rhode Island's bastardy and paternity trials will be addressed at greater length in future chapters.

The most important words in the Puritan vocabulary were covenant, family, and commonwealth.[20] Regardless of whether they were convicted or acquitted, early modern defendants were required to pay for all court costs. Most well-documented Essex County bastardy and paternity trials from the turn of the eighteenth century involved an average of eight or 10 depositions supporting the defendant's case, including appeals to justices with whom the family shared some social connection, making them expensive efforts indeed for the families involved. Providing a wide array of justices with close connections to their communities was part and parcel of the Puritan experiment. Even so, the covenanted community of the Massachusetts Bay court room only went so far. Colonists without the financial resources or social connections necessary for providing multiple deponents and a helpful Justice of the Peace could find themselves at a profound disadvantage during the trial itself. M. Michelle Jarrett

[19] All quotes from the General Court Of Trials and Goal Delivery trial for William Arnold in 1703, Newport Court Record Book, Volume A, Rhode Island Judicial Archives, Pawtucket, Rhode Island.

[20] Richard A. Bailey provides further ruminations on the importance of these words in the Puritan mindset. Bailey, *Race and Redemption in Puritan New England* (New York: Oxford University Press, 2011), 15–37.

Morris writes that "the importance of a strong family network is underlined by the experiences of those who lacked kinfolk to whom they might have turned for help ... [and] female servants, usually found that a 'family of employment' was a poor substitute for a dense network of caring kin" and this pattern was repeated throughout many of the Essex County bastardy and paternity trials.[21] The only option available to female servants impregnated by a member of their employer's family was to firmly maintain that they had had intercourse with one man and one man only and to hope that this would be enough to obtain some financial support for their children. The Sessions/Chandler trial from 1691 demonstrates that while this goal was achievable, the journey would be long and embarrassing along the way.

Community Relations and the Sessions/Chandler Bastardy and Paternity Trial

Similar to other female servants in the colonial period, the death of her father in 1689 and the dissolution of the Sessions family had reduced Andover resident Elizabeth Sessions to working as a servant in any household willing to employ her. She was living in the Christopher Osgood household when she confessed to Nathaniel Saltonstall on October 9, 1690 that she was five or six months pregnant. When Saltonstall asked when she had conceived her child, Sessions explained that she had gone to the home of Sergeant John Chandler on the evening of May 8, 1690 where several other young Andover residents were gathered. As she was walking back to the Osgood home, she was "by violence abused by Joseph Chandler" in the "open highway near to John Chandler's."[22] Some time afterward, she realized that she was pregnant. She was certain that Joseph Chandler was the father as he "had nothing to [do] with her in that kind but only that one time." Even then, she had not wanted to draw attention to the incident as "his relations [were] great men." She was only speaking now because the law required an unwed pregnant woman to name a father. Saltonstall then ordered Chandler to respond to Sessions's accusation. He denied paternity and his family, friends, and neighbors fully supported his legal fight to defend his innocence. In addition, the early stages of the trial investigation suggest that it may have been entirely possible for the Chandler family to be successful in their

21 Morris, *Under Household Government*, 177.

22 All quotes from the Essex County Quarterly Court trial for Elizabeth Sessions and Joseph Chandler in 1691, File Papers Box 2. Judicial Archives, Massachusetts State Archives, Boston.

efforts to have Chandler acquitted. As the depositions emerged in the next several months, nearly every aspect of Sessions's confession would be placed in doubt.

While the Chandlers were not among the first Andover settlers when the town was founded in the early 1640s, they rapidly achieved "something like a balance of power [by the 1690s] ... with their control of the ministry, then of the militia [and] finally in their growing control of town offices."[23] Elizabeth Sessions's parents did not move to Andover until late in the seventeenth century when most of the arable land had already been divided among the first settlers. Comparing the wills left by Joseph Chandler and Elizabeth Sessions's fathers further highlights differences between their families. When Thomas Chandler died in 1703, he left a large estate granting land and shares of his ironworks to each of his six sons. In addition to the customary widow's room in the family house, his wife, Hannah Brewer Chandler, received a yearly allowance in money and food supplies. He also added further household goods to the dowries given his two daughters at the time of their marriages. When Alexander Sessions died in 1689, he owned a house and 80 acres of land, which were promptly sold. After Sessions's debts were paid, the remaining money went to support his widow and the youngest children, with a little left over for the remaining children. Sessions's oldest son received five pounds, eight shillings and nine pence. The other children, including 23-year-old Elizabeth, received two pounds, 14 shillings and five pence each. Placing this sum in further context, Hannah Chandler received two pounds annually in money, not to mention her shelter, firewood, and food.[24]

Compounding her lack of financial resources was Elizabeth Sessions's lack of personal advocates. Neither her mother nor her brothers appear anywhere in the trial records. Sessions's bond of 20 pounds was paid by Richard Kemballs of Bradford, her maternal uncle. With her brothers still underage, he was the only male relative who could represent her in court, though he limited his representation to financial matters, rather than providing her with any legal assistance or personal support. Her vulnerability stands in sharp contrast to the other trial players. Sessions's claim that she was "by violence abused" speaks to this vulnerability. Nobody else in the trial process appears particularly concerned about how she became pregnant. Proving rape was extremely difficult

---

23 Abbot, Elinor, *Our Company Increases Apace, History, Language, and Social Identity in Early Colonial Andover, Massachusetts* (Dallas: SIL International, 2007), 147.

24 Thomas Chandler's will, in George Chandler, *The Chandler Family* (Worcester: Charles Hamilton Press, 1883), Alexander Sessions's will, in Francis Sessions, *Materials for a history of the Sessions family in America* (Albany: Munsell's Sons, 1890). Elinor Abbot also notes that in 1684, Alexander Sessions paid three shillings and 10 pence in taxes, while Thomas Chandler paid eight shillings and 11 pence, over twice as much. Abbot, *Our Company Increases Apace*, 186 and 193.

in colonial New England because conviction received the death penalty and, under Massachusetts law, this required either a confession from the perpetrator or two witnesses. With no witnesses, Joseph Chandler denying the charges, and no father to push the issue further, Sessions's rape claim was ignored by the colonial authorities and, in any event, they were more interested in paternity charges and child support than in pursuing sexual abuse.

A rape case heard in the Ipswich court a year later further highlights Elizabeth Sessions's fragile position. Peter Harris accused Mordecai Larcom of raping his daughter, Hannah Harris. Like Chandler, Larcom denied the charges. Unlike Sessions, Hannah Harris was neither pregnant nor fatherless. The court eventually ruled that Larcom would be sent to Boston to face trial.[25] Most early American families functioned as corporate households rather than as a collection of individuals. The household was represented legally, financially, and politically by the male head of the household. In the case of his death, this position could be taken on by his wife in her capacity as a deputy husband or by the oldest son.[26] If the household could not financially survive, it was dissolved. Not surprisingly, fatherless/householdless daughters appear throughout the sexual misconduct trial records. With neither secure places to live nor fathers to speak for them, they were doubly vulnerable.[27]

Nathaniel Saltonstall collected statements from 10 deponents by the time the Sessions-Chandler trial occurred in March of 1691. The first came from Joseph Chandler's family and friends. Nathaniel Lovejoy was an unmarried contemporary of Chandler, who lived at home with his parents. Like Elizabeth Sessions, Lovejoy describes spending the evening at John Chandler's house and the orchard adjoining it. While he remembers Sessions's presence in the orchard in the early evening, he states that "after [she was] gone Joseph Chandler and I and some others sat down upon the grass talking awhile and then Joseph and I went to bed together ... [I] do not remember he was gone from me in the loft that night."

The next depositions potentially changed the trial by suggesting that a different man had fathered Elizabeth Sessions's child. Thomas and Hannah Austin stated that "in the beginning of Last Summer John Russ, Jr. & Elizabeth

---

[25] See the Essex County Quarterly Court trial for Mordeca Larcom in 1692, File Papers Box 2. Judicial Archives, Massachusetts State Archives, Boston. Larcom could not be further traced in the Boston records.

[26] Laurel Thatcher Ulrich, *Good Wives: Image and Reality in the Lives of Women in Northern New England, 1650–1750* (New York: Alfred A. Knopf, 1982), 35–50 for further discussion of the concept of the deputy husband.

[27] Hambleton, *Daughters of Eve*, 24–5.

Sissions were at our house all night and the greatest part of the night together in our orchard by themselves." Russ was the 20-year-old son of John and Debora Osgood Russ and nephew to Sessions's employer, Christopher Osgood. This testimony was further supported by statements from Joseph Chandler's sister and brother-in-law, Daniel and Hannah Chandler Bixby. Sessions had spent the previous winter working for them before departing on April 26, 1690, presumably to join the Christopher Osgood household. While Sessions lived with the Bixbys, "John Russ, Jr. kept her company two or three nights in a week and some times they would be gone out of house a great part of the night." Unspoken in the records but not in the minds of the trial participants was the identity of Sessions's new employer. Russ was Christopher Osgood's nephew. However innocent the connection may have been, it added fire to arguments for Russ's guilt.

The Bixbys further added that "from the time that Elizabeth Sissions Charged Joseph Chandler with lying with her to the time of her delivery was but 37 weeks and some odd days," throwing further doubt on Sessions's claim that Joseph Chandler impregnated her in early May. Most New England colonists believed that a full-term pregnancy lasted approximately 39 weeks.[28] Pointing out the length of Sessions's pregnancy allowed the Bixbys to provide Chandler with an important alibi, at least for early May. If Sessions conceived a child with Russ in April, she could have carried it for the full 39 weeks before giving birth.

Elizabeth Sessions's birth was attended by two official witnesses, midwife Mary Barker and Mr Phibea Robinson. The presence of a male witness highlights the seriousness of Sessions's charge against Joseph Chandler. Birthing rooms were predominantly female territory in the late seventeenth century and there are no other bastardy and paternity trials in Essex County, Maine, or Rhode Island which used male birth witnesses. Barker and Robinson both stated that she had "constantly affirmed that it was Joseph Chandlers of Andover ... and no mans else." While Barker can be identified as an Andover resident in the 1690s, Robinson's identity and possible connections to the trial participants remain a mystery.[29] There were Robinson family members living in Andover at the time but his name does not appear among them. He may have been a visitor, brought in as an impartial birth witness and the title of Mr in the court records does also suggest an elevated social status.

28 Hambleton, *Daughters of Eve*, 98–100.

29 The Barker family of Andover had three sons, all of whom married women named Mary. My research suggests that the midwife in the Sessions/Chandler trial was the wife of either John or Stephen Barker. Chandler, "From Birthing Chamber to Court Room."

The final deposition came from John Russ and his first cousin, Abigail Osgood. They described seeing Joseph Chandler and Elizabeth Sessions in "an act of uncleanness ... lying together on the ground and the said Joseph Chandler said he could do well enough without us." While this account supported Sessions's claim, Russ and Osgood's testimony provided her with no further form of support.

Taken together, the 10 depositions support three plausible scenarios. The first is the simplest. Elizabeth Sessions was telling the truth, she and Joseph Chandler conceived a child on May 8, 1690, and she did not carry the child the full 39 weeks. This version is supported by testimony from the birth witnesses, Mary Barker and Phibea Robinson as well as Sessions herself.

The second scenario follows depositions from Nathaniel Lovejoy, Lida Deere and Hannah Chandler Bixby. Elizabeth Sessions became pregnant by John Russ in late March or early April of 1690. Bixby's memory of the exact date that Sessions left her household suggests some event precipitated her departure. Shortly after arriving in the Osgood household, Sessions either chose, or was persuaded, to name Joseph Chandler as the father of her child.

The third scenario is implied rather than stated outright. John Russ was the father of Elizabeth Sessions's child. Joseph Chandler learned of the pregnancy from his sister, Hannah Chandler Bixby, and decided that Sessions was fair game, already pregnant, and without family to defend her. However, for either of the latter scenarios to prevail, the justices would have to disregard unambiguous testimony from the birth witnesses.

The Ipswich court record book used in 1690 was not available to Philip Greven while he was conducting his research on community and family interactions in Andover and he concluded in 1970 that Chandler was "innocent and that John Russ ... was the more likely culprit."[30] My research in 2005 did include the Ipswich court record book, which documents that Elizabeth Sessions was charged with fornication and Joseph Chandler with being the "Reputed father of Elizabeth Sessions her Child" on March 31, 1691. Sessions was ordered to pay a fine of 40 shillings or receive 10 lashings. The Ipswich justices plainly placed more faith in the birth testimonies than in depositions from Chandler's family and friends, particularly since Sessions also had two compelling supporters who claimed to have seen her and Chandler in an "act of uncleanness." Chandler was ordered to pay a second bond of 50 pounds as well as two shillings a week in child support.

---

[30] Philip Greven, *Four Generations, Population, Land, and Family in Colonial Andover, Massachusetts* (Ithaca: Cornell University Press, 1970), 115.

Philip Greven's decision in 1970 to attribute paternity for Elizabeth Sessions's child to John Russ based on the court documents describing Sessions's time with Russ in April of 1690 and to completely disregard the birth testimonies from midwife Mary Barker and Phineas Robinson can best be described as a comment on the lack of available research on women in the early modern period in the early 1970s. Research conducted in the last 40 years on the legal roles played by midwives in both early modern Europe and the European colonies in the western hemisphere has clearly demonstrated that it was almost impossible in most communities to convict men on paternity charges without correlative testimony from the woman's midwife and this point will continue to be explored in future chapters.

Nevertheless, John Russ's complete exoneration is puzzling. The justices did not even demand that he pay court costs. Multiple witnesses had described his interactions with Elizabeth Sessions and most men named as potential fathers of illegitimate children were still charged court costs. Perhaps the justices knew more about the doings of the Andover residents than they recorded in the court documents. Not too surprisingly, a deeper investigation into the players in the Sessions/Chandler trial provides a nod to the other tales buried beneath its surface.

Andover's location on the westernmost edge of Essex County made travelers to settlements north and west of the town a frequent occurrence. Many Andover residents supplemented their incomes by keeping small taverns or inns in their households. These were carefully regulated by both town and county ordinances. Innkeepers had to apply for permission and have their licenses updated on a yearly basis. William Chandler, Joseph Chandler's uncle, received permission on February 2, 1687 to open an inn in his household. Uneasy about competition, John Osgood, another Andover innkeeper, complained to the town that Chandler was operating without a license. Chandler responded by producing the paperwork giving him permission, as well as a petition from his friends and neighbors arguing that his inn was needed. Undaunted, Osgood sent a petition signed by his friends and neighbors to the town on March 31, 1690 claiming that Chandler's inn was a disgrace.[31]

The names of the colonists supporting these petitions reinforce the community networks found in the Sessions/Chandler trial. The first name on William Chandler's petition was John Lovejoy, father to Nathaniel, who provided Joseph Chandler with an alibi for May 8, 1690. Additional names on the petition included Thomas Chandler and Ralph Farnum, whose daughter

[31] See Sarah Bailey, *Historical Sketches of Andover* (Cambridge: Riverside Press, 1880).

married into the Chandler family in 1685. In turn, Christopher Osgood, father to Abigail Osgood and uncle to John Russ, headed the list of names on John Osgood's petition. His son Thomas also signed the petition, as did members of the Fry family, relations of the Osgoods. Word of Osgood's circulating petition reached the town selectmen, which included Thomas Chandler and John Abbot, prior to its arrival. The petition was dated March 21 but the selectmen decided on March 3 to allow Chandler to stay in business. John Osgood had been outmaneuvered.

Given the amount of time John Osgood devoted to his petition, it seems unlikely that he simply allowed the matter to rest. According to the Osgood petition, William Chandler had allowed servants and children to frequent his inn "at all times unseasonable by night and day," an accusation borne out by extensive descriptions in the Sessions/Chandler trial depositions of Andover residents in their late teens and 20s trysting in orchards and roads near the Chandler households. When Elizabeth Sessions accused Joseph Chandler of fathering her child, she was living in Christopher Osgood's household. Did the Osgoods persuade her to accuse one of the Chandler offspring? And did the Chandlers retaliate by accusing John Russ, nephew to the Osgood family? Regardless of the motivations, Joseph Chandler's conviction as the father of Elizabeth Sessions's child most likely provided a sense of vindication for the collected Osgood clan.[32]

Elizabeth Sessions went on to marry Richard Carrier in 1694, a marriage suggesting she remained on the margin of respectable Andover society. Her new in-laws had a long history of making their neighbors uneasy. Local tradition held that Carrier's father, Thomas, swung the axe that beheaded Charles I.[33] Massachusetts Bay may have been a Puritan colony but that did not mean its residents condoned regicide. The Carrier family arrived in Andover in the early 1690s, having either left or been forced from neighboring Billerica. Carrier's mother, Martha Allen Carrier, immediately became involved in an extensive dispute over land boundaries with Benjamin Abbot, who was Thomas

---

[32] Elinor Abbot argues that the tensions between the Chandler-Abbot families and the Osgood-Russ families date back to Andover's early history in the 1640s when the town was settled by waves of colonists from different parts of the British isles. While the Chandlers and Abbots were both from Hertfordshire County in England, the Osgoods were from Hampshire and Wiltshire Counties. Over time, the regional English differences between these families became regional Andover differences as the Hertfordshire families settled in the southern half of Andover, while the Hampshire and Wiltshire families settled in the northern half of the town. Abbot, *Our Company Increases Apace*, 145.

[33] See unpublished Carrier family history, Andover Historical Society, Andover, Massachusetts.

Chandler's nephew and Joseph Chandler's cousin. Following the outbreak of the witchcraft hysteria in neighboring Salem Village, Abbot accused Martha Carrier of witchcraft. Abbot's accusation was supported by William Chandler's 11-year-old daughter Phebe's claim that both Martha and Richard had tried to poison her. While Richard was freed after being questioned under torture, Martha Carrier was hanged for witchcraft on August 19, 1692. Richard Carrier and Elizabeth Sessions's marriage marks yet another alliance in Andover, Massachusetts, between people wronged by the Chandler/Abbot clan.[34]

The only relief granted to Elizabeth Sessions throughout the entire experience was the knowledge that if she continued to consistently name Joseph Chandler as the father of her child through depositions, labor pains, and the eventual court trial, Chandler would almost certainly be convicted, despite his family's best efforts. The possibility that she would be punished with either a whipping or a fine she could not pay was certain to the point of being unremarked upon by either Sessions or any of the Andover community. Her willingness to submit to the trial process and, quite possibly, to have consistently lied about her certainty that Joseph Chandler was the only man who had fathered her child highlights the full extent to which understandings of the use and purposes of a rule of law existed throughout English colonial society. John Brewer and John Styles observe that "the discretion and voluntaristic nature of the legal system that aided patrician power also enabled others to exploit the law. Indeed, if this had not been the case ... then the fiction of the rule of law would not have been so potent."[35] Sessions engaged fully in the legal process and, in turn, was offered the only form of protection available to her: a modicum of financial support for her child. Her position as a potential rape victim was not part of the legal process because her pregnancy would have been seen as evidence of consent on her part and because she did not have a household head to advocate the point for her. Finally, the system in which she, and many other female servants, lived was more interested in saving the town of Andover from having to support her child if she was unable to do so than they were in providing her with any form of personal protection.

The Sessions/Chandler trial, the dispute over the Osgood and Chandler taverns and the hanging of Martha Carrier simultaneously underscore and undercut Philip Greven's argument that household tensions in Andover were

---

[34] Mary Beth Norton notes that Andover had an unusually high number of accusations. Norton, *In the Devil's Snare, The Salem Witchcraft Crisis of 1692* (New York: Alfred A. Knopf, 2002), 7.

[35] John Brewer and John Styles, "Introduction," in *An Ungovernable People: The English and their Law in the Seventeenth and Eighteenth Centuries*, Brewer and Style, eds (London: Hutchinson & Co., 1980), 19.

managed by keeping potentially wayward children under control through careful management of family lands.[36] Thomas Chandler's management of his son's sexual escapades does, indeed, support Greven's argument. What Greven did not fully address was the utter complexity of seventeenth-century familial life in Andover. The real tensions lay between families and between social classes, a point also made by Elinor Abbot.[37] Challenges to the familial honor of the landed Chandler/Abbot and Osgood/Russ clans resulted in a dual commitment of financial resources and extended community ties. Challenges to the poorer Sessions and Carrier families resulted in chaos, shame, and, occasionally, death.

Conclusion

Massachusetts Bay leaders initially hoped that the act of colonization, the sundering of geographic and societal ties, would forge a newly transformed English people. They believed instead that sexuality and sexual behavior would serve only as the emotional heart of the Puritan marriage, linking together husband and wife and producing still more Puritans to settle the new land. As their hopes for a *New* England faded, they too were forced to realize that, like England, they had societal members who sought sexual contact outside marriage and, like England, they now had to address the financial consequences of that same sexual contact. Both the 1668 amendment to *The Lawes and Liberties* adding a law mandating financial support for illegitimate children and the 1692 creation of a formalized Overseers of the Poor to help organize care for those same children brought Massachusetts law closer to English laws of the same period. If Massachusetts Bay had a more Anglicized legal system in place in 1750 because it was one mandated by the English Crown and Parliament alike, Massachusetts also had a more Anglicized legal system in place because its colonists now looked to English laws to address social problems unanticipated in the colony's early years.

Colonial leaders in Massachusetts, Maine, and Rhode Island all agreed that the desired end goal of a successful bastardy and paternity trial was the identification and conviction of the putative father so he could pay child support. They did not, however, agree on the best means of accomplishing this goal. The community-driven bastardy and paternity trials which appear in the Essex County court records were also found by M. Michelle Jarrett Morris in the

36 See Greven, *Four Generations*.

37 Godbeer, Richard, "Foreward," in Osgood, *Our Company Increases Apace*, xiii.

court records of Suffolk and Middlesex Counties during the same period, which suggests this was a Massachusetts-wide phenomenon.[38] Conducting these trials required multiple families with the financial resources needed for such trials *and* the legal infrastructure to issue warrants, collect depositions, and provide an array of justices to whom individual families could make their appeals. All these things existed in the Puritan strongholds of Massachusetts and Connecticut, though not necessarily in other parts of the region. Richard Scott Eckert writes that the Massachusetts courts "were the primary institution for the enforcement of community standards [as they] promoted an ethical unity which served to insure economic and social stability."[39] Maine had an equally active judiciary but most Maine colonists lacked the financial resources for such legal activities. In turn, many Rhode Island colonists had the financial resources but lacked the judicial networks as the Rhode Island governor and his assistants doubled as court justices until the 1720s. These factors meant that courts in Maine and Rhode Island were forced to rely on different tactics to identify men reluctant to take responsibility for their actions and these tactics will be discussed at greater length in future chapters.

Essex County's community-driven bastardy and paternity trials undoubtedly speak to the specific legal cultures created in seventeenth-century Massachusetts. They also serve as a reminder for scholars to pay attention to change over time as well as differences between geographic locations. While the community-driven bastardy and paternity trials dominate the Essex County court records in the last three decades of the seventeenth century, they vanish from the records by 1715. It is possible that documentation for community-driven trials were simply not preserved after 1715, but legal and political changes in Massachusetts suggest, instead, that they were replaced with a different system with different priorities and these changes will be discussed in future chapters.

---

[38] See Morris, *Under Household Government*.

[39] Richard Scott Eckert, *The Gentleman of the Profession: The Emergence of Lawyers in Massachusetts, 1630–1810* (New York: Garland Publishing, Inc., 1991), 88.

Chapter 5
"The Court doe Own him her Aturney": Justices, Attorneys, and the New England Court Room

New England court records contain an abundance of written accounts but few visual images of the colonists who inhabit those records. A furious Robert Swan announced in the Essex County court in 1689 that the "carrott head" justice of the peace Nathaniel Saltonstall had "upheld [Simon Wainwright] in all his roguery." The remark preserves a moment in time in which a presumably red-headed justice presided over an Essex County court room but Robert Moody also speculates that "Swan's anger was based on his belief that no ordinary citizen could get justice in an Essex County court against a Wainwright as long as a Saltonstall presided over that court."[1] Swan's belief that judiciary action stemmed directly from personal connections highlights the power and weight of the justice of the peace as well as the complexities of seventeenth-century colonial court rooms.

All colonial leaders carefully evaluated the political and legal systems of their home countries when considering whether to replicate those systems or create new ones. Medieval and early modern England's evolving sea of judicial practices provided English colonists with a wide range of models to draw from when answering these questions. The initial freedom to pick and choose from among these models contributed greatly to legal diversity in seventeenth-century New England, though this freedom would change in the eighteenth century as the region came under greater and greater English control.

Justices and Attorneys in Medieval and Early Modern England

English justices of the peace first emerged in the fourteenth century "as just one of a number of royal experiments for suppressing disorder. … [and] survived its

1 Robert Moody, *The Saltonstall Papers, 1607–1815*, Volume 1 (Portland: Anthoensen Press, 1972), 55.

rather shaky origins [to become] ... an essential part of local government" by the fifteenth century.[2] Some justices formally trained at university or apprenticed with other justices; most were simply the best educated and best connected men in their regions and, in many cases, their services were purely voluntary. Justices oversaw the early stages of court trials in the towns or city districts in which they lived, issuing warrants and subpoenas, collecting information, and notifying participants when their presence was required. Once in court, they made trial decisions based on the evidence presented to them, circumstantial or otherwise, although these rulings were also shaped by community relations and family connections. The presence of justices of the peace in rural areas meant that reports and interrogations could be conducted immediately, rather than waiting for infrequent court sessions or for justices to come from the urban legal hubs.

The concept of the paid legal professional began appearing in the sixteenth century, though J.A. Sharpe notes that "the term 'profession' is hardly applicable to the wide variety of legal practitioners existing in England" at that time.[3] These positions evolved into a system of solicitors, attorneys, and barristers in the seventeenth and early eighteenth centuries. Solicitors dealt directly with clients, attorneys "saw to the writs required, kept on top of procedural developments, and drafted the simple pleadings needed to move the case along" and barristers argued for their clients in court.[4] Traditionally, only the prosecution was allowed to ask for legal counsel but the Treason Trials Act of 1696 granted the same right to defendants on trial for treason. The right to legal counsel was also granted to felony defendants in the late eighteenth century, which widened the numbers of barristers actively employed in the court room. It also influenced the laws written for the newly formed United States of America in the 1780s.

Attorneys in Massachusetts Court Rooms

The Puritan and Separatist colonies of Massachusetts, Connecticut, and Plymouth initially barred legal professionals from providing counsel in the court room, or at least barred them from charging money for doing so. Article

---

2 J.A. Sharpe, *Crime in Early Modern England, 1550–1750* (New York: Longman Group Limited, 1984), 28.

3 Sharpe, *Crime in Early Modern England*, 146.

4 Angela Fernandez, "Record-Keeping and Other Troublemaking: Thomas Lechford and Law Reform in Colonial Massachusetts," *Law and History Review*, Volume 23, No. 2 (Summer 2005), 237.

26 of *The Bodies of Liberties* stated in 1641 that "every man that findeth himself unfit to plead his own cause in any Court shall have Libertie to imploy any man against whom the Court doth not except, to helpe him, Provided he give him noe fee or reward for his paines."[5] Nevertheless, a close reading of Article 26 suggests a loophole to anyone familiar with the workings of the English legal system in the seventeenth century. Colonists living in Massachusetts could not serve as barristers, men who earned money by serving as counsel in the court room. However, the law said nothing about the behind-the-scenes drawing-up of legal documents and arguments, the work done by solicitors and attorneys. English attorney Thomas Lechford spent a few years in Massachusetts in the late 1730s and early 1740s doing just this sort of work.[6]

The useful skills possessed by men like Thomas Lechford may explain Massachusetts's gradual transition towards accepting legal professionals in the colony. The law prohibiting payment for legal aid was removed from *The Laws and Liberties* in 1648, although the colony specified in 1663 that attorneys could not hold political office. Most of the English colonies initially blended the roles of the barrister and attorney and colonial men referred to as attorneys generally provided both counsel and the necessary legal paperwork. Clear distinctions between the two roles eventually emerged in the late eighteenth century.[7] The Dominion of New England in the 1680s and the second charter period after 1692 permanently introduced legal professionals to the Massachusetts court system and they gained both power and influence throughout the eighteenth century.

Massachusetts law initially made it impossible for colonists to seek formal legal counsel for court room proceedings and, in any event, there was no English tradition of legal counsel for defendants in the seventeenth century. Massachusetts colonists were, however, encouraged to seek out their local justices for legal advice when needed. These men were active members in their communities and the court records indicate that many colonists felt comfortable doing so. One such Massachusetts justice was Nathaniel Saltonstall who employed the "intimate knowledge possessed only by an active participant in a small town's affairs ... firm and effective in law enforcement, and yet, where allowed discretion by

---

5 Article 26, *The Bodies of Liberties*, in William Whitmore, ed., *The Colonial Laws of Massachusetts, Reprinted from the Edition of 1660, With the Supplements to 1672, Containing Also, The Body of Liberties of 1641* (Boston: Rockwell & Churchill City Printers, 1889), 39.

6 Thomas Barnes, "Thomas Lechford and the Earliest Lawyering in Massachusetts, 1638-1641," in *Law in Colonial Massachusetts, 1630–1800*, Daniel Coquilette, ed. (Boston: The Colonial Society of Massachusetts, distributed by the University Press of Virginia, 1984), 3–38.

7 See Murrin, "The Legal Transformation."

law, humane and flexible."[8] Connections between colonists and justices played a powerful role in many Essex County sexual misconduct trials and helped to reaffirm the colony's wider values and emphasis on the covenanted community.

Justices and Attorneys in Maine Court Rooms

The Reverend John Wheelwright was an ideal Massachusetts colonist on paper, having studied at the University of Cambridge, befriended Oliver Cromwell, and brought his family to Massachusetts in 1636 as part of the Great Migration. But Wheelwright was also brother-in-law to Anne Hutchison and he too exiled from Massachusetts Bay for his belief that "any true believer ... could interpret the Bible and form his own 'covenant of grace.'"[9] The Wheelwright family then moved to New Hampshire and eventually to Maine in 1643 where Wheelwright's children intermarried with the upwardly mobile Preble, Frost, Pepperell, and Hammond families. These five families dominated both colonial Maine's political and judicial systems for decades, positions they had a vested interest in maintaining. Their commitment to expanding their knowledge of their profession echoes through the extensive collection of English legal texts shared between them. Little evidence of specific titles survives but the elegy given at Charles Frost's funeral in 1724 praised Frost for his knowledge of English law and the probate inventory done for his estate valued his book collection at £120.[10] Overall, the court records suggest that like their Massachusetts counterparts, early Maine colonists believed firmly in the benefits of maintaining an active local judiciary.

The Province of Maine's initial position as a non-Puritan colony meant that Massachusetts Bay's prohibitions on paid counsel in the court room did not apply in the colony's early years. A few attorneys moved to Maine to practice law in the 1630s and 1640s. Francis Robinson probably came to Maine in 1631 with

---

8 Moody, *The Saltonstall Papers*, 50. Saltonstall was also the only Massachusetts Bay justice who refused involvement with the Salem Court of Oyer and Terminer in 1692. Francis, Richard, *Judge Sewall's Apology: The Salem Witch Trials and the Forming of an American Conscience* (New York: Harper Perennial, 2005), 123–31.

9 Julie Wheelwright, *Esther, The Remarkable True Story of Esther Wheelwright: Puritan Child, Native Daughter, Mother Superior* (Toronto: HarperCollins Publishers Ltd, 2011), 6. Wheelwright eventually apologized to Massachusetts Bay and was allowed to return, but his children refused to leave Maine.

10 Allen "Law and Authority to the Eastward," in *Law in Colonial Massachusetts, 1630–1800*, 288.

Thomas Lewis, another early settler.[11] A debt case between John Bonython and Richard Gibson tried on June 25, 1640 notes that Robinson served as Gibson's attorney and promised to "engage himselfe to the plaint[iff] that the Corne which the defend[ent] hath now growing in Saco shall remaine to the plaint[iff] for his security."[12] Robinson was also employed for trials involving debt and land disputes and for executing wills. He appears a well-respected member of Maine society and often served as a juror when he was not otherwise employed in the court room. Robinson's commercial interests took him to the Caribbean in the 1650s and Boston in the 1660s and he did not return to Maine. There were no attorneys connected to sexual misconduct trials in Maine in the seventeenth century, perhaps because they were not considered worth the financial investment. Regardless, when Maine came under Massachusetts control in the 1650s and 1670s, attorneys disappear from the court records, only to reappear in the early eighteenth century.

Attorneys in Rhode Island Court Rooms

The Rhode Island legal system functioned very differently from the ones established in both Massachusetts Bay and the Province of Maine. Unlike Massachusetts and Maine, Rhode Island did not initially use justices of the peace in its court system. Instead, similar to neighboring Plymouth Colony, the colony's legislature served as justices during court hearings until 1729 when the legal system was rearranged and lower courts using justices of the peace were introduced.[13] Legal counsel was an important part of the Rhode Island judicial system and the 1647 legal code mandated that the colony's towns maintain two attorneys at all times. The colony provided court-appointed attorneys for colonists who could not afford them by 1669. While attorneys were initially only used for civil trials, they soon played active roles in criminal trials, a transition occurring almost a century before it became common practice in England.[14]

---

11 Sybil Noyes, Charles Thornton Libby, and Walter C. Davis, *Genealogical Dictionary of Maine and New Hampshire* (Portland, ME: Anthoensen Press, 1928–39), 591.

12 All quotes from the First General Court held at Saco in the Province of Maine trial for John Bonython and Richard Gibson in 1640, in *Province and Court Records of Maine*, Volume 1, Charles Thornton Libby, ed. (Lewiston: Penmor Lithographers, 1991), 45.

13 See Patrick Conley, "The Foundations of Rhode Island's Legal System," in *Liberty and Justice: A History of Law and Lawyers in Rhode Island, 1636–1998*, Patrick Conley, ed. (East Providence: The Rhode Island Publications Society, 1998), 14–23.

14 John Murrin, "Magistrates, Sinners, and a Precarious Liberty: Trial by Jury in Seventeenth-Century New England," in *Saints & Revolutionaries, Essays on Early American History*, David Hall,

Attorneys, or, at least, the suggestion of legal counsel, appear in several of Rhode Island's sexual misconduct trials.

Justices and Essex County's Bastardy and Paternity Trial

The previous chapter established the emphasis placed on the covenanted community in Essex County's seventeenth-century bastardy and paternity trials. While it occurred in 1705, the Proctor/Choat bastardy and paternity trial highlights the crucial roles given to justices of the peace within these trials. When Ipswich resident Debora Proctor needed legal advice in 1705 to help prosecute Thomas Choat as the father of her daughter's illegitimate child, she spoke with Justice Francis Wainwright, who was related by marriage to her brother-in-law. And when Choat needed legal counsel to help confront Proctor's accusations, he spoke with family friend Justice Stephen Sewall. These relationships existed because Massachusetts Bay authorities encouraged both justices and colonists to seek them out in lieu of maintaining paid attorneys in the colony, though trials like the Sessions/Chandler trial discussed in the previous chapter also demonstrate that such relationships were not open to all Massachusetts colonists.

Family connections and the landscape around them played equally distinctive roles in the Proctor/Choat trial. Ipswich's creek-threaded marshes provided easy access to the ocean, while the remaining land was wide and flat, making farming easier than in other parts of Essex County. These resources drew dozens of settlers in the 1630s and made finding land for their children harder than in other towns. Rather than send younger son Thomas and daughter-in-law Mary Varney Choat to the uncertainties of the northern frontier in 1690, John Choat decided to buy him neighboring Hog Island as a wedding present, which gave them a stronger start for their marriage than second or third generation Massachusetts residents. The island offered land for houses and fields and relatively easy access to both Ipswich and the newly formed village of Chebacco as fair weather and a good tide meant the journey could be made in 15 minutes or so.[15]

John Murrin, and Thad Tate, eds (New York: W.W. Norton & Co., 1984), 152–206 and Catherine DeCesare, "Women and the Legal Culture of Colonial Rhode Island," in *Liberty and Justice*, 104–15.

George Lee Haskins, *Law and Authority in Early Massachusetts, A Study in Tradition and Design* (New York: The Macmillan Company, 1960), 186.

[15] Today, Hog Island has been renamed Choat Island and is owned by the Trustees of the Reservations as a nature preserve. Although the island is now uninhabited, its colonial past was revived in the late 1990s when *The Crucible* was filmed there. Chebacco has become the town of Essex, Massachusetts.

Wider tensions in eastern Massachusetts affected the Choats two years later when John Proctor, Mary Choat's maternal uncle, was hanged for witchcraft in the summer of 1692. Prior to Proctor's execution, Thomas Choat joined a group of Ipswich men who signed a petition vouching for Proctor's moral character and good name. Perhaps uneasy about his inability to save Proctor, Choat agreed to sell the northern part of Hog Island to another of his wife's uncles, Benjamin Proctor. Proctor settled on Hog Island in the mid-1690s with his wife, Debora, and their four children, Samuel, Sarah, John, and Martha. Like the Choats, their income was derived from a combination of farming and fishing. When Benjamin Proctor died suddenly in 1704, the oldest three children were unmarried, despite being in their late 20s or early 30s. Proctor's estate left debts totaling 200 pounds and it is possible the family was unable to provide the financial resources needed to attract marital partners.[16] Regardless, the settling of the estate left just enough money to allow Debora to remain in her home on the island and one of the sons to rent a mainland farm on Castle Neck in Ipswich.

Debora Proctor's troubles were further compounded the following year when Martha became pregnant out of wedlock and refused to name the father of her child, although local rumor held that Thomas Choat was the father. There was no doubt that Martha would face fornication charges in the Essex County Court of General Sessions. However, Proctor's position as a female head of household since Benjamin Proctor's death put certain limitations on her legal options. She could neither represent Martha in court, nor force her daughter to name a father during the birth. Nor could she afford to pay for multiple deponents from her community to help verify who had fathered Martha's child. Consequently, Proctor devised a third method for addressing the problem. Before her daughter's trial in September of 1705, she sent a lengthy statement to the Essex County court justices describing her interpretation of the events leading to Martha's pregnancy.

---

[16] They may also have suffered from the social stigma of close family ties with multiple Salem witch trials suspects. Debora's mother, Elizabeth Hutchins Hart, was arrested for witchcraft on May 14, 1692, imprisoned in Boston, and released without trial late in 1692. Benjamin Proctor's debts at the time of his death seem odd, given that Proctor had inherited and sold a 200-acre farm in the 1670s and purchased a farm on Hog Island in the 1690s. He may have provided financial support for John Proctor's family following Proctor's execution for witchcraft. See James Hart, *Genealogical history of Samuell Hart from London, England, to Lynn, Mass., 1640 and descendants, to 1903, Nicholas Hart, from London to Taunton, Mass., 1642, at Boston, Mass., 1643, and Warwick, R.I., 1648, and descendants, Isaac Hart from Scratby, England, to Watertown, Mass., 1636, later of Reading, Mass., and several short lines and their descendants up to 1903* (Concord: Rumford Print. Co., 1903).

Debora Proctor's "Declaration of the Case concerning Thomas Choat" survives today as the most extensive description of a sexual crime in colonial Essex County. Well-documented bastardy and paternity trials usually produced depositions and warrants, subpoenas and bills each approximately 750 to 1,000 words in length. Proctor's "Declaration," by contrast, measures 12 by 24 inches in size and contains approximately 2,000 words. In addition to detailing the pregnancy, Proctor describes her attempts to mitigate the extensive persecution her family had suffered since Martha's conception. Without birth testimony from Martha, Choat was unlikely to be convicted, which would leave the Proctors financially responsible for supporting her child. Instead, Proctor gambled that a careful documentation of Choat's "wickedness" would encourage the Essex County justices to take a second look at the evidence relating to her daughter's trial.

Thomas Choat entered the legal proceedings on a very different footing. His morality may have been called into question but his legal and financial position as a head of household remained intact. Choat filed a preemptive complaint with family friend Justice Stephen Sewall against Martha Proctor on July 12, 1705; Martha's uncle, Joseph Proctor, did not name Choat as the father of her child until the next day. Choat also guaranteed the court fees necessary to provide 10 depositions supporting his claim of innocence. Four of these deponents were directly related to Choat, and others may have been linked through no-longer-traceable social or economic ties.

The specificity provided by most Essex County paternity trial depositions makes them read rather like accusations made in the board game of *Clue*: so and so did it, in the orchard, at midnight. The Proctor/Choat depositions are, by contrast, extremely vague. Rather than describe the details of Martha Proctor's sexual activities, they document conversations with Martha regarding the father's identity. Josiah Burnham testified that "she never said so in her life nor never thought that [Choat] was the father of her child for he was not she would clear him before a hundred men."[17] The most crucial, and most cryptic, testimony came from midwife Elizabeth Low, who stated that Martha Proctor had initially said that the father was "the married man that hath fetcht you on to the Island severall times before." Low had likely attended Martha Proctor's cousin, Mary Varney Choat, at the births of one or more of the seven children that she had borne by this time and Proctor appears to have been hinting that Thomas Choat was the father. However, according to Low, her patient did not

[17] All quotations from the Essex County Court of General Sessions Trial for Martha Proctor and Thomas Choat trial in 1705. File Papers, Box 3. Judicial Archives, Massachusetts State Archives, Boston.

mention "any mans name and this she held to before all that were thare present thoe I told her often it was her duty to tell yet this she said to the very last."

Another oddity about the Proctor/Choat depositions is the lack of calendar dates. Many of the well-documented Essex County bastardy and paternity trial depositions speculated about the length of the unwed woman's pregnancy. Elizabeth Low testified on July 19, 1705 but did not say when Martha's child was born, nor did any other deposition mention possible conception dates. The first instinct may be to blame the vagueness on Hog Island's isolation, but the depositions suggest frequent contact between the island and the mainland. Deponent Josiah Burnham mentions being at work on Hog Island. A deposition given by Joseph Choat, Thomas Choat's son, details his travel by boat to the island along with the Proctors and other members of the Ipswich community. The Choat and Proctor families routinely attended church on Sundays in neighboring Essex, Massachusetts. In contrast to these vague depositions, Debora Proctor's "Declaration" provides concrete details, although Proctor is equally imprecise in dating its events.

The "Declaration" documents that Martha Proctor had gone to visit one of her brothers on his rented farm. Early in the morning, Thomas Choat arrived with a warning that 100 cattle were loose in the corn field. After Martha's brother had gone outside, "the said Choat came to [Martha's] bed and insinuated as to ly with her and having done his will he rose up [and left]." While the "Declaration" stops short of calling Choat's actions rape, it firmly suggests that Martha did not welcome his sexual advances. Realizing no cattle were loose, the brother returned to the house just as Choat departed. No doubt hoping that she would not become pregnant, Martha did not tell her brother that she had had intercourse with Choat. At some later point, she realized that she was with child.

When Martha informed Choat of the pregnancy, he offered to strike a bargain with her. If she remained silent, he would give her money to pay the fine and support the child. He would also find a midwife who would not question Martha during the birth regarding the father of her child. This particular piece of information was potentially the most damning for Choat as midwives were required by law to question unwed mothers. Since testimony from midwife Elizabeth Low clearly demonstrates that she did question Martha during the birth, it is impossible to know whether Choat were unable to find a midwife willing to break the law for him or whether Debora was making false allegations, hoping that something would persuade the justices to investigate Choat more fully. Finally, Choat also threatened both Martha and the unborn child's lives if she were to name him, a threat made more potent by their shared residence on Hog Island.

Debora Proctor's "Declaration" raises a number of questions. A woman in her 50s by the time of her daughter's trial in 1705, she would have been familiar enough with the ritualized process of the early modern bastardy and paternity trial to know the Proctor family stood no chance of having Thomas Choat convicted without sworn testimony from Martha's midwife verifying Choat as the father. Producing her "Declaration" required considerable time and means: acquiring paper and ink, taking the time to write it out, or arranging to have it written for her, and then delivering it to a justice on the Massachusetts mainland. The text of the "Declaration" itself provides some clues as to its origins. In the penultimate paragraph, Proctor notes that "the forsaid threatnings made me for my safety to complain to Justice Wainwright." Justice Francis Wainwright was the man to whom Joseph and Martha Proctor had made their statements on July 13, 1705. Wainwright was also Joseph Proctor's brother-in-law as Joseph had married Wainwright's sister, Martha, in the early 1670s. Given this connection, it seems likely that Wainwright provided Proctor with legal advice regarding the composition of the "Declaration."

The Proctor declaration continually emphasizes Proctor's role as the head of the Proctor household. With the usual channels for convicting a man of impregnating a woman out of wedlock foreclosed to her, Proctor needed another method to persuade the remaining Essex County justices to consider her story with the seriousness she felt it deserved. The initial paternity accusation had come as a direct challenge to Choat, and he met it with a barrage of depositions swearing that he had not fathered Martha's child. Anne S. Lombard argues that early New Englanders believed that "[m]anliness ... implied not only moral qualities but also ... sexual potency, [and] required that a man be able to ... maintain control over his dependents."[18] Now Proctor needed to provide further evidence that Choat's inability to control himself was potentially damaging to the communities of Ipswich and Essex as a whole. The suggestion that Choat was willing to work outside Massachusetts law to find a midwife who would not question her daughter while she was giving birth was an excellent start, not to mention the description of him as a man willing to kill his cousin and aunt by marriage. In short, Proctor portrays Choat as a man willing to upset the Puritan bonds of family and household to cover his own misdeeds. If Essex County justices were, indeed, concerned about Debora Proctor's ability to run a household, the "Declaration" suggests that perhaps they should first examine her neighbor.

---

[18] Anne S. Lombard, *Making Manhood: Growing Up Male in Colonial New England* (Cambridge: Harvard University Press, 2003), 68.

Debora Proctor's willingness to pursue writing her "Declaration" places her in the tradition of the colonial-era "deputy husband" described by Laurel Thatcher Ulrich: "Under the right conditions any wife not only *could* double as a husband, she had the responsibility to do so."[19] Proctor's husband was dead; therefore, she needed to speak for her daughter and for her household as a whole. The "Declaration" also serves as a reminder of the caveats placed by Ulrich on the role of the deputy husband, namely, that actions matter more to their participants than to their observers. Proctor saw herself as possessing the same ability as Thomas Choat legally to represent her household but the Essex County court system clearly did not. This particular chain of events suggests a further limit to the role of the deputy husband: women could stand in their husband's places for economic reasons, but not necessarily for legal ones. And, in the end, Debora Proctor's "Declaration" failed. Martha Proctor was convicted of fornication and bastardy, while Thomas Choat received a full acquittal. Like Choat, Proctor had the ability and the connections to appeal to an Essex County justice of the peace on her behalf, but the other limitations placed on her rendered her as connectionless as Elizabeth Sessions had been in 1691.

Attorneys and Essex County's Bastardy and Paternity Trials

Community driven bastardy and paternity trials like the Proctor/Choat trial disappear from the court records around 1715, a disappearance most likely triggered by overall changes in both Massachusetts and its legal system. The close relationships with local justices present in so many of the Essex County court trials, not just the sexual misconduct ones, were replaced in the early eighteenth century with financial contracts with paid attorneys. These new relationships were encouraged by both the growing acceptance of paid legal counsel in Massachusetts Bay in the 1720s and 1730s and the growing presence of a wide array of lawyers available for hire. Increasingly, men who would have studied for the ministry in previous generations were now acquiring legal training, whether through informal apprenticeships or through formal education, particularly in London. And once trained, they were eager to translate their educations into paid employment and there was no shortage of colonists in need of their services.[20]

---

[19] Laurel Thatcher Ulrich, *Good Wives: Image and Reality in the Lives of Women in Northern New England, 1650-1750* (New York: Knopf, 1980), 38. Italicized emphasis is Ulrich's from the original text.

[20] Murrin, "The Legal Transformation: The Bench and Bar of Eighteenth-Century Massachusetts."

A vivid example of Massachusetts's changing society comes from a trial conducted in the Court of General Sessions in Salem on July 9, 1734 for Elisabeth Lynch of Beverly, who was ordered to pay a fine of 50 shillings for committing both fornication and bastardy. There is no mention of the man who fathered her child in the court record book. Lynch's parents were, most likely, Eugene and Martha Eliott Lynch. Eugene Lynch was of Irish descent and came to New England sometime in the early eighteenth century. He declared his intentions to marry Martha Eliot of Rowley on October 17, 1714. Genealogist Michael O'Brien speculates that "Eugene Lynch was the local schoolmaster [in 1718] at Kittery, Maine, and as his wife's name was Martha, I believe the abovementioned was the Irish pedagogue."[21] Whether Lynch was Catholic or Protestant is unclear from the records. Approximately 2,600 Scots-Irish colonists from Northern Ireland arrived in Boston around 1718 and moved to Maine that same winter. The following year they left Maine for the Merrimack River valley, where most of them settled along the newly formed Massachusetts/New Hampshire border.[22] While there is no direct evidence that Lynch was part of this group, the timing of his movements suggests, at the very least, a connection between Lynch and these settlers. There is no information available on Martha Eliot's family but her last name suggests her family was English rather than Irish.

Eugene and Martha Lynch settled in Beverly by the early 1720s and their children were born there, including Elisabeth. The Lynch's last child was a daughter named Mary who was born on May 11, 1729 to "Eugena, deceased, and Martha," indicating that Eugene died before his last child was born.[23] As was stated previously, the court record book makes no mention of the man who fathered Elisabeth Lynch's child. However, there is a legal document signed by both Martha and Elisabeth Lynch which names "Jonathan Gillbard of Gloucester or Cape Ann" as the father of Elisabeth's child.[24] As a side note, this document verifies that Eugene Lynch died before 1734 as Martha Lynch was acting as the primary legal representative for the Lynch family. For his part, there are equally few records about Jonathan Gillbard in the records but he most

[21] Michael O'Brien, "Some Traces of the Irish Settlers in the Colony of Massachusetts Bay," in *The Journal of the American Irish Historical Society*, Volumes 19–20, New York: Published by the Society, 1919, 154.

[22] Kerby A. Miller, Arnold Schrier, Bruce D. Boling, and David N. Doyle, eds, *Irish Immigrants in the Land of Canaan: Letters and Memoirs from Colonial and Revolutionary America, 1675–1815* (New York: Oxford University Press, 2003).

[23] *Vital records of Beverly, Massachusetts, to the end of the year 1849* (Topsfield: Topsfield Historical Society, 1906), 220.

[24] All quotes from the Essex County Court of General Sessions trial for Elisabeth Lynch in 1734, File Papers Box 12. Judicial Archives, Massachusetts State Archives, Boston.

likely was the Jonathan Gilbert born to John and Martha Gilbert in Gloucester on March 28, 1713.[25]

Elisabeth Lynch was pregnant, presumably with Jonathan's child, in the summer of 1734. Some two months after her conviction on fornication and bastardy charges on July 9 in the Salem court, Martha Lynch employed attorney Jonathan Dodge of Beverly to negotiate a settlement with Gilbert. A legal document states that Lynch had "received of Jonathan Gillbard fower Pounds and of Mr. Jonathan Dodge Said Atturney thee summ of two pounds likewise said Dodge hath given me a bound for fowerteen pounds" and that these were "in Relation of the said Child above named to Discharge said Gillbard from any trouble or charges that may come after." In exchange for this settlement, the Lynch women were henceforth prevented by law from ever troubling Gilbert again.

Martha and Elisabeth Lynch received a total of 20 pounds from Jonathan Gilbert. The going rate for weekly child support fees in the early 1730s was four shillings which makes 20 pounds approximately the equivalent of two years of child support. Very few paternity convictions in Massachusetts specify the length of time that child support payments had to be paid. However, there are petitions submitted from convicted fathers asking to stop making payments after one year.[26] Since most of these petitions were granted, two years' worth of payments was generous by the standards of the time and this may explain Martha Lynch's motives in hiring Jonathan Dodge to negotiate the financial settlement. If she was going to raise her illegitimate grandchild, she wanted the best terms possible. Elisabeth and Gilbert's conception of an illegitimate child in 1734 appears to have done no damage to either of their long-term marital prospects as Elisabeth married Edward Fitsgerald on June 27, 1740 in Beverly and Gilbert married Abigail Rogers on April 17, 1740 in Gloucester.

Martha Lynch's actions demonstrate that she was as comfortable with using the legal options available to her as Debora Proctor had been some 30 years earlier when confronted with the same challenge of being a widow with a daughter pregnant out of wedlock. While a signature is not absolute proof of literacy, Martha and Elisabeth Lynch and Debora Proctor all signed their documents with their names rather than using the mark which usually denotes illiteracy.

---

[25] *Vital records of Gloucester, Massachusetts, to the end of the year 1849* (Topsfield: Topsfield Historical Society, 1917), 280. I am assuming that Gillbard is a misspelled form of Gilbert as there are no Gillbards in Gloucester but there are Gilberts.

[26] See both the Essex County Quarterly Court Records, 1636–92 and the Essex County Court of General Sessions Records, 1692–1750, Judicial Archives, Massachusetts State Archives, Boston.

Lynch's ultimate success (as opposed to Proctor's failure) stems largely from two core differences between the Lynch/Gilbert trial and the Proctor/Choat trial: the presence of verifiable dates and a putative father's confession. Elisabeth Lynch was convicted on July 9, 1734. The settlement promising Lynch 20 pounds for raising her grandchild was signed on September 20, 1734. Elisabeth gave birth on December 29, 1734 to a son named Jonathan, presumably for his father. In order for the financial settlement to be made two months before the child was born, Jonathan Gilbert had to have willingly acknowledged his guilt even before Elisabeth was questioned by her midwife during labor.

Martha Eliot Lynch's actions also speak to other changes occurring in Massachusetts in the 1730s and 1740s. Everything about the Lynch family indicates they were on the margins of Essex County society. They appear only in the records to give birth, marry, or die and sometimes not even that. Lynch was the widow of an Irish-born colonist. Elisabeth's husband's last name suggests she also married a man of Irish descent, which implies that the family maintained an ongoing Irish cultural identification after Eugene Lynch died. Nevertheless, Lynch appears thoroughly comfortable with employing an attorney from a well-established Beverly family, particularly since she did not even bother to wait for the additional security of a midwife's testimony that her daughter had, indeed, named Jonathan Gilbert as the father of her child during her birth pains. Richard Scott Eckert writes that the "operation of the courts [between 1720 and 1745] continued to be responsive to local needs both in their administrative functions and as judicial bodies."[27] Increasingly, attorneys like Jonathan Dodge were replacing justices as the conduits between the colony and its colonists. From the perspective of long-standing Massachusetts Bay officials, this was further evidence that "the rise of the bar was the secular counterpart for the decline of the New England way."[28] Martha Lynch, however, probably saw the new system as an improvement on the old one.

The Dodge family was among Beverly's first settlers as William Dodge, Jonathan's grandfather, established a farm there in 1629, predating the founding of Massachusetts Bay Colony in 1630.[29] Male members of the family routinely served as justices and jurors throughout the seventeenth century, not to mention multiple political and ecclesiastical positions. The services of Jonathan Dodge, attorney, were available to whomever could pay his fee; it seems unlikely that his earlier family members who served as justices would have been quite as helpful to

---

27 Eckert, *The Gentleman of the Profession*, 187.

28 Murrin, "The Legal Transformation: The Bench and Bar of Eighteenth-Century Massachusetts," 551.

29 See Joseph Thompson Dodge, *Genealogy of the Dodge Family of Essex County, Mass. 1629–1894* (Madison: Democrat Printing Company, 1894).

the widow Lynch. John Winthrop and the other early founders of Massachusetts Bay most likely would argue that the new system put colonists like the Lynch family at a disadvantage because it required them to pay for legal counsel. While this may be true, the multiple layers of socio-economic communities present in the colonial bastardy and paternity trials make clear that social connections were as important as economic means and that it was now possible to have one without the other. Like Elisabeth Lynch and Martha Proctor, Elizabeth Sessions had also been a young woman pregnant out of wedlock with a dead father and a living mother. Unlike Lynch and Proctor, Sessions's mother had had neither social connections nor financial means.

Attorneys and Maine's Bastardy and Paternity Trials

Attorneys returned to Maine early in the eighteenth century and there are two York County sexual misconduct trials which clearly identify attorneys serving in their professional capacity. The first such trial was the bastardy and paternity trial conducted for Joanna Gilford and John Brown, Jr of Falmouth, Maine, in 1745. The records note that Brown employed "N. Emory [as] His attorney" and enough trial records survive to document the arguments Emery used to defend Brown. Emery was almost certainly Noah Emery, who was born to Daniel and Margaret Emery on December 11, 1699 in Berwick, Maine. He originally trained as a cooper but was admitted to the bar in Massachusetts in 1725 by taking the mandatory oath of office. There are no records documenting Emery's training but it probably came from reading all the legal texts available to him and by observing members of the legal profession. Genealogist Charles Emery writes that "he appears to have been a man of bookish tastes ... [with] a library of his own. By his will he bequeathed to his sons in equal shares his 'books of law, physic, divinity, and history,'" which included one of the earliest copies of *The Laws and Liberties of Massachusetts*.[30] Emery was recognized as "King's Attorney" for York County between 1741 and 1759 and would have been at the height of his career in 1745.[31] Emery also served as a captain in the Kittery militia and letters between Sir William Pepperell and Emery indicate social and professional connections between Emery and the Wheelwright, Preble, Frost, Pepperell, and Hammond families who still dominated Maine's political and legal offices.

---

30 Charles Emery Stevens, *Noah Emery of Exeter: Member of the Provincial Congress and Clerk of the Assembly in New Hampshire in the Revolution* (Privately printed, 1886), 8.

31 William Willis, *A History of the Law, the Courts, and the Lawyers of Maine, From its First Colonization to the Early Part of the Present Century* (Portland: Bailey and Noyes, 1863), 82.

Joanna Gilford was convicted on fornication and bastardy charges on November 5, 1745 and ordered to either receive seven whippings or pay a fine of 20 shillings. When asked on November 23, 1744 who had fathered her child, she told Justice of the Peace Christopher Strout that "John Brown Juner of Falmouth Labourer ... had the Carnal Knowledge of her body ... and that the said Brown and no other person is the father of the said Bastard."[32] There are no surviving records about Joanna Gilford or her family so it is impossible to know anything about her socio-economic standing in Falmouth. Brown is a common enough surname to make absolute verification difficult but a John Brown who was born in 1664 purchased land in Falmouth in the 1730s. He had a son named John who was probably born in the 1680s or 1690s and was listed as a shipwright in Gloucester in the 1720s. The John Brown, Jr mentioned in this trial was probably his son as the Brown family appears to have settled in Falmouth by the 1740s.[33] Following Joanna Gilford's accusation, John Brown's family employed Noah Emery to serve as his attorney. Emery's notes for the trial lay out a series of four separate arguments for why Brown should not be convicted as the father of Gilford's child and it seems likely that he then used the argument or arguments he found most persuasive in the court room at the time.

The first two points made by Emery focused on Joanna Gilford's marital status. According to Emery, the "Complainant is a Married woman [who] o[ught]t not to recover any support for child from any Man but her husband." Emery may have been relying on the sexual misconduct trial conducted for Sarah Simson in 1724 when launching this particular defense for Brown. On being asked who had fathered her child, Simson replied that "it was no matter who was the father of said child she had a husband to maintain it & leett the Court do as they pleased she was ready to answer her fine."[34] The justices were clearly not amused by this response as Simson was ordered to either be whipped "Ten stripes on her naked back at the post" or to pay a fine of five pounds, though they did cease asking who should support her child.

It is difficult to tell whether Joanna Gilford was married when she became pregnant. Her original testimony notes that she conceived her child while "gowing from mr Browns home to hir fathers," a reference suggesting she lived in

[32] All quotes from the York County Court of General Sessions trial for Joanna Gilford and John Brown, Jr in 1745, York County Courts of Common Pleas and General Sessions File Papers, Box 99, Maine State Archives, Augusta.

[33] Noyes, *Genealogical Dictionary of Maine and New Hampshire*, 116.

[34] All quotes from the York County Court of General Sessions trial for Sarah Simson in 1724, York County Court of Common Pleas and General Sessions Record Book, 1718–27, Volume 7. Maine State Archives, Augusta.

her father's house, rather than her husband's. While colonial documents usually refer to married women's husbands by name, none of the documents connected to this trial mention Gilford's husband. The confusion regarding Gilford's exact marital state may have led to Emery's second point, which questions how the justices would rule if Gilford was not married. "If she were a single woman & the Child a Bastard," writes Emery, "the Justices of the peace and Inhabitants of the Town of Falmouth aforesaid such are liable to pay support of a Bastard child born in said Town and ought not to sit in Judgement in this Case [as] their estates being so liable." In other words, if Gilford were single and the justices were unable to convict anyone for fathering her illegitimate child, the town of Falmouth would be responsible for supporting her child and, therefore, the justices would be more apt to rule against Brown because they did not want the town to be financially responsible than because they actually thought he was guilty, which would render them anything but impartial conveyers of justice.

This particular argument directly referenced the changing social world of the eighteenth century. An emphasis on the needs of the community over the needs of the individual runs throughout early modern European social and legal practices. While the Puritans of England and New England developed this emphasis into an art form, it also appears in other places and in other forms. Barbara Shapiro writes that the selection of medieval era trial jurors and their resulting deliberations were based on "a mixture of their own personal knowledge of events and the testimony of others" and that trial outcomes could reflect the wider needs of the community involved, rather than the individual's guilt or innocence.[35] This last factor is particularly apparent in the handful of incest trials conducted in colonial New England in which the justices and jury did their utmost to prevent accused fathers from being convicted on incest charges because this meant they would almost certainly be executed, thereby potentially leaving their family members without a means of financial support.[36] This practice disappeared in the early modern period as "judicial charges to juries came to emphasize the duty of jurors to [document] some sort of firm assurance of guilt based [solely] on the evidence."[37] Jurors working only with the facts at hand who were discouraged from considering the wider context of

35 Barbara Shapiro, *"Beyond Reasonable Doubt" and "Probable Cause": Historical Perspectives on the Anglo-American Law of Evidence* (Berkeley: University of California Press), 1.

36 See the Plymouth Colony General Court trial for Mary Atkins and Thomas Atkins in 1660 and the Plymouth Colony General Court trial for Martha Winter and Christopher Winter trial in 1668, in *Records of the colony of New Plymouth, in New England*, Volume 1, Nathaniel B. Shurtleff, ed. (Boston: W. White Press, 1855–61).

37 Shapiro, *"Beyond Reasonable Doubt,"* 1.

crimes committed were less likely to rule based on community needs. Noah Emery wanted to make certain that the York County justices thought only about whether John Brown had fathered Joanna Gilford's child and not about who would eventually have to support the child.

Noah Emery's third and fourth points revolved around two interlinked legal technicalities. Point three states that an unidentified Justice of the Peace issued a warrant for John Brown's arrest as the putative father of Joanna Gilford's child in November of 1744 but that Brown was not served with the warrant until November of 1745 and "the justice if he had a Right to Act in that affair ought to have Bound over the Complainent to the Next Court of General Sessions of the Peace as the Law directs." The question of whether the Justice in question had the right to "Act in that affair" appears a reference to Emery's first point that the only man who should be held responsible for Gilford's child was her husband. Point four adds that "no accusation [was] made or brought before the Court of Generall Sessions of peace untill nine months after the birth of said Child." In short, Emery appears to have asked that the case be dismissed as the justices had not behaved "as the Law directs." The 1650 law intended to "suppress the detestable sins of incest, adultery, and fornication" had also specified that "no person or persons shall incur any of the penalties in this Act mentioned, unless the said person or persons be thereof indicted within twelve Moneths after the offence committed" and Emery's argument on this point was clearly a reference to this section of the 1650 law or other laws like it.[38] Maine justices could just as easily have argued that many bastardy and paternity trials dragged on for years after the initial conception between the need for waiting until after the woman had given birth and the difficulties of tracking down putative fathers, though this raises the inevitable question of why more men did not attempt this particular means of trying to have themselves acquitted. Perhaps they lacked Emery's faith in his own rhetorical skills and extensive knowledge of the inner workings of English law.

Noah Emery's actions in this stage of the trial further illuminate the growing tension between justices and attorneys in the early to mid-eighteenth century discussed by John Murrin, who writes that lawyers' educations "included the intensive and systematic study of the law itself. Consequently, many lawyers knew a good deal more than some judges about English law, and they betrayed no embarrassment in revealing this to the public."[39] Local justices of the peace in

[38] "May 1650: An Act for suppressing the detestable sins of Incest, Adultery and Fornication," *Acts and Ordinances of the Interregnum, 1642–1660* (1911), 389. URL: http://www.british-history.ac.uk/report.aspx?compid=56399 Date accessed: July 7, 2014.

[39] Murrin, "The Legal Transformation: The Bench and Bar of Eighteenth-Century Massachusetts," 558.

both England and New England generally gained their positions through their social and political connections rather than any legal formal training. While the Wheelwright, Preble, Frost, Pepperell, and Hammond families routinely passed legal texts among themselves as a means of preparing their sons for future offices, their knowledge of the law was still contained to themselves and their libraries.[40] Attorneys were expected to gain their legal knowledge through more formal training, whether apprenticeships or university educations, and a growing number of New England men studied at London's Inns of Court in the early eighteenth century.[41]

The document concludes with Noah Emery asking "that the whole process may be Quashed" The court records for November 5, 1745 note that "after a full hearing of both Parties and the midwife Rebecca Sayer on oath face to face in Court this Cause was Committed to the Jury Sworn ... [who] sade that said John Brown Junior is not guilty." This suggests that midwife Rebecca Sayer did testify that Gifford had named Brown during the birth since Emery's notes do not mention Sayer and he would have seized on any evidence to the contrary. So what happened in this particular trial to result in John Brown's acquittal? Unfortunately, the jury's reasoning was not recorded so we do not know the grounds on which they based their ruling. Given the strong likelihood that Sayer confirmed that Gifford named Brown during her labor pains, it seems most likely that Brown was acquitted using one of the legal technicalities suggested in Noah Emery's third and fourth arguments. This particular legal gambit enjoyed fairly high success rates in the English colonies and its use in Rhode Island will be discussed at greater length later in this chapter. Regardless, the Gifford/Brown trial marks a major turning point in colonial New England court trials as it was one of the first trials to place an individual man's needs and interests over the needs and interests of his community.

Noah Emery is also mentioned in another York County bastardy and paternity trial which took place the following year. On realizing that she was pregnant out of wedlock in 1746, Elizabeth Benson accused Charles Frost of fathering her child. The Benson family moved to Maine in the 1690s and lived along Spruce Creek in Kittery. Elizabeth was probably the daughter of John Benson, who married Hannah Brown in 1724, and may have been named for John's sister Elizabeth. The family was not indigent but they were not wealthy either. By contrast, Charles Frost was a member of the collective Wheelwright, Preble, Frost, Pepperell, and Hammond families, York County's colonial elite.

---

40 Allen, "Law and Authority to the Eastward," 288.

41 Eckert, *The Gentlemen of the Profession*, 133–5.

The name Charles was a common one in the Frost family but he probably was the grandson of the first Charles Frost who moved to Maine as a child in 1634.[42]

The York County Court of General Sessions record book notes that "Charles being a minor the Court appointed Mr. Noah Emery his guardian to plead for him."[43] There are no documents from Emery connected with this trial so it is impossible to tell how Emery "plead[ed]" for Frost, though it seems likely that decision to appoint Emery as Frost's guardian was made by justices looking out for a younger family member. Regardless, Benson accused Frost of fathering her child and he was convicted on paternity charges and ordered to pay one shilling and six pence a week in child support. This was the same amount specified for other men convicted on paternity charges in the 1740s, which suggests that having Emery "plead" for Frost made no difference in the trial outcome. Perhaps, unlike Brown, Frost had confessed to fathering Benson's child, which made conviction almost inevitable. For her part, Benson was convicted on fornication and bastardy charges and ordered to choose between receiving five lashes or paying a fine of 15 shillings. Attorneys like Emery were successfully introducing the use of legal technicalities into New England court rooms but acquittals still required material for them to work with.

Attorneys and Rhode Island's Bastardy and Paternity Trials

Rhode Island's open acceptance of attorneys in the court room created the earliest sexual misconduct trials in New England in which the defendants relied on legal counsel. The first of these trials offers a few details regarding what actually occurred in the court room. Samuel Legg was accused of fornication with Ezable (presumably Isabel) Scase in 1664. His unnamed attorney argued that he was not guilty and the jury agreed, resulting in an acquittal for Legg. Scase did not have an attorney and was convicted on fornication charges and ordered to pay 40 shillings.[44] The May 11, 1668 session of the Rhode Island Court of Trials placed Mr John Porter and Horrud, or Herodias, Long on trial for incontinency with each other. Porter successfully pleaded for his own acquittal and returned

[42] Noyes, *Genealogical Dictionary of Maine and New Hampshire*, 88 and 246.

[43] All quotes from the York County Court of General Sessions trial for Elizabeth Benson and Charles Frost, Jr in 1746, York County Court of Common Pleas & General Sessions Record Book, 1733–57, Volume 10, Maine State Archives, Augusta.

[44] All quotes from the Court of Trials of the Colony of Providence Plantations trial for Ezable Scase and Samuell Legg trial in 1664, in *Rhode Island Court Records[:] Records of the Court of Trials of the Colony of Providence Plantations* (Buffalo: Dennis Prince Co., 1946), 27.

to court on October 21 for the following session where he presented the court with a piece of paper authorizing him to serve as Long's attorney. The jury found Long not guilty, and the court agreed to acquit her as well.[45]

The 1668 court session was not Horrud Long's first appearance in a Rhode Island court room. Long had married John Hicks on March 14, 1637 when she was approximately 13 or 14 years old, and the couple moved to Newport, Rhode Island, in 1640.[46] As Hicks was almost immediately made a freeman, he was financially well off and, presumably, much older than his wife. Their marriage was clearly unstable as Hicks was charged with beating her in 1645. Shortly afterwards, he moved to Long Island where he petitioned to divorce her because she had committed adultery with George Gardiner, while Long argued that she had been abandoned and had only taken up with Gardner for financial reasons. Hicks was granted his divorce and Long remained with Gardner. She eventually petitioned the colony for a legal separation from Gardner on May 8, 1665. The court agreed, although both Long and Gardiner were fined 20 pounds for their irregular arrangements.

That same court session featured a petition from Margaret Porter, wife to John Porter. Margaret wanted the court to order her husband to support her as "he is destitute of all congugall love towards her, and sutable care for her."[47] The court agreed, declaring all Porter's financial affairs void since the time of his desertion. The Porters were divorced shortly afterwards, with John Porter making lifelong arrangements for his ex-wife's financial support. Porter and Horrud Long married in the early 1670s, at which point he also took on financial support for her children from John Hickes and George Gardiner.

John Porter's success at acquitting both Horrud Long and himself highlights the weight legal counsel was given in the Rhode Island court room. Women with reputations like Long's were rarely given the benefit of the doubt in early modern court systems. It is unfortunate that the records do not document exactly how he managed to persuade justices and jury that both he and Long were innocent when the circumstantial evidence clearly suggested otherwise. The fact that both Porter and Long were charged with incontinency suggests legal technicalities may have been employed in both their charging and their defense. Incontinency had been used as a flexible sexual misconduct charge in England in the sixteenth and

---

45 All quotes from the Court of Trials of the Colony of Providence Plantations trial for Horrud Long and John Porter in 1668, in *Rhode Island Court Records*, 35.

46 Archer, Richard, *Fissures in the Rock, New England in the Seventeenth Century* (Hanover: University Press of New England, 2001), 124.

47 All quotes from the Court of Trials of the Colony of Providence Plantations trial for Margaret Porter in 1665, in *Rhode Island Court Records*, 31.

early seventeenth centuries and in southern New England in the 1640s and 1650. However, with the exception of the Maine court system, the term had fallen out of use by the 1660s and the Long/Porter trial is the only time it was ever used in a Rhode Island sexual misconduct trial. The acquittal probably also speaks to Porter's position in the colony as a landed gentleman who served as an Assistant throughout the 1640s. Rhode Island may have been a "livelie experiment" in early democracy but economic and social status still mattered enormously there.

Acquittals rooted in legal technicalities appear in five other Rhode Island sexual misconduct trials. Grace Bailey Lawton committed adultery in 1670 with Thomas Lawton, while still married to William Bailey. Bailey appears to have then divorced his wife as Grace married Lawton while Bailey was still alive, although there is no record of the divorce. Grace married Thomas early in 1671 and was tried for adultery on October 18, 1671. Circumstantial evidence did not play in Grace's favor, particularly since she was now married to the man with whom she was accused of having an adulterous affair. Unsurprisingly, both jury and justices found her guilty. However, her attorney "declar[ed] that there was a failer in the Testimony" and the court ordered her acquitted.[48] The other four trials were all fornication trials.[49] John Coggeshall and William Hall of Portsmouth were accused of fornication with unspecified women on November 11, 1671. Both men pleaded "informality of the bill" and were swiftly acquitted. Finally, Mary Moone and Dennis Lannegan successfully used the same plea on October 23, 1673 when they were accused of fornication.

None of the Rhode Island court records preserve the details of these trials and it is impossible to know exactly how these acquittals were accomplished. William Eckert notes that "the use of legal technicalities to sabotage litigation dates from the last quarter of the seventeenth century. In contrast to anti-lawyer tracts that condemned the practice as a subversion of justices, colonists often found legal fine points that could serve their interests."[50] The use of legal counsel was still infrequent enough that attorneys who paid close attention to both linguistics and procedure could easily trump a witness or justice who misused them with a reminder of the correct method. However, colonial lawmakers began fighting back against this process and a 1701 Pennsylvania law "proclaimed that defects in pleas or other clerical errors should not suspend or abort the judicial process."[51]

---

[48] All quotes from the Rhode Island General Court of Trials for Grace Lawton in 1671, Newport Court, Volume A, 1671–1724, Rhode Island Judicial Archives, Pawtucket, Rhode Island.

[49] See Fiske, *Rhode Island General Court of Trials* for transcripts of these four trials.

[50] Eckert, *The Gentleman of the Profession*, 81.

[51] Jack D. Marietta and G.S. Rowe, *Troubled Experiment: Crime and Justice in Pennsylvania, 1682–1800* (Philadelphia: University of Pennsylvania Press, 2006), 161.

The overall numbers also make clear that colonists who used this defense were few and far between as the court trials described here were outnumbered by 148 successful Rhode Island prosecutions for sexual misconduct between 1650 and 1750.

Conclusion

Massachusetts, Maine, and Rhode Island's initial uses of justices and attorneys in their court rooms highlight early differences between their social and legal systems. Puritan concerns about the dangers of paid legal counsel made justices central figures in seventeenth-century Massachusetts court rooms, while Rhode Island's dual emphasis on attorneys and juries lessened the role of the justice of the peace throughout the colony's history. Maine, by contrast, developed a hybrid system, blending the community-centered justice of the peace with the use of paid legal counsel in the 1640s. These distinctions blurred in the early eighteenth century when attorneys were first allowed to practice in Massachusetts courts and allowed to practice again in Maine's courts.

Surviving documentation from the legal defenses used in colonial New England sexual misconduct trials also points to wider transitions taking place throughout the eighteenth-century Anglo-American world. Noah Emery's 1745 defense for John Brown asked the justices to consider Brown's individual integrity and needs over the needs of a community uninterested in providing financial support for the illegitimate children conceived within its bounds. This new emphasis on the needs of individuals versus their communities will be explored further in the following chapter as it appeared in a growing number of eighteenth-century sexual misconduct trials. These documents also demonstrate that colonists in both Massachusetts and Maine responded positively to the introduction of attorneys to their court rooms. Colonists like Martha Lynch plainly saw the new system which offered legal counsel for hire as preferable to one offering legal advice only to the well connected.

Transitions like this also serve as reminders of the need for comprehensive study of court records over an extended period of time. M. Michelle Jarrett Morris's research on sexual misconduct trials in Suffolk and Middlesex Counties for the years between 1660 and 1700 found the same types of community driven bastardy and paternity trials which appear in the Essex County court records between 1670 and 1715. Had her research continued into the eighteenth century, it would be interesting to see whether Middlesex and Suffolk experienced equivalent legal transitions in the early eighteenth century.

Chapter 6

"The said Margaret Prays Process against Him": Public and Private Lives in New England Court Rooms

Hester Prynne's public humiliation, eternally forced to wear a scarlet 'A' sewn to her clothing, remains the image most commonly associated with punishing sexual misconduct in colonial New England. Early modern leaders believed taking part in the community ritual of the sexual misconduct trial punished defendants while providing examples for would-be transgressors, though long-term punishments like Prynne's were rare. Most defendants convicted on sexual misconduct charges were simply whipped or fined. Instead, their humiliation took other forms which reflected the immediate legal and political needs of the jurisdiction conducting the trial. These practices would change in the eighteenth century as new understandings of privacy for the middling and upper classes became a growing part of the Anglo-American world.

Alternative Methods for Identifying Putative Fathers in Maine and Rhode Island

The specific rituals and burdens of proof used in Massachusetts, Maine, and Rhode Island to identify putative fathers were closely tied to each colony's own social circumstances. Seventeenth-century Massachusetts was farther away from English law than either Maine or Rhode Island but the colony's method for identifying men who had fathered illegitimate children was virtually identical to English practice during the same period. Unwed mothers in Essex County were expected to submit to their midwife's questioning during labor and were rewarded, in turn, with child support payments for naming their partners.[1] Relying on midwives to reliably identify putative fathers required sustained

1 See Merry E. Weisner, "Early Modern Midwifery: A Case Study," in *Women and Work in Preindustrial Europe*, ed. Barbara Hanawalt (Bloomington: Indiana University Press, 1986) and

networks of trained midwives who lived within short distances of their clients, circumstances traditionally available in England and apparently cultivated within the initial settlement years in Massachusetts. By contrast, Maine and Rhode Island appear to have either lacked a network of midwives or deliberately decided not to involve midwives in court trials because both colonies used court room identification as the final determination when convicting male colonists on paternity charges. These circumstances created very different experiences for the women in question. Birthing chambers were feminine, private spaces; court rooms were public, male-dominated spaces. The quarterly court sessions conducted throughout New England attracted dozens of people beyond the immediate justices, juries, defendants, plaintiffs, and witnesses. Isolated settlements and restrictions on public entertainment made opportunities to see one's neighbors publicly disgraced or triumphant, depending on the circumstances, irresistible to most colonists. Justices and ordinary colonists alike shared long memories, reaching back into the individual defendants' histories. Whether in the birthing chamber or the court room, colonial authorities relied heavily on unwed mothers' ability to name their sexual partners in front of their neighbors, who were expected to know whether or not a lie had been uttered in their presence and to protest vigorously if they believed this to be the case.

Bastardy and Paternity Trials in Maine

Maine experienced its own rising numbers of illegitimate children in the early eighteenth century. While there were only 19 bastardy and paternity trials conducted in Maine from 1675 to 1699, there were 59 between 1700 and 1724 and 133 trials between 1725 and 1750. Over time, the colony devised its own method for extracting child support payments from reluctant fathers, one which, similar to the Massachusetts' community-driven bastardy and paternity trials, suited Maine leaders' specific social and political needs. Margaret Chearen was pregnant and unmarried in the fall of 1738 when she told Justice Nicholas Shapleigh that Captain John Heard was the father of her child and that she "prays prosess against the said John Heard & that he may be proceeded with according to Law."[2] Heard was from a Kittery family who had lived in Maine

---

Hilary Marland, *The Art of Midwifery: Early Modern Midwives in Europe* (New York: Routledge Press, 1993).

[2] All trial quotes are from the York County Court of General Sessions trial for Margaret Chearen and John Heard in 1739, York County Court of Common Pleas & General Sessions, Box 78. Maine State Archives, Augusta.

since the 1630s. Born around 1667 near Sturgeon Creek, he would have been in his early 70s at the time of the trial. The York County court records document that Heard was given a license to maintain a tavern in his home in Kittery during the 1720s and 1730s and Chearen may have been employed as a servant.[3]

The phrase "prays prosess" commonly appears in the Maine court records after 1700, though it was not used in either Essex County or Rhode Island. The very specificity of the words suggests there was a "process" for prosecuting bastardy and paternity charges and that it was familiar to most Maine colonists. None of the Maine paternity trial documents specify how the accusation process worked, though this lack of information reinforces its commonality in York County court rooms rather than otherwise. The repeated "Face to Face in Court" notations in the court records suggest a shorthand used by overworked court clerks to save themselves from describing events deemed too familiar to their participants to be worthy of further documentation. If doubt lingered afterwards as to whether the proper ritual had been followed, justices could call on dozens of witnesses for verification. Fortunately, there are enough bastardy and paternity trial records surviving from this period to piece together just what this process entailed in York County. The early stages of the process resembled ones used in Essex County. Maine midwives did also question unwed mothers about the identity of their children's fathers during labor. Midwife Katherine Neal's deposition makes clear that "when the said Margaret was in ... in the greatest Extremity, she examined the said Margaret ... [who] declared that the said Captain John Heard was the Father of her same." Once the midwife had given her testimony, Maine justices asked unwed mothers to look "face to face" at their sexual partners and name them as the fathers of their children in front of the crowded court room.

Margaret Chearen was first convicted on fornication and bastardy charges and ordered to either receive seven lashes or pay a fine of 50 shillings. She then "declared upon Oath Face to Face in Court, That he ... is the Father of said child"

3 The Chearen family do not appear in either *The Genealogical Dictionary of Maine and New Hampshire*, *New England Marriages Before 1700* or *Old Kittery and Her Families*. The Heards can be found in Noyes, Sybil, Charles Thornton Libby, and Walter Goodwin Davis, *The Genealogical Dictionary of Maine and New Hampshire* (Portland, ME: Anthoensen Press, 1939), 323. Heard also had a long history of disregarding both Maine law and the men who enforced it. The York County Court of General Sessions records document that on March 12, 1721, John Heard told Major Joseph Hammond that "he could tell that Said Hammond was the Son of a whore and that he could prove it." Editor Neal Allen notes that "there was some substance to [the charge], even if the epithet used seems too strong. Hammond's mother was Catherine Frost ... at a County court held 5 July 1670, she and Joseph Hammond, father of the justice here, were presented for fornication." Allen, *Province and Court Records of Maine*, Volume VI, 98.

and John Heard was consequently convicted on paternity charges. The emphasis on the accusation being made "upon Oath" in all of these trials suggests the woman may have been asked to swear a second oath to tell the truth just before the accusation process began. The rising pattern of questioning depending on the woman's labor pains conducted by the midwives during birth suggests that the court room accusation process may have worked in a similar fashion, with the justices reminding women of the dangers of lying, while repeatedly exhorting them to name their sexual partners "face to face." Midwives also often asked unwed mothers when and where their children were conceived and it seems likely that the justices did the same during these trials. Sixty-four Maine men were convicted on paternity charges in the years between 1700 and 1750 and at least 35 of these men can be documented as having been publicly accused by their partners in the court room. Only nine of these convictions mention testimony from a midwife and there were no convictions in Maine for the years between 1700 and 1750 based solely on testimony from a midwife.[4]

The power of Maine's "process" by which putative fathers were identified and convicted during a face-to-face court room accusation is further reinforced by the October 5, 1736 trial for Susannah Brown of North Yarmouth who was convicted on fornication and bastardy charges and ordered to receive seven whippings or pay a fine of 50 shillings. Both female and male willingness to fully submit to the sexual misconduct trial process played a role during the eventual court hearings. Unwed mothers navigated particularly narrow paths when questioned about their sexual activities as they were expected to be forthcoming with the details regarding where and when they became pregnant. The most important question was whether sexual contact with their partners had occurred only once or had happened multiple times. Women who only had limited contact with their partners were looked upon more favorably than women who had had sex multiple times. Another common question was whether a marriage proposal had been part of the initial decision.

Susannah Brown was questioned by Justice of the Peace Samuel Seabury on July 1, 1736. The transcript documents that she responded promptly to Seabury's first questions, telling him that she wished to charge Edmund Chandler as the father of her child and that he had "carnal knowledge of [her] body ... in October

---

4 Martha Ballard's diary of her years as a midwife in Hallowell, Maine, suggests the practice of having the midwife question unwed mothers about who had fathered their children lingered into the early nineteenth century. Further research on bastardy and paternity trials for the years between this study and 1785, the first year documented by Ballard's diary, still needs to be conducted. See Laurel Thatcher Ulrich, *A Midwife's Tale: The Life of Martha Ballard, Based on Her Diary, 1785–1812* (New York: Vintage Books, 1991).

last past the nineteenth or twentyeth day."[5] When Seabury asked her "What was the reason of Iniquity or what enticement brought you to this sin did he promise to marry you," the transcript notes "no answer." In response to the question, "Where was the place that he commited this sin with you," the transcript notes "silence" and it appears there were no further questions. Brown's unwillingness to discuss the exact terms under which she had had intercourse with Chandler suggests that Brown knew she could not provide the court with any kind of narrative which might induce them to look favorably upon her. The trial record then goes on to note that she "in Court Face to Face made Oath that the said Edmund is the Father of the said Child" and Chandler was convicted on paternity charges and ordered to pay her four shillings a week in child support costs. Brown's refusal to play along with the usual script used for unwed mothers in Anglo-American society was tempered by her willingness to follow local custom.

Maine Justices and Bastardy and Paternity Trials

Birthing rooms and court rooms alike provided a form of social theater in the early modern period. Most women gave birth attended by five to eight other women who generally included a midwife, if available, and attendants chosen based on their relationship to the mother, social position in the community, and familiarity with the birthing process.[6] Unwed mothers often chose women who could serve as reliable birth witnesses capable of verifying that they had been properly questioned regarding the father of their children. For their part, the quarterly courts drew dozens, if not hundreds, of spectators, eager to share in the communal process of trying their neighbors for a wide array of crimes. The role of the early modern court room as public theater is well documented by A.G. Roeber and Robert Blair St George, who notes that "at times courtrooms and theaters *were* interchangeable seats of personation and judgment in British culture."[7] This particular emphasis on face-to-face-contact between mothers

5 All trial quotes are from the York County Court of General Sessions trial for Susannah Brown and Edmund Chandler in 1736, York County Court of Common Pleas & General Sessions, Box 64. Maine State Archives, Augusta.

6 See Adrian Wilson, "Participant or Patient? Seventeenth Century Childbirth from the Mother's Point of View," in *Patients and Practitioners, Lay Perceptions of Medicine in Pre-industrial Society*, ed. Roy Porter (Cambridge: Cambridge University Press, 1985).

7 See A.G. Roeber. *Faithful Magistrates and Republican Lawyers: Creators of Virginia Legal Culture, 1680–1810* (Chapel Hill: The University of North Carolina Press, 1981) and Robert Blair St George. "Massacred Language: Courtroom Performance in Eighteenth-Century Boston," in *Possible Pasts, Becoming Colonial in Early America*, ed. Robert Blair St George (Ithaca: Cornell

and putative fathers reflects Maine justices' deft manipulation of their own circumstances. Both Essex County justices and their English counterparts could rely on an extensive network of midwives to question unwed mothers regarding the fathers of their children and there may simply not have been enough midwives in Maine to render their birthing-room questioning a reliable means of identifying putative fathers.[8]

However, the Wheelwright, Preble, Frost, Pepperell, and Hammond families who served as Maine's political leaders and justices were also masters of political theater and face-to-face court room accusations allowed them to take center stage. They could ask the questions and they could make the process as publicly humiliating as they chose. In the end, the process reinforced their power and their control over their court rooms, elements they had been cultivating since the late seventeenth century. The direct break from the methods used to identify putative fathers in Massachusetts also comments on their growing confidence in the eighteenth century. Maine's abrupt transition from incontinency trials to fornication trials in the 1670s had suggested a willingness to accommodate Massachusetts' legal practices but now they appear comfortable taking any judicial action deemed appropriate to the situation at hand.

The need for such very public displays of judicial power most likely stemmed from the sheer size of York County in the early eighteenth century, which spanned approximately 100 miles between the Piscataqua and Kennebec Rivers. A decision was made in the mid-1730s to rotate the court between Falmouth and York, though this posed further challenges to defendants ordered to attend court sessions in the place further from them. Elizabeth Gray was ordered to appear in the Falmouth court in 1737 on fornication and bastardy charges. She petitioned the Falmouth justices, saying that as she lived "in the Westernmost part of said County and being poor is not able to hire a horse and [must] ... Travel afoot Seventy mile," she wanted to have her trial moved to the York court in January of 1738.[9] No evidence of the Falmouth justices' response to her petition survives but

University Press, 2000). Justices in both England and New England were well aware of the benefits of the court room as judicial theatre and J.M. Beattie notes that "the deliberate theatricality of [early modern English] criminal courts has been frequently commented on." Beattie, *Crime and the Courts in England, 1660–1800* (Princeton: Princeton University Press, 1986), 316.

[8] My research on midwives in Essex County has documented 71 women who were recognized as midwives in active practice during the period between 1650 and 1750. So far, I have only found 10 midwives for the equivalent period in Maine. More research needs to be done but this suggests that there were fewer midwives in Maine during this time.

[9] All trial quotes are from the York County Court of General Sessions trial for Elizabeth Grey in 1738, York County Court of Common Pleas & General Sessions, Box 71. Maine State Archives, Augusta.

her presence at the York Court of General Sessions on January 1, 1738 suggests that her request, and others like it, was granted. The York County Courts of General Sessions and Common Pleas remained the lone judicial system in Maine until Massachusetts recognized the creation of Cumberland and Lincoln Counties and their respective court systems in 1760. Knowing their colonists were spaced so far apart from each other and from their justices, York County justices needed the court room experience to be as memorable as possible so that it would provide a vivid reminder of their own existence.

Bastardy and Paternity Trials in Rhode Island

Public court room interactions took multiple forms in the sexual misconduct trials conducted in Rhode Island between the mid-seventeenth century and the early eighteenth century. Rhode Island experienced only a minor increase in the numbers of children conceived out of wedlock in the late seventeenth century, with five bastardy and paternity trials conducted between 1650 and 1674 and 22 bastardy and paternity trials between 1675 and 1699. Trial numbers fell in the early eighteenth century and there were only 12 such trials conducted between 1700 and 1724 and none between 1725 and 1750. Rhode Island justices did, however, also require the unwed mothers who were put on trial in the colony to name their partners in front of the court room, though the phrase "prays process" was never used in Rhode Island.

Two such bastardy and paternity trials occurred in Rhode Island on March 25, 1684. The first trial was for Priscilla Knight and William Foster.[10] Knight's parents were Richard and Sarah Rogers Knight who moved to Rhode Island in 1646 where he became a carpenter and was given a grant for 100 acres in the new town of East Greenwich, located on the western shore of Narragansett Bay.[11] Richard Knight then died in 1680, leaving a widow and six children, almost all of whom were of age. Fatherless daughters were especially vulnerable in colonial America as their lack of financial resources and fatherly advocacy made gaining child support via the judicial process doubly difficult. Foster was the son of William Foster, who moved to Rhode Island in 1638 after being ordered to leave Massachusetts for his religious beliefs and was admitted to the colony as a freemen in the 1640s.

---

[10] All trial quotes are from the Rhode Island General Court of Trials trial for Priscilla Knight and William Foster in 1684, Newport Court, Volume A 1671–1724, Rhode Island Judicial Archives, Pawtucket, Rhode Island.

[11] Moriarty, G. Andrews, "The Early Knights of Rhode Island," *New England Historical and Genealogical Register*, 87 (1933), 264.

Priscilla Knight was first convicted on fornication and bastardy charges and ordered to either receive 15 lashes or pay a fine of 26 shillings and eight pence. Then the court records document that "Precilla Knight unto him before the Court affirming that he was the person by whome she was begotten with childe, and the only father of that childe by her born into the world." Similar to the Maine bastardy and paternity trials, Knight made her accusation in front of a court room filled with people scrutinizing her every statement and every physical gesture for any signs of doubt that Foster had actually fathered her child. She was consistent in her accusations and Foster did not challenge her charge. Since the child had died shortly after birth, the court ruled that he was to pay 13 shillings and four pence for the costs of both childbirth and burial.

The trial for Rebeckah Saxbey and James Kinion reads almost identically to the Knight/Foster trial.[12] Like Priscilla Knight, Saxbey was convicted on fornication and bastardy charges and was ordered to be whipped 15 times in Newport or pay a fine of 26 shillings and eight pence. Also like Foster, Saxbey testified "in open Court ... that he was the person by whome she was begotten with child and the only father of that child by her born into the world."[13] As the child was still alive, Kinion was ordered to pay two shillings weekly to Saxbey in child support until the court decided otherwise.

Jury Trials in Rhode Island

A third bastardy and paternity trial from Rhode Island provides a further reminder of the benefits afforded to women who could rely on male heads of household to represent them in the court room. Susannah Talman of Portsmouth accused Roger Goulding of fathering her bastard child in October of 1672.[14] Talman's father was Peter Talman, who moved to Rhode Island in 1648 with his wife, children, assorted in-laws, an English indentured servant, three African slaves, and numerous trade goods. He opened an apothecary shop shortly afterwards and was made a freeman in Portsmouth, Rhode Island. Talman took

---

[12] No further information regarding Rebeckah Saxbey and James Kinion's social and economic backgrounds is available.

[13] All trial quotes are from the Rhode Island General Court of Trials trial for Rebeckah Saxbey and James Kinion in 1684, Newport Court, Volume A, 1671–1724, Rhode Island Judicial Archives, Pawtucket, Rhode Island.

[14] All trial quotes are from the Rhode Island General Court of Trials trial for Susannah Talman and Roger Goulding in 1672, Newport Court, Volume A, 1671–1724, Rhode Island Judicial Archives, Pawtucket, Rhode Island.

part in numerous lawsuits involving both his business and property interests throughout the 1650s and 1660s. He was elected as Solicitor for the General Court of Rhode Island in 1662 and served as a Deputy between 1662 and 1665. For his part, Roger Goulding also came from a comfortable Newport family.

The trial opened by convicting Susannah Talman on fornication and bastardy charges and ordering her to either receive 15 lashes at the whipping post in the center of Newport or to pay a fine of 26 shillings and eight pence. Roger Goulding was then brought into the room and Tallman was ordered to identify whether he was the father of her child. Holding her baby in her arms, Talman looked him in the eye and repeatedly accused him of fathering her child.

Roger Goulding denied the charges and asked to be tried by a jury. Unlike other New England colonies where juries were only used for extreme crimes such as rape or murder, Rhode Island residents could request trial by jury if they felt it would better aid their cases. The full extent to which sexual misconduct defendants chose to take advantage of this legal right is unclear but the records indicate that at least nine such trials employed a jury. Since these trials ranged from the severe charges of rape and adultery to the lesser charges of paternity and fornication before marriage, it seems likely that juries were more commonly used than the records would suggest. Whether or not defendants benefited from having juries decide their verdict rather than justices is unclear. Elaine Forman Crane notes that the way juries "perceived testimony depended on how the judges permitted it to be presented and what commentary they might offer."[15] Disagreements between juries and justices were always decided in favor of the justices. Five of the nine defendants known to have been tried by jury were acquitted but their acquittals cannot be definitely attributed to their juries.

Roger Goulding's jury declared him not guilty, based on lack of evidence. This may have been the case but the potential identity of one of the jurors raises questions for modern audiences about this decision. The final juror listed was a Thomas Gould and clerks often shortened names by removing the final letters. There is little or no documentation regarding Goulding's parentage or family connections but his first son was named Thomas, which suggests a family name.[16] Elaine Forman Crane argues that colonial Rhode Islanders "believed that knowledge of a defendant's history and character assisted in determining

15 Elaine Forman Crane, *Killed Strangely, the Death of Rebecca Cornell* (Ithaca: Cornell University Press, 2002), 49.

16 John Osborne Austin, *The Genealogical Dictionary of Rhode Island* (Baltimore: Genealogical Publishing Co., 1978), 150. His wife does not appear to have had any relations named Thomas.

whether or not he or she was capable of committing a particular crime."[17] Rhode Island jurists were also encouraged to do further case research prior to the trial, whether interviewing witnesses, talking to the defendants or considering the family's history in the colony.

The use of trial by jury and the central role played by Rhode Island jurors may also explain a core difference between court records from Essex County and Maine and court records from Rhode Island. Court records for both Essex County and Maine include dozens of depositions, warrants, and other legal forms, all of which were recorded separately from the court record books. While relatively few of these documents survive, they plainly played an active role in helping justices prepare for the resulting court trials. The only trial with surviving depositions from colonial Rhode Island was the 1673 matricide trial for Thomas Cornell and these depositions were copied into the court record book, rather than existing as separate documents.[18] Encouraging jurors to do their own research before the trial may have made it easier to dispense with the preparatory documents used in trials in both Essex County and Maine.

Susannah's father, Peter Talman, took immediate action after the jury's decision was announced and demanded that the court reconsider the matter. The justices ruled that "upon Consideration of the motion made in Court by Peter Talman, and the Law, That she having upon oath charged the said Roger Goulding to be the ffather of the saide childe," Goulding now had to "cleere himself" to avoid paying child support charges for Talman's child. Talman's public charging of Goulding as the father of her child was clearly seen by the justices as trumping the jury's decision. Goulding was now ordered to pay bail of 50 pounds against the promised child support. He later filed an appeal which most likely was unsuccessful as there is no further mention of Goulding in the trial records.

The record noting "the motion made in Court by Peter Talman" suggests Talman's close familiarity with the law. Unlike other New England colonies, Rhode Island's political leaders served as justices well into the eighteenth century. Talman had probably experienced the Rhode Island court system from a justice's perspective and knew how best to appeal to them. The Talman/Goulding trial also demonstrates that if Susannah Talman's father had not argued for the jury to be overruled, Goulding would have been acquitted, leaving her responsible for the child's upkeep.

---

17 Crane, *Killed Strangely*, 150.

18 For more information about Thomas Cornell's trial, see Crane, *Killed Strangely*.

Peter Talman also had reason to be personally familiar with the workings of Rhode Island sexual crime trials. He had brought a suit against Thomas Durfee in 1664, complaining that Durfee was too familiar with Talman's wife and Susannah's mother, Ann. The court ordered Durfee to avoid Ann and considered the matter closed. Talman then filed for divorce from Ann a year a later, citing adultery as the cause. Ann confessed her infidelity and explained that her youngest child was not Talman's. The court asked whether she was willing to repent and reconcile with her husband. Ann responded that "she would rather caste herselfe on the mercy of God if he take away her life, than to returne."[19] The court ordered her to be whipped 30 times, 15 lashes in Portsmouth and 15 lashes in Newport. They also fined her 10 pounds and granted Talman his divorce request. Two months later, he filed a nuptial contract with Joan Briggs, giving her a house, property, and half his household goods. Ann then fled the colony, going either to her brother Robert in Virginia or to Plymouth Colony for a two-year period. She returned in 1667 when a warrant was issued for her arrest. Both Ann and Durfee were convicted on fornication charges on May 11, 1668. Although they were legally unable to marry, circumstantial evidence suggests that they remained together.[20]

Multiple convictions for sexual crimes within one family were relatively common in colonial New England, though it is unclear whether such colonists actually were engaging in more illicit activities. What is certain is that their neighbors were less apt to give them the benefit of the doubt. Ann Talman's adultery and fornication trials probably affected her daughter's trial. The jury's initial decision to acquit Goulding suggests that he may have tapped into the jury's memories of Ann Talman's trials. Paternity trial acquittals usually occurred when there were multiple possibilities of who the father was and Goulding may have hinted at other partners for Susannah Talman. If the mother was capable of adultery, then there was no telling about the daughter's morals. Regardless, Goulding's presumed guilt was not held against him for long as he married Governor Benedict Arnold's daughter Penelope three months later on January 1, 1673. It is unclear when Susannah Talman married but later family records refer to her as Susannah Beckitt.

---

19 All statements from the Court of Trials of the Colony of Providence Plantations trial for Ann Talman in 1665, published in Rhode Island Historical Society, *Rhode Island Court Records[:] Records of the Court of Trials of the Colony of Providence Plantations* (Buffalo, NY: Dennis Prince Co., 1946), 30.

20 See William F. Reed, *The Descendents of Thomas Durfee of Portsmouth, Rhode Island* (Washington, DC: Gibson Brothers Press, 1902).

Public Repentance in Rhode Island

Justices in both Maine and Rhode Island found face-to-face accusations of putative fathers in the court room effective methods for identifying and convicting men in order to extract child support payments from them. Rhode Island justices also used court room performances in other ways when prosecuting colonists on sexual misconduct charges. A crucial element in Ann Talman's adultery trial in 1667 was the choices given to her by the justices. First, the court gave her an opportunity to publicly repent for her actions. When she refused to do so, she was ordered to receive 15 lashes in Newport, 15 lashes in Portsmouth and a fee of 10 pounds. The trial records note that Talman petitioned the court for mercy and saw her sentence reduced to 15 lashings in Newport and no fine, a sizable reduction. Two years later, the October 20, 1669 adultery trial for Margaret Colwell of Providence noted that her "Ingenioues Confestion" lowered her fine from 10 pounds to five, although it does not specify precisely what Colwell said to warrant the reduced fine.[21] Wife to Robert Colwell of Providence, Margaret Colwell ran away with Thomas Walling sometime around 1666. Walling was whipped 15 times in Providence and 15 times in Newport, though he did not pay a monetary fine and it is unclear whether a fine was imposed or dropped. Robert Colwell divorced Margaret on July 2, 1668 and Colwell and Walling were married on June 19, 1669.

Couples unwilling to publicly confess and repent paid a steep price in Rhode Island court rooms. Mary Stockes and William Timberlake were placed on trial for adultery charges on October 20, 1699.[22] Stockes was, most likely, an orphan who maintained close ties to her grandparents, Richard and Mary Morris. Stockes pleaded not guilty and refused to ask for clemency. The court convicted her on adultery charges and ordered her to be "sevearly whipt at newport with fifteen stripes and shall then haver her Choyce to pay five pound or to be whipt soe againe at portsmouth." The court then considered the "grevious Cryes of mrs. Mary morris for mercy or some mercy to be shown to her grandchild," but the extent of their mercy was to allow Stockes to delay her punishment for a month. Unfortunately, no details of Marry Morris's plea for a reduced sentence for her granddaughter have survived. Nevertheless, her actions resemble

---

[21] All quotes from the Court of Trials of the Colony of Providence Plantations trial for Margaret Colwell in 1669, published in Rhode Island Historical Society, *Rhode Island Court Records*, 38. The record does not detail what Colwell said to the court.

[22] All trial quotes are from the Rhode Island General Court of Trials trial for Mary Stockes and William Timberlake in 1699, Newport Court, Volume A, 1671–1724, Rhode Island Judicial Archives, Pawtucket, Rhode Island.

the ones undertaken by Deborah Proctor and Martha Lynch, both of whom were widows who sought legal defenses for their daughters. Ann Talman and Margaret Colwell's punishments for adultery were both drastically reduced after the women publicly repented. Most likely, the justices believed Stockes needed to be pleading directly to them rather than through her grandmother.

William Timberlake also pleaded not guilty during his trial and was asked "what hee had yett to say for himselfe to give the Court grownd to show any favor to him." Timberlake then informed the court that "hee had sayd all that was with him to say" and was promptly informed that he was to be imprisoned until he was whipped 15 times at Portsmouth, 15 times at Newport and had paid a 10 pound fine. The decision to imprison Timberlake until his punishment speaks to the justices' frustration with his refusal to repent or apologize for his actions. Most defendants who were convicted on sexual misconduct charges paid their surety and were sent home to wait for conviction or punishment. The justices' wariness appears justified as the record goes on to add that Timberlake had "mad an Escape from Justice at presant by volent breaking the Collony preson." He was eventually recaptured and forced to face further charges. Similar patterns can be found in trials where reduced fines were given. A public acknowledgement of guilt accompanied by a promise to marry left Rhode Island courts with the reassurance that the couple were now ready to take legitimate part in colonial society.

The discrepancies between the sentencing used in the Talman/Durfee and Colwell/Walling trials and the Stockes/Timberlake trial raise the cynical question of whether certain colonial Rhode Islanders were taking advantage of the benefits wrought by public displays of repentance. Mary Hicke, the wife of Gabriel Hicke, and James Woodward of Portsmouth were tried on October 8, 1661 for "being in Bead together Contrary to Law," rather than adultery. Convicting couples for adultery required two witnesses and there was only one underage witness, presumably one of Hicke's children. The court record book documents that the couple "out of the Conviction of their Conscieneces did freely Confese the ofence."[23] The court then sought someone who could provide the evidence necessary to "Convict the Sayd persons" but nobody came forward. Based on the lack of witnesses and the couple's obvious repentance, the court convicted them on fornication charges and ordered them to pay the standard fine of 40 shillings each. While this was a far less severe punishment than they could have received, they also could have sought an acquittal based on the legal

[23] All statements from the Court of Trials of the Colony of Providence Plantations trial for Mary Hicke and James Woodward in 1661, published in Rhode Island Historical Society, *Rhode Island Court Records*, 76.

technicality. Woodward and Hicke were either sincerely penitent or lacked the services of a good attorney, a common theme among the Rhode Island sexual misconduct trials discussed in the previous chapter.

Court Room Performances in Rhode Island

Reduced sentences were rare occurrences in colonial New England court rooms and there is no immediate explanation as to why Rhode Island allowed its convicted defendants to plea for reduced sentences. The combination of the face-to-face paternity accusations and the reduced sentences for defendants who publicly repented their crimes in Rhode Island suggests the colony placed a greater emphasis on court room performance than its New England counterparts. This emphasis highlights a core difference between Rhode Island and its Puritan neighbors. Authorities in all three colonies believed communities should be bound together by common, vocally expressed values, including the belief that sexual intercourse should only happen within marriage. Rhode Island colonists willing to demonstrate sincere repentance in front of their communities were usually granted the privilege of receiving a reduced sentence. Defendants who refused to do so were treated harshly, with William Timberlake as a pointed example. The decision to provide their colonists with this opportunity reflects the needs of Rhode Island's leaders as much as the use of the "face-to-face" accusations benefited justices in Maine. Until the reorganization created by the second charter in 1692, Puritan leaders relied on the knowledge that requiring their colonists to attend the Puritan Church on Sundays created certain commonalities between them. Ministers could preach sermons, congregants could publicly repent for their actions, and all members of Massachusetts society heard the results.[24] Secular Rhode Island had no such common bond and so Rhode Island leaders needed its court rooms and its town meetings to provide points of commonality between its colonists. Encouraging sexual misconduct defendants to publicly repent helped invest them in the Rhode Island system. Maine's decision to force unwed mothers to name their partners in public court rooms may reflect similar political traditions, though Maine was firmly under the control of Massachusetts by the time the "prays process" method emerged in the court records.

[24] Richard Godbeer notes the use of meeting day confessions and repentance in Puritan churches in Massachusetts, along with the threat of excommunication for church members who did not take such actions. Godbeer, *The Sexual Revolution in Early America* (Baltimore: The Johns Hopkins Press, 2002), 230–31.

Sexual Misconduct Trials in the Eighteenth Century

Seventeenth- and early eighteenth-century New England court records make clear that sexual misconduct charges could be brought against anyone, whether male or female, rich or poor, white or non-white. Maine court records document that Abraham and Mary Bragdon Preble were charged with fornication before marriage on April 2, 1695. Preble's uncle was one of the court justices and Mary was from an equally prominent family. Nineteen years later, Abraham Preble, now a highly respected local sheriff, took his daughter, Mary Preble Bray, to face fornication before marriage charges with Samuel Bray in 1714. In both cases, all members of the Preble family received the same punishment as their less-connected neighbors.[25] The concept that all members of New England society should be publicly punished for engaging in sex outside marriage gradually disappeared in the eighteenth century. This transition has been well documented by many historians including Cornelia Hughes Dayton who notes that the decision "to withdraw certain matters of 'private behavior' from the purview of the courts ... [indicates] a growing ethic of privacy, a desire among the genteel to place responsibility for moral behavior squarely within the middle class family."[26] By contrast, the sex lives of poor and non-white colonists remained on display for their communities throughout the eighteenth century.

Gender and Bastardy and Paternity Trials

Economic and racial distinctions were not the only factors deciding whose behavior warranted public court trials and gender also played a role. Similar to *The Lawes and Liberties*, Massachusetts' 1692 *The Acts and Resolves* instructed unwed mothers to "continu[e] constant in such an accusation, being examined upon oath, and put upon the discovery of the truth in the time of her travail." Convicted fathers were still charged with "the maintenance thereof, with the

---

25 A desire to actively prove that political and judicial leaders were not above the law can be traced in at least one other colony as William Offut's research indicates that while most Quakers who committed crimes, including sexual misconduct, were tried within the Quaker community itself, Quaker leaders who committed crimes deliberately chose to be tried in the Pennsylvania court system as a way of legitimizing both the Pennsylvania court system and their control in the colony. Offut, *Of "Good Laws" and "Good Men:" Law and Society in the Delaware Valley, 1680–1710* (Champaign: University of Illinois Press, 1995).

26 Cornelia Hughes Dayton, "Turning Points and the Relevance of Colonial Legal History," *The William and Mary Quarterly* 50, No. 1 (1993), 12.

assistance of the mother ... and to save the town or place where such child is born, free from charge for its maintenance."[27] But while the numbers of children conceived out of wedlock continued to climb in the eighteenth century, the numbers of men prosecuted for fathering illegitimate children fell. Between 1700 and 1724, there were 134 Essex County women convicted on bastardy charges and 58 men convicted on paternity charges; between 1725 and 1750, there were 157 women convicted and only 23 men. The same disparity also existed in Maine and Rhode Island, albeit on a much smaller scale in Rhode Island. Maine had 39 women and 20 men convicted between 1700 and 1724 and 89 women and 44 men convicted between 1725 and 1750, while Rhode Island convicted 8 women and 4 men for conceiving children out of wedlock between 1700 and 1724 and none between 1725 and 1750.

The growing disparities between the numbers of women and men convicted for conceiving illegitimate children the New England colonies has been read by many historians as evidence of a rising double standard for men and women. Elaine Forman Crane observes that "the biased treatment that many women experienced as their cases were adjudicated reflects an attitude that permeated the larger community."[28] A close reading of all the Essex County court records supports Crane's conclusions, but with certain qualifications. It seems unlikely that Massachusetts authorities completely lost interest in identifying financial support for illegitimate children. Convicted women were still being whipped or fined, which suggests their punishments did not include financial responsibility for their children. In addition, actual child support payments were on the rise. The standard child support fee in the 1670s was two shillings and six pence per week, to be paid either to the woman's family or to the town where the child resided if the woman was unable to care for her child. Inflation first affected child support fees in 1725 when they were raised to three shillings weekly. Two years later, the fee was raised to three shillings and six pence weekly. The fee was raised to four shillings in 1734 and then to four shillings and six pence weekly in 1737. The early 1740s introduced a new system whereby the father paid an initial down payment of four or five pounds and then paid 15 pence weekly. The constantly increasing fees between the 1720s and the 1740s demonstrates that Massachusetts authorities still cared deeply about the issue, even while the numbers of men actually prosecuted in the courts on paternity charges were decreasing.

[27] *The Acts and Resolves, Public and Private, of the Province of the Massachusetts Bay, to which are prefixed The Charters of the Province with Historical and Explanatory Notes, and an Appendix*, Volume I (Boston: Wright & Potter Printers, 1869), 52.

[28] Elaine Forman Crane, *Ebb Tide in New England: Women, Seaports, and Social Change, 1630–1800* (Boston: Northeastern University Press, 1998), 197.

A handful of records suggest that justices may have devised a different method at the turn of the eighteenth century for identifying and convicting fathers. Naomi Lovejoy attended court in Salem on June 26, 1683 where she was convicted for conceiving an illegitimate daughter. The Salem court records do not specify whether she named her child's father in court but Lovejoy arranged for her daughter's name to be entered in the Andover records as "BenNaomie Abbot, ye illegitimate Daughter of Benjamin Abbot and Naomie Lovejoy."[29] Unwed mothers entering their children's names in local town records nearly always named the child for the putative father, thereby providing an additional accusation available for anyone willing to look at the entry. Lovejoy was ordered to pay court fees and an unspecified fine. Abbot was not charged in court. However, nine months later, Justice Nathaniel Saltonstall noted in his journal that Thomas Chandler, Benjamin Abbot's maternal uncle, had acknowledged Abbot's paternity by paying a 40 shilling fine, presumably intended to go towards financial support for BenNaomie.[30] Since Abbot was not contesting the charges, his family was allowed to settle the matter out of court.[31]

Other court records follow similar patterns. Hannah Green was convicted in the Salem court on fornication and bastardy charges on December 27, 1737 and ordered to pay a fine of 40 shillings. Similar to the Abbot trial, there is no mention of the man who fathered her child in the court record book. However, a secondary document from the Salem court records shows that she charged Robert Manning "with being the Father of a bastard child born of her body" and that he "appeared and confest the fact."[32] Manning was then ordered to pay Hannah half the costs for delivering her child and four shillings and six pence weekly in child support costs as well as a 50 pound bond "to save the Town of Salem free from any charge towards the maintenance of the said child." Elizabeth Dean was later convicted in the Salem court on fornication and bastardy charges

---

29 "A List of Births, Marriages & Deaths in the Town of Andover in the year 1683–1684," Essex County Court Papers, Series II, Volume 43, Judicial Archives, Massachusetts State Archives, Boston.

30 Thomas Chandler was also father to the Joseph Chandler discussed in an earlier trial and was Benjamin Abbot's maternal uncle.

31 The Saltonstall journal documents the years 1682 to 1685. During those four years, 56 colonists were arraigned on sexual misconduct charges in the Ipswich court where Saltonstall was a justice. The Salem court had slightly fewer, with 41 colonists charged. By contrast, Saltonstall's journal mentions only four colonists in connection with sexual misconduct charges. Nathaniel Saltonstall, *Records of the Magistrate's Court at Haverhill, Massachusetts* (Boston: Massachusetts Historical Society, 1979).

32 All trial quotes are from the Essex County Court of General Sessions trial for Hannah Green in 1737, File Papers Box 12. Judicial Archives, Massachusetts State Archives, Boston.

on December 28, 1743 and ordered to pay a fine of 10 shillings.[33] A document from the Salem court records that "John Gray ... freely offered to become bound in a bond of fifteen pounds with suretie to the overseers of the poor of the town of Salem Conditioned to save the said town of Salem harmless & free from any charges that may arise on the maintenance of a male bastard born of the body of Elizabeth Dean."[34] Richard Godbeer also found similar documents in other colonies and notes that "men who chose to settle out of court and so avoid public embarrassment would never appear in the court records."[35]

The utter disparity between the numbers of women and men convicted for conceiving illegitimate children suggests that growing numbers of men were, indeed, settling out of court because it seems so unlikely that Massachusetts Bay towns would agree to the presence of so many illegitimate children with no form of financial support. Cornelia Dayton and Elaine Crane are correct in saying that there was a rising sexual double standard in the eighteenth century. However, Essex County men did not escape total responsibility for their actions. What they appear to have been offered was the chance for their actions to remain largely undisclosed to their communities as a whole. The ability to settle the financial burden incurred by fathering illegitimate children out of court preserved both these men's privacy and the increasingly popular image of middle- and upper-class men as genteel creatures divorced from their sexual passions, a point that will be further discussed later in this chapter.

These trials may also point to changes in Massachusetts society as a whole. All four trials hinge on the willingness of Benjamin Abbot, Jonathan Gilbert, Robert Manning, and John Gray to acknowledge their children. The stigma of fathering an illegitimate child was decreasing to the point that Essex County families no longer saw the financial investment needed to fight such charges as a worthwhile investment because it was generally cheaper to pay child support charges for a year or two than to mount the full-scale court battles found in the earlier bastardy and paternity trials records. There are no documents indicating that men in either Maine or Rhode Island were settling child support payments out of court but the equivalent disparities between the numbers of women and men convicted for conceiving illegitimate children suggests similar practices occurred in these colonies as well.

---

33 Fines for fornication and bastardy charges abruptly dropped from 40 or 50 shillings to 10 or 15 shillings around 1740, although it is unclear from the records why this was the case.

34 All trial quotes are from the Essex County Court of General Sessions trial for Elizabeth Dean in 1743, File Papers Box 13. Judicial Archives, Massachusetts State Archives, Boston.

35 Godbeer, *Sexual Revolution in Early America*, 256.

Punishing Sexual Misconduct in Eighteenth-Century Essex County

Allowing putative fathers to settle out of court when unwed mothers still had to face the embarrassment of a public trial undoubtedly created a sexual double standard – which would continue until women also ceased to be tried for sexual misconduct around the turn of the nineteenth century. One particular concern about privacy and gentility was applied equally for Essex County men and women in the first half of the eighteenth century. The punishment for both men and women convicted on fornication before marriage charges usually was a choice between a fine and a whipping, and the same choice was offered to women convicted on both fornication and bastardy charges. Elaine Forman Crane notes the fact that many convicted couples were "required to strip 'from the girdle upwards' for this public spectacle suggests that her punishment included a greater degree of humiliation."[36] Whipping punishment for sexual misconduct disappeared completely from the Essex County court records during the years between 1650 and 1750.

There were 37 defendants ordered to be whipped for sexual misconduct charges, 33 ordered to pay a fine, and 48 colonists given a choice between a whipping and a fine between 1650 and 1674.[37] Between 1675 and 1699, there were six defendants whipped for sexual misconduct charges, 93 fined, and 76 colonists given a choice between a whipping and a fine. By the early eighteenth century, the differences were even starker: 23 defendants were whipped, 241 were fined, and 65 were given a choice between 1700 and 1724. Finally, between 1725 and 1750, only two colonists were whipped, 335 were fined, and two were given a choice between a whipping and a fine. All four defendants ordered to be whipped or choose between a whipping or a fine were women convicted on fornication and bastardy charges and it is unclear why the justices recommended they be whipped, though perhaps they knew that the four women in question were unable to pay their fines. In addition to concerns about shielding colonists from the humiliation of a public whipping, it seems likely that local governments saw fines as more useful than physical punishment, particularly when it came to maintaining the ever larger infrastructures demanded by a rapidly commercializing society.

---

36 Crane, *Ebb Tide in New England*, 200.

37 Unfortunately, the court records almost never document which punishment was chosen which makes it impossible to know how many colonists preferred physical punishment to financial punishment.

Punishing Sexual Misconduct in Eighteenth-Century Maine

A very different pattern appears in the Maine court records as the numbers of Maine colonists ordered to be whipped or given a choice between a whipping or a fine remained consistent throughout the period from 1650 to 1750. There were 11 defendants whipped for sexual misconduct charges, 14 ordered to pay a fine, and 19 colonists given a choice between a whipping and a fine between 1650 and 1674 in Maine. Between 1675 and 1699, one defendant was whipped for sexual misconduct charges, 19 were fined, and 40 colonists were given a choice between a whipping and a fine. Another 43 colonists were sentenced with alternate punishments which ranged from appearing in public in a white sheet to sitting in the stocks between 1650 and 1674 and eight colonists had equivalent punishments between 1675 and 1679.[38] The only real difference in the early eighteenth century punishments was the complete disappearance of the alternate punishments after 1700. Nine defendants were whipped, six were fined, and 65 were given a choice between 1700 and 1724. Finally, between 1725 and 1750, no colonists were ordered to be whipped, seven were fined and 128 were given a choice between a whipping and a fine. The high rates of defendants given a choice between a whipping or a fine throughout this period meant Maine colonists could avoid the humiliation of a public whipping if they could afford to pay their fines. The fact that York County officials kept whipping as a stated possible punishment suggests they recognized that many Maine colonists could not afford to pay fines in hard currency. It also suggests that York County did not have Essex County's ever growing social and political infrastructure to maintain.

Punishing Sexual Misconduct in Eighteenth-Century Rhode Island

Maine's decision to continue using whipping as a punishment for sexual misconduct aside, sexual misconduct prosecutions in both Essex County and Maine remained consistent throughout the first half of the eighteenth century. Both colonies continued to convict colonists for fornication before marriage charges and bastardy and paternity charges, as well as the occasional rape or incest charge. Rhode Island, by contrast, was the first New England colony to abandon trying its colonists on sexual misconduct charges. The numbers of colonists

[38] See Appendix B for a complete list of Alternate Punishments found in colonial New England court records.

prosecuted in the colony's court plummeted in the period between 1650 and 1750. Rhode Island prosecuted 75 colonists on all sexual misconduct charges between 1650 and 1674, 52 colonists between 1675 and 1699, 20 colonists between 1700 and 1724, and just a single colonist between 1725 and 1750. The numbers of colonists prosecuted on fornication before marriage charges followed the same pattern, going from eight prosecutions to one to none in the eighteenth century. Adultery, incest, and rape charges all followed the same pattern. The only charge to rise in this period was bastardy and paternity, but even these trials were miniscule compared to the equivalent trials in both Essex County and Maine. Rhode Island conducted five bastardy and paternity trials between 1650 and 1674, 22 trials between 1675 and 1699, 12 trials between 1700 and 1724, and none after 1725.

The fall in the numbers of sexual misconduct trials conducted in the Rhode Island colony court may reflect the 1721 decision to divide the Rhode Island court system into county courts, with the original court in Newport now serving as an Inferior Court of Common Pleas and Superior Court.[39] Ordinary sexual misconduct trials were now tried in the local courts, as they were in Massachusetts. Nevertheless, the drop in sexual misconduct trials in the Rhode Island colony court record books occurred in the 1690s, some 30 years before the creation of the county courts, which suggests there are very few such trials even in the county record books. A more compelling argument for the decreasing numbers of sexual misconduct trials in the Rhode Island colony court is the corresponding rise in the numbers of civil trials in the early eighteenth century. The numbers of civil and criminal trials conducted in the Rhode Island court in the first court of the year in 1720, 1730, 1740, and 1750 provide vivid snapshots of a society in transition. The Generall Court of Trials and General Goal Delivery conducted 48 civil and six criminal trials in March of 1720, 346 civil and six criminal trials in March of 1730, 72 civil, and no criminal trials in March of 1740 and 67 civil and one criminal trial in March of 1750.[40]

Rhode Island courts were increasingly used to collect financial damages rather than expecting colonists to answer for their transgressions. The growing emphasis on mercantile affairs was largely due to the swift rise of Newport, ever

[39] See Jane Fiske, *Gleanings from Newport Court Files, 1659–1783* (Boxford: Jane Fletcher Fiske, 1998). For the sake of consistency, I used the Rhode Island Superior Court record book after 1721, rather than switching to the county court books.

[40] These statistics came from the Newport Court, 1671–1724, Volume A, the General Court Of Trials and Goal Delivery, 1725–30 and the Judicature Court of Assize 1730–41, Volume B and the General Court Of Trials and Goal Delivery and the Judicature Court of Assize, 1747–50, Volume D, Rhode Island Judicial Archives, Pawtucket, Rhode Island.

tuned to trade opportunities available in the Anglo-American Atlantic world. The early presence of attorneys in the colony reflected Rhode Island's English legal influences but they were equally connected to Rhode Island's commercial interests. Lawyers survive only where their services are paid for. The rest of New England would eventually make the same commercial and moral transitions but these movements remained a few decades away in the early eighteenth century. For the moment, an overwhelming attention paid to legal procedure and financial affairs was still suspect in the Puritan colonies.[41]

Conclusion

The use of fornication trials rather than the more explicit incontinency trials discussed in Chapter 2 was the first salvo towards protecting the privacy of colonists engaging in sexual acts outside the marriage bed. At their most basic level, fornication trials provided fewer details to be broadcasted from the court room which made them less humiliating experiences for their participants. They also reduced the sexual act to a clinical term in keeping with the changing sensibilities of the eighteenth century. Kenneth Lockridge writes that the "ever increasing *aversion* to the bodily self and to strong emotions [was] coupled with a powerful *internalization* of restraint on the body and on feelings."[42] Sexual misconduct trials would eventually be removed altogether from the public court room, lest their very existence remind denizens of the early modern period of the messy realities of the human body. These changes also reflected the broader transitions towards distinct understandings of public and private lives in the eighteenth-century Anglo-American world, as even the Massachusetts court system came to accept illicit sex as an economic transgression rather than a moral one. Nevertheless, the factors determining whose sex lives were private were clearly shaped by economic class, gender, and racial identities. While both poor and non-white men and women continued to have their sex lives on display for their communities into the early nineteenth century, wealthier white women were tried in court long after their male counterparts.

---

[41] See Richard Bushman, *From Puritan to Yankee: Character and the Social Order in Connecticut, 1690–1765* (Cambridge: Harvard University Press, 1967).

[42] Kenneth Lockridge, "Colonial Self-Fashioning: Paradoxes and Pathologies in the Construction of Genteel Identity in Eighteenth-Century America," published in *Possible Pasts, Becoming Colonial in Early America*, ed. Robert Blair St George (Ithaca: Cornell University Press, 2000), 279.

Conclusion

Laws prohibiting sexual contact outside the marriage bed existed throughout early modern England and its expanding numbers of North American colonies. Seventeenth-century definitions and punishments for such behavior reflected a wide range of local needs and interests and colonial officials reserved the right to decide when to model their laws directly on English legal practices and when to develop laws alongside English legal practice. The eighteenth-century disappearance of localized distinctions in sexual laws stemmed equally from the growing political, legal, and social Anglicization of the North American colonies and changing understandings of extramarital sex during the Enlightenment period. Nevertheless, this transition flowed both ways as a growing emphasis on racialized sexual misconduct laws in the wider British Empire reflected an equally colonial influence.

While this study is focused particularly on colonial New England, a wide variety of sexual misconduct laws can be found in the other English colonies as well. Male colonists in seventeenth-century South Carolina accused of impregnating female colonists "had no right to a jury trial ... unless the chief judge of the Sessions Court upon a bench trial found [them] innocent."[1] Heavily dependent on labor from indentured servants, the seventeenth-century Chesapeake colonies preferred extended indenture contracts as punishments for sexual misconduct rather than the fines or whippings used in both England and the other English colonies.[2] Prosecuting sexual misconduct in Pennsylvania varied depending on whether the defendant was tried in Pennsylvania's court system or by the justice systems used within the Quaker courts. The colony courts emphasized both the privacy and the interests of the individuals and tried to avoid outright prosecution unless the sexual misconduct in question financially affected the local community, while the

---

1 William Nelson, *The Common Law in Colonial America: The Middle Colonies and the Carolinas, 1660–1730*, Volume 2 (New York: Oxford University Press, 2013), 81.

2 John Ruston Pagan, *Anne Orthwood's Bastard, Sex and Law in Early Virginia* (Oxford: Oxford University Press, 2003), 83–5.

Quaker courts remained equally interested in both morality and the needs of the Quaker community.[3]

Despite these differences, certain patterns and similarities appear throughout colonial sexual misconduct trial legal practices. The growing emphasis on the economic ramifications posed by illicit sex rather than the moral implications which first appeared in sixteenth-century English sexual misconduct law is also present throughout the colonial trials. Likewise, the colonial sexual misconduct trials also demonstrate growing disparities in the ways in which male and female, rich and poor, white and non-white societal members were viewed in Anglo-American society. Men were punished with child support payments for their illegitimate children, while their female partners continued to be punished with fines or whippings for the original sexual acts which created those children. Most English colonies also introduced laws specifying different punishments for sex between partners of different races, though white men who had sex with non-white women generally fared better than white women who had sex with non-white men.

Pennsylvania's efforts to preserve both the privacy and the individual interests of defendants on trial for sexual misconduct charges was an early salvo towards another larger societal transition in the eighteenth century. Seventeenth-century Anglo-American justices considered the needs of the immediate community before the needs and interests of trial defendants, while eighteenth-century justices began to consider defendants as individuals whose needs might be separate from the best interests of their communities. Once again, a caveat must be attached to this transition as it applied more often to male defendants than female, a point demonstrated by Maine attorney Noah Emery who argued in 1745 that the justices should not convict John Brown simply because they did not want their town to be financially responsible for the child Brown was accused of fathering.

In turn, the presence of attorney Noah Emory in the 1745 bastardy and paternity trial for John Brown and Joanna Gilford points to the growing professionalization of the Anglo-American court room. Justices of the Peace, who often gained their positions through social and economic connections, traditionally held center stage in English court rooms. While justices remained part of the judicial process, university-educated attorneys and barristers brought a new emphasis on legal precedent and procedure to the eighteenth-century

3 Nelson, *The Common Law in Colonial America*, Volume 2, 113–15 and Jack D. Marietta and G.S. Rowe, *Troubled Experiment: Crime and Justice in Pennsylvania, 1682–1800* (Philadelphia: University of Pennsylvania Press, 2006), 82–6.

court room. Whether in Rhode Island, where attorneys were part of the legal system from the beginning, or Massachusetts, which deliberately opposed their presence in the seventeenth century, their collective presences helped shift the prosecution of sexual misconduct towards a greater emphasis on method and discourse alongside the older consideration of communal outcome.

These components, whether an emphasis on the economic rather than moral implications of extramarital sex, the rights of the individual versus the rights of a larger community, or the growing professionalization of the legal profession, all point towards a growing political, legal, and social convergence between England and its North American colonies. In some respects, these changes reflect the greater political control exercised over their colonies by the later Stuart kings and their successors. The reorganization of the Massachusetts and, by extension, the Maine courts which led to the creation of General Sessions courts for criminal trials and Common Pleas courts for civil trials in 1692 stemmed from changes mandated by the second Massachusetts charter in 1691. Changes in the sexual misconduct trials also reflect the wider influences and growing contradictions of the Enlightenment period, whose growing emphasis on the rights of the individual rather than the community was tempered and shaped by rising racial, gender, and class distinctions. These components affected how individuals experienced the judicial process and eventually led to illicit sex becoming a crime committed only by non-whites and by the working classes.

This particular story of colonial divergence moving towards greater convergence with England is not a new one for the British North American colonies. While John Murrin called this process "Anglicization," other scholars have named it "re-Anglicization," "Imperialization," "Royalization," or "Centralization."[4] My study of New England's sexual misconduct trials adds a necessary legal and social nuance to this political approach. Concerns about sexual misconduct were common enough across the Anglo-American world to make its prosecution a consistent presence in most court dockets. In turn, the precise details of dates and geographic locations provided by court records

---

4 John M. Murrin, "Anglicizing an American Colony: The Transformation of Provincial Massachusetts" (PhD diss., Yale University, 1966), Joseph A. Conforti, *Saints and Strangers: New England in British North America* (Baltimore: The John Hopkins University Press, 2006), 164, Meranze, Michael, "Penality and the Colonial Project: Crime, Punishment, and the Regulation of Morals in Early America," in *The Cambridge History of Law in America*, Volume 1, Michael Grossberg and Christopher Tomlins, eds (New York: Cambridge University Press, 2008), 200, Richard R. Johnson, *Adjustment to Empire: The New England Colonies, 1675–1715* (New Brunswick: Rutgers University Press, 1981), 419, and James A. Henretta, "Magistrates, Common Law Lawyers, Legislators: The Three Legal Systems of British America," in *The Cambridge History of Law in America*, Volume 1, 581.

allows for the precision needed to track legal and societal changes, however subtle, alongside political evolutions, and the very subtlety of these transitions is what led me to add the phrase "Alternating Anglicization" to the growing vocabulary of the Anglicization thesis.

Colonial New England is best known for the Puritans' efforts to create a new political and legal structure for themselves, including trying to end the growing practice of using paid legal counsel in court trials. Nevertheless, attorneys were part of both Rhode Island and Maine's legal systems from the 1640s, only to disappear from the Maine courts in the mid-seventeenth century when the colony was absorbed into Massachusetts, and then reappear when Massachusetts came under closer English scrutiny in the 1690s. Anglicization became a political mandate in the eighteenth century but it was a personal choice for colonial leaders in the seventeenth century and this is an important distinction in our understanding of how a group of disparate colonies could become a highly disparate country in 1776. John Murrin observes that "only by imitating Great Britain throughout the eighteenth century did the colonies grow sufficiently alike to embark on a common Revolution."[5] The Anglicization process did, indeed, help in the forming of the United States as a collection of colonies with just enough elements in common to conceive of themselves as a united country. However, the colonies came to these moments of convergence at different times and for different reasons, and paying attention to these moments says as much about American similarities as it does American differences.

This point is further highlighted by another example from the Maine courts. The professionalization of the Anglo-American court room led to a change from the use of the more colorful, and more specific, terms of "incontinency" or "loose carriage" to describe sexual misconduct in the court room to the far more clinical term "fornication." Most Anglo-American courts made this transition gradually, with the descriptive charges continuing to appear long after the first fornication charge had been used. Maine's transition from descriptive sexual misconduct charges to fornication charges took place almost overnight in the mid-1670s, a period in which Maine was also coming under the permanent control of Massachusetts Bay. The speed at which the language in Maine's sexual misconduct trials changed suggests judicial deliberation rather than gradual evolution. Using fornication as the only sexual misconduct charge in their court rooms was an easy way for Maine justices to demonstrate compliance with their changed status as a newly identified Massachusetts county, not to mention their

---

5 John M. Murrin, "Anglicizing an American Colony: The Transformation of Provincial Massachusetts" (PhD diss., Yale University, 1966), 300.

familiarity with contemporary legal terminology and customs. They may have lived in Maine but they wanted it known that they were modern practitioners of the legal profession.

This particular transition struck me as an illuminating one. The decision to change the terminology used to describe sexual misconduct almost certainly occurred for political reasons in Maine. By contrast, the gradual evolution towards the use of fornication charges in other jurisdictions suggests they experienced a more organic process. The end result for all members of Anglo-American society was the same as fornication charges were universally used in eighteenth-century English court rooms. However, those same court rooms came to use those terms at different times and for different reasons. The Anglicization of daily life in the English colonies was not solely desired by royal officials in England or even colonial officials. It was also negotiated and navigated by ordinary colonists on a daily basis in their homes and court rooms, taverns and churches.

Appendix A: Alternate Sexual Misconduct Charges

1. Uncleanness
2. Unseemly behavior
3. Unchaste words
4. Carriage
5. Unseemly carriage
6. Kissing
7. Attempting chastity
8. Incontinency
9. Lascivious speeches
10. Wanton dalliance
11. Miscarriages
12. Keeping/Frequenting company
13. Staying overnight
14. Unclean speeches
15. Soliciting adultery
16. Obscene and filthy speeches
17. Abusing woman's body in foul manner
18. Relations after contract and before marriage
19. Profane and foolish dancing, singing and wanton speeches
20. Suspicious carriages
21. Making love
22. Seeking marriage without friends' consent
23. Lascivious carriage
24. Uncivil carriage
25. Unproper relations
26. Attempted abasement
27. Too much/unlawful familiarity
28. Acted lasciviously
29. Being together in scandalous manner on Sabbath in husband's absence

30. Light carriage
31. Bigamy
32. Lying together
33. Coming together
34. Breached separation
35. Too much familiarity
36. Carnall fellowship
37. Putting hand in codpiece
38. Scandalous carriage
39. Unseemly speeches and misbehaviors
40. Soliciting adultery
41. Unseemly glorying in the abuse of his own and his wife's chastity
42. Carnal copulation
43. Bedding with each other as man and wife
44. Abuse out of bed naked on the floor
45. Unseemly practices
46. Filthiness
47. Unlawful enticing
48. Defiling the marriage bed
49. Offering violence to the body, tending toward uncleanness
50. Abusive carriages
51. Assault
52. Suffering a young man to lie with her
53. Great offences
54. Heinous, lascivious, and adulterous carriages
55. Carnal knowledge
56. Boasting about lascivious and unclean practices
57. Filthy lascivious carriage divers times
58. Filthy carriage
59. Being unchaste before marriage
60. Unchastity
61. Keeping company at an unseasonable time of day
62. Being naught and unseemly being together
63. Offer to lie with another man's wife and abuse her with uncleanness
64. Using dalliance divers times
65. Suffering a man's attempt to abuse her body by uncleanness
66. Lying in bed with brother
67. Lude carriages
68. Unclean practices

69. Lascivious and uncleane carriages
70. Fornication in unlawfull companying before their marriage
71. Uncleane speeches and carriages/lascivious speeches and misbehavior
72. Abusing himself with now wife by committing uncleanness before marriage
73. Carnal knowledge/copulation before marriage contract
74. Attempting chastity of diverse women by lascivious words and carriages
75. Knowledge of each other before public marriage
76. Lewd behavior each with other upon a bed
77. Offering an attempt of boddyly uncleanes
78. Vain, light and lascivious carriage at an unseasonable time of the night
79. Idle and lascivious behavior
80. Lascivious going in the company of young men
81. Misdemeaning of himself in words and carriages
82. Lascivious carriages and unchast in attempting chastity to serve fleshly, beastly lust without intention of marriage
83. Keeping company with each other in an undecent manner at unseasonable time and place before marriage
84. Unseemly carriage at an unseasonable time, being at night
85. Unclean and filthy behavior
86. Unclean and lascivious behavior
87. Attempting chastity by offering violence
88. Disorderly coming together without consent of parents and lawful marriage
89. Lascivious and unnatural practices
90. Adulterous practices and attempts, so far as the strength of nature would permit
91. Obscene and lascivious behavior
92. Drawing his wife in an uncivil manner upon the snow
93. Committing whoredom agrevated with divers circumstances
94. Sundry attempts to abuse her, by attempting by force to lie with her and other lascivious carriages
95. Conceived child before marriage but after contract
96. Lascivious, obscene and wild expressions and actions
97. Uncivil words and carriages towards/giving writings to intice despite being married
98. Whoredom
99. Lascivious and light behavior
100. Found in bed together

101. Lascivious attempts
102. Carnally know and ravish by force
103. Light behavior
104. Desiring and divers times attempting to lye with her

Appendix B: Alternate Punishments

1. Stocks in one town
2. Stocks in two towns
3. Confession after church
4. Warned away from other party
5. Admonished
6. Bound for good behavior
7. Indenture extended for one year
8. Imprisoned
9. Punishment delayed until after childbirth
10. Fine paid to servant's master
11. Referred to next court
12. Pay costs to husband
13. "Stand in a white sheete publiquely in the congregation"
14. Wearing sign labeled "Convicted for speaking words in a boasting manner of his lascivious and unclean practices" on meeting day
15. Wearing sign labeled "For my Lacivious and Wanton Carriages" in Salem and in Beverly on meeting day or to be whipped
16. Pay costs for a "hue and cry"
17. If marriage was contracted within next two days, fine would be reduced
18. Wearing sign describing crime in meeting house
19. Give security or marry
20. Imprisoned while deciding what to do/no further records
21. General Assembly will decide punishment

Appendix C: Preservation and Publication of Colonial New England Legal Sources

Colonial New England's laws and legal cultures were shaped by the individual colonies' origins and intentions. The preservation and publication of these same records has followed an equally diverse trajectory, one that has often (and not coincidentally) reflected the original legal cultures of the respective colonies. While nothing can replace examining the original records, I also offer this guide to working with published court records for Essex County, Massachusetts, the Province of Maine, and Rhode Island.

Massachusetts Bay was New England's dominant colony throughout the seventeenth century. Following decades of challenges ranging from King Philip's War in the 1670s to the Dominion of New England in the 1680s and the coming of a new royal charter in the 1690s, Puritan leaders faltered before rebirth in the eighteenth century as the independent-minded colonists who would help drive the fervor behind the American Revolution. Essex County judicial records for the years between 1636 and 1686 were edited by George Francis Dow in the early twentieth century and published by the Essex Institute in a nine volume series titled *Records and Files of the Quarterly Courts of Essex County, Massachusetts*, though these volumes should be approached with care as Dow may have been overly zealous in his editing work. In addition, a Works Project Administration project in the 1930s transcribed Essex County court records for the years between 1636 and 1691. By contrast, colonial court records for Essex County after 1692 remain unpublished and untranscribed and are now held at the Judicial Archives division of the Massachusetts State Archives in Boston, Massachusetts, along with the original records for the period between 1636 and 1691.[1]

1 *Records and Files of the Quarterly Courts of Essex County, Massachusetts*, ed. George Francis Dow (Salem: Essex Institute, 1911), Volumes 1–9. Both the "Work Progress Administration Transcriptions for Essex County Court Records," Volumes 1–55 and all of the record books and file papers for the Essex County Court Records are held at the Judicial Archives division of the Massachusetts State Archives in Boston.

Like Maine's colonial courts, the publication of its legal records has also been a vibrant, homespun affair. Under the guidance of Charles Thornton Libby, Robert Moody, and Neal Allen, the Maine Historical Society published Maine's judicial records for the years between 1636 and 1727 in a five volume series titled *Maine Province and Court Records*. Unlike the published court records for Essex County, Maine's published records were thoroughly annotated, thereby providing readers with additional historical contexts understanding the events described in the trials. All of Maine's original colonial court records are held at the Maine State Archives in Augusta, Maine.[2]

The Colony of Rhode Island and Providence Plantations struggled to create unity between its incongruent towns and religious congregations throughout the seventeenth century. Given this history, the lack of consistency in the publication and preservation of Rhode Island's legal records is unsurprising. Transcriptions for the courts conducted between 1641 and 1646 were published by Howard Chapin in a volume titled *Documentary History of Rhode Island*, while the Rhode Island Historical Society published records for the years between 1647 and 1662 in *Rhode Island Court Records[:] Records of the Court of Trials of the Colony of Providence Plantations*. Jane Fiske has also transcribed and published various colonial court records in two volumes titled *Rhode Island General Court of Trials, 1671–1704* and *Gleanings from Newport Court Files, 1659–1783*. All of Rhode Island's original colonial court records are held at the Rhode Island Judicial Archives in Pawtucket, Rhode Island.[3]

---

2 *Maine Province and Court Records*, Volumes 1–6, Charles Thornton Libby, Robert Moody and Neal Allen, eds (Portland: Maine Historical Society, 1928–75). All of the record books and file papers for the colonial Maine courts are held at the Maine State Archives in Augusta.

3 *Documentary History of Rhode Island*, Volumes 1–2, Howard Chapin, ed. (Providence: Preston and Rounds Co., 1920), *Rhode Island Court Records[:] Records of the Court of Trials of the Colony of Providence Plantations*, Rhode Island Historical Society, ed. (Buffalo: Dennis Prince Co., 1946), *Rhode Island General Court of Trials, 1671–1704*, Jane Fletcher Fiske, ed. (Boxford: Fiske Press, 1998), and *Gleanings from Newport Court Files, 1659–1783*, Fiske, ed. (Boxford: Fiske Press, 1998). All of the record books and file papers for the colonial Rhode Island courts are held at the Rhode Island Judicial Archives in Pawtucket, Rhode Island.

Appendix D: Colonial Court Systems in Massachusetts, Maine, and Rhode Island

Massachusetts Bay Courts

"Greate and Generall Court" of Massachusetts Bay, March 4, 1629–March 3, 1636.
Court of Assistants, under the Charter of the Governor and Company of the Massachusetts Bay in New England, 1629–92
Superior Court of Judicature, under the Province Charter, 1692–1780

Essex County

Essex County Inferior Quarterly Court in Salem, 1636–92
Essex County Inferior Quarterly Court in Ipswich, 1641–92
Essex County Court of General Sessions of the Peace at Salem, Ipswich, and Newbury, 1692–1780
Essex County Court of Common Pleas at Salem, Ipswich, and Newbury, 1692–1780

Maine Courts

New Somersetshire, Province Court, 1636
Province of Maine General Court, 1640–51
York County Court, 1653–64
York County Court of Associates, 1658–61, 1663–64, 1668–79
Province of Maine Court, Eastern and Western Divisions, 1665–67
York County Court, 1668–79

York County Court of Pleas 1680–92
York County Court of Sessions, 1680–92
York County Court of General Sessions of the Peace, 1692–1780
York County Inferior Court of Common Pleas, 1692–1780

Rhode Island Courts

Rhode Island Circuit Courts, 1640–46
Rhode Island General Court of Trials at Newport, Portsmouth, Providence, and Warwick, 1647–63
Rhode Island General Court Of Trials and Goal Delivery at Newport, 1664–1730
Rhode Island Judicature Court of Assize and General Goal Delivery at Newport, 1731–80

References

Secondary Sources

Abbot, Elinor. *Our Company Increases Apace, History, Language, and Social Identity in Early Colonial Andover, Massachusetts.* Dallas: SIL International, 2007.

Allen, Neal. "Law and Authority to the Eastward: Maine Courts, Magistrates and Lawyers, 1690–1730," in *Law in Colonial Massachusetts, 1630–1800.* Daniel Coquilette, ed. Boston: The Colonial Society of Massachusetts, 1984.

Amory, Hugh. "Printing and Bookselling in New England, 1638–1713," in *A History of the Book in America*, Volume I. Hugh Amory and David D. Hall, eds. Chapel Hill: University of Carolina Press, 2007.

Anderson, Ruth Alice. "Peter Talman, a footnote in history." M.A. Thesis, University of Rhode Island, 1986.

Archer, Richard. *Fissures in the Rock, New England in the Seventeenth Century.* Hanover: University Press of New England, 2001.

Austin, John Osborne. *The Genealogical Dictionary of Rhode Island.* Baltimore: Genealogical Publishing Co., 1978.

Bailey, Richard. *Race and Redemption in Puritan New England.* New York: Oxford University Press, 2011.

Bailey, Sarah. *Historical Sketches of Andover.* Cambridge: Riverside Press, 1880.

Baker, Emerson et al., eds. *American Beginnings: Exploration, Culture and Cartography in the Land of Norumbega.* Lincoln, NE: University of Nebraska Press, 1995.

———. "A Scratch with a Bear's Paw: Anglo-Indian Deeds in Early Maine." *Ethnohistory* 36, No. 3 (1989): 235–56.

Barnes, Thomas. *Shaping the Common Law: From Glanvill to Hale, 1688.* Redwood City: Stanford University Press, 2008.

———. "Thomas Lechford and the Earliest Lawyering in Massachusetts, 1638–1641," in *Law in Colonial Massachusetts, 1630–1800.* Daniel Coquilette, ed. Boston: The Colonial Society of Massachusetts, 1984.

Barnes, Viola Florence. *The Dominion of New England: a Study in British Colonial Policy*. New York: F. Ungar Publishing Company, 1960.

Beattie, J.M. *Crime and the Courts in England, 1660–1800*. Princeton: Princeton University Press, 1986.

Berman, Harold. *Law and Revolution II: The Impact of the Protestant Reformations on the Western Legal Tradition*. Cambridge: The Belknap Press of Harvard University Press, 2003.

Berry, Helen and Elizabeth Foyster. *The Family in Early Modern England*. New York: Cambridge University Press, 2007.

Bilder, Mary Sarah. *The Transatlantic Constitution, Colonial Legal Culture and the Empire*. Cambridge, MA: Harvard University Press, 2004.

Black, Maggie. *A Taste of History: 10,000 Years of Food in Britain*. London: British Museum Press, 1993.

Block, Sharon. *Rape and Sexual Power in Early America*. Chapel Hill: University of North Carolina Press, 2006.

Boyer, Allen. *Sir Edward Coke and the Elizabethan Age*. Stanford: Stanford University Press, 2003.

Bradford, William. *Of Plymouth Plantation, 1620–1647*. Samuel Eliot Morison, ed. New York, Knopf Press, 1952.

Brewer, Holly. "The Transformation of Domestic Law," in *The Cambridge History of Law in America*, Volume 1. Michael Grossberg and Christopher Tomlins, eds. New York: Cambridge University Press, 2008.

Brewer, John and John Style, eds. *An Ungovernable People: The English and Their Law in the Seventeenth and Eighteenth Centuries*. London: Hutchinson & Co., 1980.

Bridenbaugh, Carl. *Fat Mutton and Liberty of Conscience, Society in Rhode Island, 1636–1690*. Providence: Brown University Press, 1974.

Brown, Irene Quenzler and Richard Brown. *The Hanging of Ephraim Wheeler: a Story of Rape, Incest, and Justice in Early America*. Cambridge: Belknap Press of Harvard University Press, 2003.

Brown, Kathleen. *Good Wives, Nasty Wenches, & Anxious Patriarchs*. Chapel Hill, NC: University of North Carolina Press, 1996.

Bucke, Byron. *Isaac Buck of Scituate, Plymouth Colony, and Some of his Descendants, Generations 1–5*. Hightstown, NJ: B. Buck, 1998.

Chandler, E.J. *Ancient Sagadahoc, A Story of the Englishmen who welcomed the Pilgrims to the New World*. Thomaston: Conservatory of American Letters, 1998.

Chandler, George. *The Chandler Family*. Worcester: Press of Charles Hamilton, 1883.

Chapin, Bradley. *Criminal Justice in Colonial America, 1606–1660*. Athens, GA: University of Georgia Press, 1983.

Chu, Jonathon. "The Social and Political Contexts of Heterodoxy: Quakerism in Seventeenth-Century Kittery." *The New England Quarterly* 54, No. 3 (1981): 365–84.

Churchill, Edwin. "Too Great the Challenge: The Birth and Death of Falmouth, ME, 1624–1676." Ph.D. diss., University of Maine, 1979.

———. "English Beachheads in Seventeenth-Century Maine," in *Maine, The Pine Tree State from Prehistory to Present*. Richard Judd, ed. Orono: University of Maine Press, 1995.

Clark, Anna. *Desire: A History of European Sexuality*. New York: Routledge, 2008.

Clark, Charles. *The Eastern Frontier, The Settlement of Northern New England, 1610–1763*. Hanover: University Press of New England, 1983.

Coleman, Emma Lewis. *New England Captives Carried to Canada Between 1677 and 1760 During the French and Indian Wars*. Portland: Southworth Press, 1925.

Conforti, Joseph. *Saints and Strangers: New England in British North America*. Baltimore: The John Hopkins University Press, 2006.

Crane, Elaine Forman. *Ebb Tide in New England, Women, Seaports, and Social Change, 1630–1830*. Boston: Northeastern University Press, 1998.

———. *Killed Strangely: The Death of Rebecca Cornell*. Ithaca: Cornell University Press, 2002.

———. *Witches, Wife Beaters, & Whores: Common Law and Common Folk*. Ithaca: Cornell University Press, 2011.

Crawford, Katherine. *European Sexualities, 1400–1800*. New York: Cambridge University Press, 2007

Cressy, David. *Birth, Marriage & Death: Ritual, Religion, and the Life-Cycle in Tudor and Stuart England*. Oxford: Oxford University Press, 1997.

Dabhoiwala, Faramerz. *The Origins of Sex: A History of the First Sexual Revolution*. Oxford: Oxford University Press, 2012.

Dalrymple, William. *White Mughals: Love and Betrayal in Eighteenth-Century India*. New York: Penguin Books, 2004.

Daniels, Christine and Michael Kennedy, eds. *Negotiated Empires: Centers and Peripheries in the Americas, 1500–1820*. New York: Routledge Press, 2002.

Dayton, Cornelia. "Turning Points and the Relevance of Colonial Legal History." *The William and Mary Quarterly* 50, No. 1 (January 1993): 7–17.

———. *Women Before the Bar, Gender, Law & Society in Connecticut, 1639–1789*. Chapel Hill: University of North Carolina Press, 1995.

DeCesare, Catherine. "Women and the Legal Culture of Colonial Rhode Island," in *Liberty and Justice: A History of Law and Lawyers in Rhode Island, 1636–1998*. East Providence, RI: Rhode Island Publications Society, 1998.

Dodge, Joseph Thompson. *Genealogy of the Dodge Family of Essex County, Mass. 1629–1894*. Madison: Democrat Printing Company, 1894.

Drake, James. *King Philip's War, Civil War in New England, 1675–1676*. Amherst: University of Massachusetts Press, 1999.

Eckert, Richard Scott Eckert. *The Gentleman of the Profession: The Emergence of Lawyers in Massachusetts, 1630–1810*. New York: Garland Publishing, Inc., 1991.

Farber, Hannah. *The Rise and Fall of the Province of Lygonia, 1643–1658. The New England Quarterly* 82, No. 3 (2009): 490–513.

Fernandez, Angela. "Record-Keeping and Other Troublemaking: Thomas Lechford and Law Reform in Colonial Massachusetts." *Law and History Review* 23, No. 2 (Summer 2005): 235–77.

Finlay, Roger. *Population and Metropolis, The Demography of London, 1580–1650*. Cambridge: Cambridge University Press, 1981.

Fischer, Kirsten. *Suspect Relations, Sex, Race and Resistance in Colonial North Carolina*. Ithaca, NY: Cornell University Press, 2002.

Flaherty, David, ed. *Essays in the History of Early American Law*. Chapel Hill: Institute of Early American History and Culture, 1969.

Fletcher, Anthony. *Gender, Sex and Subordination in England, 1500–1800*. New Haven: Yale University Press, 1995.

Foster, Thomas. *Sex and the Eighteenth-Century Man, Massachusetts and the History of Sexuality in America*. Boston: Beacon Press, 2006.

Francis, Richard. *Judge Sewall's Apology: The Salem Witch Trials and the Forming of an American Conscience*. New York: Harper Perennial, 2005.

Friedman, Lawrence. *A History of American Law*. New York: Simon and Shuster, 1973.

Galenson, David W. *Traders, Planters, and Slaves: Market Behavior in Early English America*. Cambridge: Cambridge University Press, 1986.

Gerber, Scott Douglas. *A Distinct Judicial Power: The Origins of an Independent Judiciary, 1606–1787*. New York. Oxford University Press, 2011.

Godbeer, Richard. *Sexual Revolution in Early America*. Baltimore: The Johns Hopkins University Press, 2002.

Goebel, Julius and T. Raymond Naughton. *Law Enforcement in Colonial New York: A Study in Criminal Procedure*. Montclair: Patterson Smith, 1970.

Gowing, Laura. *Domestic Dangers, Women, Words and Sex in Early Modern London*. Oxford: Clarendon Press, 1996.

———. *Common Bodies: Women, Touch and Power in Seventeenth-Century England*. New Haven: Yale University Press, 2003.

Greenberg, Douglas. *Crime and Law Enforcement in the Colony of New York, 1691–1776*. Ithaca: Cornell University Press, 1974.

Greene, Jack. *Creating the British Atlantic: Essays on Transplantation, Adaptation and Continuity*. Charlottesville: University of Virginia Press, 2013.

Greven, Philip. *Four Generations, Population, Land, and Family in Colonial Andover, Massachusetts*. Ithaca: Cornell University Press, 1970.

Gura, Philip. *A Glimpse of Sion's Glory: Puritan Radicalism in New England, 1620–1660*. Middletown: Wesley University Press, 1984.

Hambleton, Else. *Daughters of Eve, Pregnant Brides and Unwed Mothers in Seventeenth-Century, Massachusetts*. New York: Routledge Press, 2004.

Hamilton, Frederick. *A Brief History of Printing in England*. Chicago: United Typothetae of America, 1918.

Harkness, Deborah. *The Jewel House: Elizabethan London and the Scientific Revolution*. New Haven: Yale University Press, 2008.

Harrington, Virginia. *American Population before the Federal Census of 1790*. New York: Columbia University Press, 1932.

Hart, James. *Genealogical history of Samuell Hart from London, England, to Lynn, Mass., 1640 and descendants, to 1903*. Concord: Rumford Print. Co., 1903.

Hartog, Henrik. "The Public Law of a County Court: Judicial Government in Eighteenth Century Massachusetts." *The American Journal of Legal History* 20, No. 4 (1976).

Haskins, George Lee. *Law and Authority in Early Massachusetts, A Study in Tradition and Design*. New York: The Macmillan Company, 1960.

Hawthorne, Nathaniel Hawthorne. *The Scarlet Letter*. New York, Barnes and Noble Classics, 2003.

Hellinga, Lotte. *William Caxton and Early Printing in England*. London: British Library, 2010.

Henretta, James, "Magistrates, Common Law Lawyers, Legislators: The Three Legal Systems of British America," in *The Cambridge History of Law in America*, Volume 1. Michael Grossberg and Christopher Tomlins, eds. New York: Cambridge University Press, 2008.

Herndon, Ruth. *Unwelcome Americans: Living on the Margin in Early New England*. Philadelphia: University of Pennsylvania Press, 2001.

Herrup, Cynthia. *The Common Peace: Participation and the Criminal Law in Seventeenth-Century England*. Cambridge: Cambridge University Press, 1987.

Hirsh, Adam Jay. *The Rise of the Penitentiary: Prisons and Punishment in Early America*. New Haven: Yale University Press, 1992.

Hitchcock, Tim. "Paupers and Preachers: The SPCK and the Parochial Workhouse movement," in *Stilling the Grumbling Hive: The Response to Social and Economic Problems in England, 1689–1750*. Lee Davison, Tim Hitchcock, Tim Keirn and Robert Shoemaker, eds. New York: St Martin's Press, 1992.

Houston, R.A. *The Population History of Britain and Ireland, 1500–1750*. Cambridge: Cambridge University Press, 1992.

Ingram, Martin. *Church Courts, Sex, and Marriage in England, 1570–1640*. New York: Cambridge University Press, 1987.

Jackson, Mark. *New-Born Child Murder, Women, Illegitimacy and the Courts in Eighteenth-century England*. New York: Manchester University Press, 1996.

James, Sydney. *Colonial Rhode Island: a History*. New York: Scribner, 1975.

———. *John Clarke and His Legacies, Religion and Law in Colonial Rhode Island, 1638–1750*. University Park: Pennsylvania State University Press, 1999.

Jameson, E.O. *Choats of America*. Boston, Alfred Mudge & Sons Printers, 1896.

Johnson, Herbert. *Imported Eighteenth-Century Law Treatises in American Libraries, 1700–1799*. Knoxville: University of Tennessee Press, 1978.

Johnson, Richard. *Adjustment to Empire: The New England Colonies, 1675–1715*. New Brunswick: Rutgers University Press, 1981.

Kamensky, Jane. *Governing the Tongue, the Politics of Speech in Early New England*. Oxford: Oxford University Press, 1997.

Kawashima, Yasuhide. *Puritan Justice and the Indian, White Man's Law in Massachusetts, 1630–1763*. Middletown, CT: Wesleyan University Press, 1986.

Kermode, Jenny and Gartine Walker. *Women, Crime and the Courts in Early Modern England*. Chapel Hill, NC: University of North Carolina Press, 1994.

Konig, David. *Law and Society in Puritan Massachusetts, Essex County, 1629–1692*. Chapel Hill, NC: University of North Carolina Press, 1979.

Levy, Leonard. *The Palladium of Justice: Origins of Trial by Jury*. Chicago: Ivan R. Dee, 1999.

Littlefield, George Emery. *Early Boston Booksellers, 1642–1711*. Burt Franklin: New York, 1969.

Lockridge, Kenneth. "Colonial Self-Fashioning: Paradoxes and Pathologies in the Construction of Genteel Identity in Eighteenth-Century America," in

Possible Pasts, Becoming Colonial in Early America. Robert Blair St George, ed. Ithaca: Cornell University Press, 2000.

Lombard, Anne S. *Making Manhood, Growing Up Male in Colonial New England*. Cambridge: Harvard University Press, 2003.

Lyons, Clare. *Sex among the Rabble: An Intimate History of Gender and Power in the Age of Revolution, Philadelphia, 1730–1830*. Chapel Hill: University of North Carolina Press, 2006.

Magnalia Christi Americana or the Ecclesiastical History of New England. Hartford: Silas Andrus and Son, 1853.

Main, Gloria. *Peoples of a Spacious Land: Families and Cultures in Colonial New England*. Cambridge: Harvard University Press, 2001.

Mandell, Philip. *King Philip's War: Colonial Expansion, Native Resistance, and the End of Indian Sovereignty*. Baltimore: The Johns Hopkins University Press, 2010.

Marietta, Jack and G.S. Rowe. *Troubled Experiment: Crime and Justice in Pennsylvania, 1682–1800*. Philadelphia: University of Pennsylvania Press, 2006.

Marland, Hilary, ed. *The Art of Midwifery: Early Modern Midwives in Europe*. New York: Routledge Press, 1993.

Martin, John Frederick. *Profits in the Wilderness, Entrepreneurship and the Founding of New England*. Chapel Hill, NC: University of North Carolina Press, 1991.

Mather, Cotton. *The Fisher-mans Calling A Brief Essay, to Serve the Great Interests of Religion among our Fisher-men*. Boston: T. Green, 1712.

McConville, Brendan. *The King's Three Faces: The Rise and Fall of Royal America, 1688–1776*. Chapel Hill: The University of North Carolina Press, 2006.

McLoughlin, William G. *Rhode Island: A Bicentennial History*. New York: W.W. Norton, 1978.

McManus, Edgar. *Law and Liberty in Early New England: Criminal Justice and Due Process, 1620–1692*. Amherst: University of Massachusetts Press, 1993.

McWilliams, James. *Building the Bay Colony: Local Economy and Culture in Early Massachusetts*. Charlottesville: University of Virginia Press, 2007.

Meranze, Michael Meranze. "Penality and the Colonial Project: Crime, Punishment, and the Regulation of Morals in Early America," in *The Cambridge History of Law in America*, Volume 1. Michael Grossberg and Christopher Tomlins, eds. New York: Cambridge University Press, 2008.

Miller, Kerby, Arnold Schrier, Bruce Boling and David Doyle, eds. *Irish Immigrants in the Land of Canaan: Letters and Memoirs from Colonial and

Revolutionary America, 1675–1815. New York: Oxford University Press, 2003.

Miller, Marla. *The Needle's Eye, Women and Work in the Age of Revolution*. Amherst: University of Massachusetts Press, 2006.

Montrose, Louis. "The Work of Gender in the Discourse of Discovery." *Representations* 33 (Winter 1991): 1–41.

Moody, Robert, ed. *The Saltonstall Papers, 1607–1815*. Portland: Anthoensen Press, 1972.

Morey, David. *The Voyage of Archangell: James Rosier's Account of the Waymouth Voyage of 1605, a True Relation*. Gardner: Tilbury House Publishers, 2005.

Morison, Samuel Eliot. *The European Discovery of America, the Northern Voyages*. New York: Oxford University Press, 1971.

Morris, M. Michelle Jarret. *Under Household Government: Sex and Family in Puritan Massachusetts*. Cambridge: Harvard University Press, 2013.

Murray, John and Ruth Herndon, eds. *Children Bound to Labor: The Pauper Apprentice System in Early America*. Ithaca: Cornell University Press, 2009.

Murrin, John. "Anglicizing an American Colony: The Transformation of Provincial Massachusetts." Ph.D. diss., Yale University, 1966.

———. "The Legal Transformation: The Bench and Bar of Eighteenth-Century Massachusetts," in *Colonial America: Essays in Politics and Social Development*. Stanley Katz and John Murrin, eds. New York: Alfred A. Knopf, 1983.

———. "Magistrates, Sinners, and a Precarious Liberty: Trial by Jury in Seventeenth-Century New England," in *Saints & Revolutionaries, Essays on Early American History*. David Hall, John Murrin and Thad Tate, eds. New York: W.W. Norton & Co., 1984.

Nellis, Eric and Anne Decker Cecere, eds. *The Eighteenth-Century Records of the Boston Overseers of the Poor*. Eric Nellis and Anne Decker Cecere, eds. Boston: The Colonial Society of Massachusetts, 1984.

Nelson, William. *The Common Law in Colonial America: The Chesapeake and New England, 1607–1660*, Volume 1. New York: Oxford University Press, 2008.

———. *The Common Law in Colonial America: The Middle Colonies and the Carolinas, 1660–1730*, Volume 2. New York: Oxford University Press, 2013.

Norton, Mary Beth. *Founding Mothers & Fathers: Gendered Power and the Forming of American Society*. New York: Alfred A. Knopf, 1996.

———. *In the Devil's Snare, The Salem Witchcraft Crisis of 1692*. New York: Alfred A. Knopf, 2002.

Noyes, Sybil, Charles, Thornton Libby and Walter C. Davis, eds, *Genealogical Dictionary of Maine and New Hampshire*. Portland, ME: Anthoensen Press, 1928–39.

Offut, William, *Offut. Of "Good Laws" and "Good Men:" Law and Society in the Delaware Valley, 1680–1710*. Champaign: University of Illinois Press, 1995.

Pagan, John Ruston Pagan. *Anne Orthwood's Bastard, Sex and Law in Early Virginia*. New York: Oxford University Press, 2003.

Parent, Anthony. *Foul Means: The Formation of a Slave Society in Virginia, 1660–1740*. Chapel Hill: University of North Carolina Press, 2003.

Parnes, D.C. *Plymouth and the Common Law, 1620–1775*. Kingston: Pilgrim Publishers, 1971.

Plaine, Ann Marie. *Colonial Intimacies, Indian Marriage in Colonial New England*. Ithaca: Cornell University Press, 2000.

Pole, J.R. *Contract and Consent, Representation and the Jury in Anglo-American Legal History*. Charlottesville: University of Virginia Press, 2010.

Pulsipher, Jenny Hale. *Subjects unto the Same King: Indians, English and the Contest for Authority in Colonial New England*. Philadelphia: University of Pennsylvania Press, 2005.

Reed, William. *The Descendents of Thomas Durfee of Portsmouth, Rhode Island*. Washington, DC: Gibson Brothers Press, 1902.

Reid, John. *Acadia, Maine, and New Scotland: Marginal Colonies in the Seventeenth Century*. Toronto: University of Toronto Press, 1981.

Reid, John Philip, *Rule of Law: The Jurisprudence of Liberty in the Seventeenth and Eighteenth Centuries*. DeKalb: Northern Illinois University Press, 2004.

Rice, Douglas Walthew, *The Life and Achievements of Sir John Popham, 1531–1607: Leading to the Establishment of the First English Colony in New England*. Madison: Fairleigh Dickinson University Press, 2005.

Richter, Daniel. *Before the Revolution: America's Ancient Pasts*. Cambridge: Harvard University Press, 2011.

Roeber, A.G. *Faithful Magistrates and Republican Lawyers: Creators of Virginia Legal Culture, 1680–1810*. Chapel Hill: The University of North Carolina Press, 1981.

Ross, Richard. "The Legal Past of Early New England: Notes for the Study of Law, Legal Culture, and Intellectual History." *The William and Mary Quarterly* 50, No. 1 (1993), 28–41.

Shammas, Carole. *A History of Household Government in America*. Charlottesville: University of Virginia Press, 2002.

Shapiro, Barbara, *Probability and Certainty in Seventeenth-Century England: a Study of the Relationships between Natural Science, Religion, History, Law, and Literature*. Princeton: Princeton University Press, 1983.

———. *"Beyond Reasonable Doubt" and "Probable Cause": Historical Perspectives on the Anglo-American Law of Evidence*. Berkeley: University of California Press, 1991.

———. *A Culture of Fact: England, 1550–1720*. Ithaca: Cornell University Press, 2003.

Sharpe, J.A. *Crime in Early Modern England, 1550–1750*. New York: Longman Group Limited, 1984.

Smith, Joseph, "The English Criminal Law in Early America," in *The English Legal System: Carryover to the Colonies*. Joseph Smith and Thomas Barnes, eds. Los Angeles: University of California Press, 1975.

Stackpole, Everett. *Old Kittery and Her Families*. Lewiston, ME: Press of Lewiston Journal Co., 1903.

Stanwood, Owen. *The Empire Reformed: English America in the Age of the Glorious Revolution*. Philadelphia: University of Pennsylvania Press, 2011.

Stavely, Keith and Kathleen Fitzgerald, *America's Founding Food: The Story of New England Cooking*. Chapel Hill: University of North Carolina Press, 2004.

St George, Robert Blair, "Massacred Language: Courtroom Performance in Eighteenth-Century Boston," in *Possible Pasts, Becoming Colonial in Early America*. Robert Blair St George, ed. Ithaca: Cornell University Press, 2000.

Stone, Lawrence Stone. *The Family, sex and Marriage in England, 1500–1800*. New York: Harper and Row Publishers, 1977.

Stratton, Eugene Aubrey, *Plymouth Colony: Its History and People, 1620–1691*. Salt Lake City: Ancestry Publishing, 1986.

Taves, Ann, *Religion and Domestic Violence in Early New England: the Memoirs of Abigail Abbot Bailey*. Bloomington: Indiana University Press, 1989.

Teichman, Jenny Teichman. *Illegitimacy: An Examination of Bastardy*. Ithaca: Cornell University Press, 1982.

Thomas, Isiah. *The History of Printing in America, with a Biography of Printers & an Account of Newspapers*. New York: Weathervane Books, 1970.

Thomas, Keith, "The Puritans and Adultery: The Act of 1650 Reconsidered," in *Puritans and Revolutionaries: Essays in Seventeenth-Century History*. Donald Pennington and Keith Thomas, eds. Oxford: Oxford University Press, 1978.

Tomlins, Christopher. *Freedom Bound: Law, Labor and Civic Identity in Colonizing English America, 1580–1685*. New York: Cambridge University Press, 2010.

Tomlins, Christopher and Bruce Mann, eds. *The Many Legalities of Early America*. Chapel Hill: University of North Carolina Press, 2001.

Ulrich, Laurel Thatcher. *Good Wives: Image and Reality in the Lives of Women in Northern New England, 1650–1750*. New York: Alfred A. Knopf, 1980.

———. *A Midwife's Tale, the Life of Martha Ballard, Based on Her Diary, 1785–1812*. New York: Vintage Books, 1990.

Varney, George. *History of Scarborough, Maine, From A Gazetteer of the State of Maine*. Boston: B.B. Russell Press, 1886.

Vaughan, Alden and Edward Clark, eds. *Puritans among the Indians: Accounts of Captivity and Redemption, 1676–1724*. Cambridge: Harvard University Press, 1981.

Weisner, Merry, "Early Modern Midwifery: A Case Study," in *Women and Work in Preindustrial Europe*. Barbara Hanawalt, ed. Bloomington: Indiana University Press, 1986.

Wheelwright, Julie Wheelwright, *Esther, The Remarkable True Story of Esther Wheelwright: Puritan Child, Native Daughter, Mother Superior*. Toronto: HarperCollins Publishers Ltd, 2011.

White, G. Edward White. *Law in American History*. Oxford: Oxford University Press, 2012.

Williams, Daniel. *Pillars of Salt, Monuments of Grace: New England Crime Literature and the Origins of American Popular Culture, 1674–1860*. Boston: University of Massachusetts Press, 2006.

Willis, William. *A History of the Law, the Courts, and the Lawyers of Maine, From its First Colonization to the Early Part of the Present Century*. Portland: Bailey & Noyes Press, 1863.

Wilson, Adrian. "Participant or Patient? Seventeenth Century Childbirth from the Mother's Point of View," in *Patients and Practitioners, Lay Perceptions of Medicine in Pre-industrial Society*. Roy Porter, ed. Cambridge: Cambridge University Press, 1985.

Worden, G.B. "The Rhode Island Civil Code of 1647," in *Saints and Revolutionaries: Essays on Early American History*. David D. Hall, John M. Murrin and Thad W. Tate, eds. New York: W.W. Norton, 1984.

Wroth, Lawrence. *The Colonial Printer*. Portland: Southworth-Anthoensen Press, 1938, Second Edition.

Primary Sources: Published

Chapin, Howard. *Documentary History of Rhode Island.* Providence: Preston and Rounds Co., 1920.

Cushing, John D. ed. *The Earliest Acts and Laws of the Colony of Rhode Island and Providence Plantations, 1647–1719.* Wilmington, DL: M. Glazier Press, 1977.

Dalton, Michael. *The Countrey Justice, Conteyning the practise of the Justices of the Peace out of their Sessions, Gathered for the better helpe of such Justices of Peace as have not beene much conversant in the studie of the Lawes of this Realme.* Clark: The Lawbook Exchange, Ltd., 2004. Original edition, London: Societie of Stationers, 1618.

———. *The Countrey Justice.* New York: The Legal Classics Library, Division of Gryphon Editions. Original edition, London: Company of Stationers, 1655.

———. *The Countrey Justice.* Provo: Repressed Publishing Company, 2012. Original edition: London: Printed by Henry Lintot, 1746.

Dow, George Francis, ed. *Records and Files of the Quarterly Courts of Essex County, Massachusetts.* Salem: Essex Institute, 1911.

———. *The Probate Records of Essex County, Massachusetts, 1635–1664,* Volume 1. Salem: Newcomb & Gauss, 1916.

———. *The Probate Records of Essex County, Massachusetts, 1675–1681,* Volume 3. Salem: Newcomb & Gauss, 1920, 424.

Fiske, Jane Fletcher, ed. *Gleanings from Newport Court Files, 1659–1783.* Boxford: Fiske Press, 1998.

Fiske, Jane Fletcher, ed. *Rhode Island General Court of Trials, 1671–1704.* Boxford: Fiske Press, 1998.

Gorges, Thomas. *The Letters of Thomas Gorges, Deputy Governor of the Province of Maine, 1640–1643.* Robert E. Moody, ed. Portland: Maine Historical Society, 1978.

Libby, Charles Thornton, Robert Moody and Neal Allen, eds. *Province and Court Records of Maine.* Portland: Maine Historical Society, 1928.

Rhode Island Historical Society, *Rhode Island Court Records[:] Records of the Court of Trials of the Colony of Providence Plantations.* Buffalo, NY: Dennis Prince Co., 1946.

Shurtleff, Nathaniel, ed. *Records of the colony of New Plymouth, in New England.* Boston: W. White Press, 1855–61.

T.E., *The Lawes Resolutions of Womens Rights, or, The Lawes Provision for Woemen: a Methodicall Collection of Such Statutes and Customes, with the Cases, Opinions, Arguments, and Points of Learning in the Law, as doe properly*

concerne Women. Clark: The Lawbook Exchange Ltd, 2006. Original edition: London: Printed by John More, 1632.
The Laws and Liberties of Massachusetts, Reprinted from the Copy of the 1648 edition in the Henry E. Huntington Library. San Marino: The Henry E. Huntington Library and Art Gallery, 1998.
Whitmore, William, ed. *The Colonial Laws of Massachusetts, Reprinted from the Edition of 1660, With the Supplements to 1672, Containing Also, The Body of Liberties of 1641*. Boston: Rockwell & Churchill City Printers, 1889.

Primary Sources: Unpublished

Records and File Papers for the Essex County Inferior Quarterly Court, Judicial Archives division of the Massachusetts State Archives, Boston, Massachusetts.
Record Books and File Papers for Essex County General Sessions of the Peace, Judicial Archives division of the Massachusetts State Archives, Boston, Massachusetts.
Records and File Papers for the York County Court of Associates, Maine State Archives, Augusta, Maine.
Records and File Papers for the Province of Maine Court, Eastern and Western Divisions, Maine State Archives, Augusta, Maine.
York County Court of Sessions, Maine State Archives, Augusta, Maine.
York County Court of General Sessions of the Peace, Maine State Archives, Augusta, Maine.
"Newport Court Book A," Rhode Island Judicial Archives, Pawtucket, Rhode Island.
Judicature Court of Assize and General Goal Delivery, Newport County, Volumes B, C and D, Rhode Island Judicial Archives, Pawtucket, Rhode Island.

Index

For Product Safety Concerns and Information please contact our EU representative GPSR@taylorandfrancis.com Taylor & Francis Verlag GmbH, Kaufingerstraße 24, 80331 München, Germany